MW00655477

ArtScroll Series

Rabbi Nosson Scherman / Rabbi Meir Zlotowitz
General Editors

Published by
Mesorah Publications, ltd

SERVICE of the HEART

Rabbi Shimon Finkelman

The beauty and essence of Tefillah
based on the teachings of
RABBI MOSHE WOLFSON

FIRST EDITION
First Impression . . . July 2012

Published and Distributed by
MESORAH PUBLICATIONS, Ltd.
4401 Second Avenue
Brooklyn, New York 11232

Distributed in Europe by
LEHMANNS
Unit E, Viking Business Park
Rolling Mill Road
Jarrow, Tyne & Wear NE32 3DP
England

Distributed in Israel by
SIFRIATI / A. GITLER — BOOKS
6 Hayarkon Street
Bnei Brak 51127

Distributed in Australia & New Zealand by
GOLDS WORLD OF JUDAICA
3-13 William Street
Balaclava, Melbourne 3183
Victoria Australia

Distributed in South Africa by
KOLLEL BOOKSHOP
Ivy Common 105 William Road
Norwood 2192, Johannesburg, South Africa

THE ARTSCROLL SERIES®
SERVICE OF THE HEART

4401 Second Avenue / Brooklyn, N.Y. 11232 / (718) 921-9000 / www.artscroll.com

---

ISBN 10: 1-4226-1303-8
ISBN 13: 978-1-4226-1303-0

Printed in the United States of America by Noble Book Press Corp.
Bound by Sefercraft Quality Bookbinders, Ltd., Brooklyn, N.Y.

לכבוד מורי ורבי

הרה"ג המשגיח שליט"א

ולעילוי נשמת

אבי מורי הרה"ח ר' משה בן ר' יונה ווייס ז"ל

נלב"ע י"ט אייר תש"ס

מורי חמי הרה"ח ר' ארי' יהודה בן ר' יצחק ז"ל

נלב"ע ט"ז חשון תשס"ז

מורתי חומתי מרת אדל בת ר' ראובן ע"ה

נלב"ע כ"ה אדר תשס"ד

ת.נ.צ.ב.ה.

מאת

ר' יונה יששכר דוב ווייס ומשפחתו לאס אנגליס

נדבת האחים

יונה וישראל בלומענפרוכט ומשפחותיהם

לזכר נשמות הוריהם וזקניהם ז"ל

ת.נ.צ.ב.ה.

In honor of our dear parents

Mr. and Mrs. Yissochor Hasenfeld עמו"ש

who were the first supporters of Beis Medrash Emunas Yisroel. We are proud to follow in their footsteps as sponsors of this collection of *divrei Torah* of the Mashgiach, Harav Wolfson שליט"א.

Mr. and Mrs. Hertzy Hasenfeld

לעילוי נשמת

ר׳ יוסף בן ר׳ נפתלי בנימין פערלמאן ע״ה

נלב״ע ח׳ שבט תשס״ה

ת.נ.צ.ב.ה.

לעילוי נשמת

הרה״ח ר׳ יונה צבי ב״ר יוחנן ז״ל

נפ׳ ליל ש״ק י״ב תשרי תשנ״ה לפ״ק

וזוג׳ מרת שרה ע״ה ב״ר משה יהושע ז״ל

נפ׳ ליל ש״ק כ״ח טבת תשמ״ב לפ״ק

ת.נ.צ.ב.ה.

לעילוי נשמת

הרה״ח ר׳ אפרים ב״ר שמואל חיים ז״ל

נפ׳ י״ג מנחם אב שמו״ת לפ״ק

וזוג׳ מרת רבקה ע״ה הי״ד בת הרה״ח משה אהרן ז״ל

נעקה״ש כ׳ תמוז תש״ד לפ״ק

ת.נ.צ.ב.ה.

בס"ד

משה וואלפסאן
משגיח רוחני, ישיבה תורה ודעת
ורב דביהמ"ד אמונת ישראל

RABBI MOSHE WOLFSON
1574 43RD STREET
BROOKLYN, NEW YORK 11219

ב"ה

ערב ראש חודש סיון, תשע"ב

אל כבוד אהובי ידידי הרב שמעון פינקעלמאן, שליט"א

תשואות חן חן על שסידרת את שיחותי על ענייני תפילה בשפת אנגלית. ושמעתי שבעזה"י הספר "ואני תפילה" בלשון הקודש נתקבל ברצון בין אחינו ב"י וקובעים בו שיעורים בישיבות. ויה"ר שנזכה לעשות נחת רוח לאבינו שבשמים.

ברוב ידידות
משה וואלפסאן

Preface to Rabbi Wolfson's *sefer* אמונת עתיך on the Torah and Festivals

פתיחה

מה אודה לד׳ כל תגמולוהי עלי, אשר מעודי שם חלקי בין כותלי ביהמ״ד במשכנות הרועים. ויביאני המלך חדריו לרעות צאן קודש תשב״ר, ואח״כ מאחר עלות הביאני לשמש במשרת משגיח בביהמ״ד של המתיבתא תורה ודעת, ושם נקבצו אגודות לשמוע בקול דברי בעניני מוסר ואגדה. וחלק מאותם התלמידים, כאשר הגיעו לפרשת ויצא ונפרדו מכותלי הישיבה עדיין נשארו קשורים בה ובאורחות חייה ע״י שנקבצו יחדו ונתקשרו כאחד בבית הכנסת מיוחד אשר כאיש אחד ובלב אחד ימשיכו להתחזק בהתמדת התורה וכונת התפלה ואהבת חברים כבימי קדם. אתה ד׳ תשמרם מכל מכשול ומוקש, ולא יפלו בנופלים ח״ו רק יזכו להגביר חיילים בעבודת ד׳ באורח חיים למעלה למשכיל ולעשות נחת רוח.

והנה עתה עלה על רוחם של אחוזת מהחברים לאסוף בספר מן המאמרים אשר הגדתי בישיבה וגם מה ששמעו ממני בביהכנ״ס מדי שבת בשבתו ומועד במועדו. כי כמה מאמרים נכתבו באר היטב ע״י חברים מקשיבים. וגם ביקשו ממני שאמציא להם ממה שיש אתי בכתבים שרשמתי כשמצאתי פנאי, כדי לחברם על סדר הפרשיות והזמנים.

ועתה אתנצלה נא, שכאשר הציעו לי ענין זה, יראתי מלעמוד במקום גדולים ומחברי חיבורים, ומה לי להסתכן ח״ו וללכת בגדולות ובנפלאות ממני. ומ״מ, כאשר דרכי ב״ה לשאול בעצת רבותי בכל ענין חשוב העומד על הפרק, לכן גם עכשו היתה נפשי בשאלתי לפני חכמי וצדיקי הדור, והם עודדוני וזרזוני והבטיחוני, ועל דעתם הסכמתי להדפסת הספר. ומי כמוני יודע שיש רבים וטובים ממני אשר קטנם עבה ממתני בחכמה ויראה שלא הגיע אליהם שיהיו דבריהם נשמעים לרבים ונכתב בספר. אולם אלה וכאלה הם כבשי דרחמנא ונסתרות שמבראשית. ואין זה תלוי רק בכשרון המעשים, אלא בתפקידו של כל איש ואיש כפי אשר נגזר עליו בספרו של אדה״ר (כדאיתא בב״מ פ״ה ע״ב). ונאמן הוא אלקינו אדון כל הנשמות רבון כל המעשים, שממציא ומזמין לכל נפש ונפש, אופני תיקוניו הפרטיים.

ובהזדמנות זאת אביע תודות להנהלת הישיבה תורה ודעת והמתיבתא, אשר שם גודלתי ונתחנכתי. וכאשר הגעתי אני לפרק האיש מקדש, הגיעו הם לפרק השוכר את הפועלים ומשם פרנסתי ופרנסת אנשי ביתי בגזירת הזן ומפרנס לכל. ויותר אסיר תודה אני להנהלת הישיבה, לרבות ועד הדירקטורים והנהלת משרד הכלכלי אשר עכשו שאין כוחי עתה כבוחי אז, עדיין ממציאים לי את פרנסתי בכבוד ובטובת עין, והכל בחסדי הבורא ית׳ המגלגל זכות ע״י זכאים. תהא משכורתם שלמה, מאת ד׳ אלקי ישראל.

ולך ד׳ החסד כי אתה תשלם לאיש כמעשהו תריק נא טובך ותשפיע חסדך לתת חיים וחסד וחנינה לאיש היקר באנשים הרבני הרודצו״ח זרע קודש מחצבתו ר׳ שמוא׳ יוסף ריעדר נ״י אשר נדבה רוחו אותו לקבל עליו כל ההוצאות של ההדפסה. ברך ד׳ חילו להדרו ולנשאו ולשמרו אותו ואת ביתו מכל צרה וצוקה רח״ל, ויראה נחת יהודי מכל צאצאיו, וימלא ד׳ כל משאלות לבו לטובה.

ואוחילה לבוראי ואשאלה ממנו שיהי׳ הספר הזה לתועלת למעיינים בו לחיזוק באמונה ובייר״ש ובכל מדה נכונה, וימצאו בו דברים המתקבלים, ואבנה גם אנכי ממנה. ותמכתי יתידותי במה שכתוב בס׳ צדקת הצדיק (קמ״ח) שלפעמים יש דברי תורה יקרים בפי מי שהוא. ומי שיש לו שייכות הנפש לדברים כאלו (עיין ספר התניא בהקדמת הרב ז״ל) יהיו הדברים שמחים אצלו בעזה״י.

ויה״ר מלפני הבורא ית׳ שיעזור ויושיע ויגן על כל הכותבים והמסייעים, ואת כל בני חבורתנו ובני ביתם נ״י, ואת כל בית ישראל, ונזכה כולנו לעבוד את הבורא ית׳ באמת ובתמים מתוך שמחה ונחת והרחבה ובאהבה וידידות עד ביאת גואל צדק במהרה בימינו בקרוב.

משה וואלפסאן

A NOTE TO THE READER

In this book, the Hebrew term for prayer, *tefillah,* and Yiddish term, *davening* [to *daven,* etc.], are often used.

Minyan is the quorum of 10 adult Jewish males needed for one's prayers to be considered *tefillah b'tzibbur* (prayer with a congregation).

Table of Contents

PART TWO
Expositions on the Siddur 87

Preface

I cannot adequately express my feelings as, with the help of Hashem, I present this collection of essays on tefillah based on the *shmuessen* (ethical discourses) of my revered rebbi, Harav Moshe Wolfson, שליט"א.

We became his talmidim as young *bachurim* in Mesivta Torah Vodaath, where he serves as *Mashgiach Ruchani*. Ever since, we refer to him with awe and love as "the Mashgiach."

It was the Rosh Yeshivah, Harav Yaakov Kamenetsky, זצ"ל, who took Rav Wolfson from his classroom as a fifth-grade rebbi and appointed him as Mashgiach. Reb Yaakov would later say that this appointment was one of his most important achievements as Rosh Yeshivah of Torah Vodaath.

Talmidim who had the Mashgiach as their rebbi in the second and fifth grade still recall the exceptional love for Hashem and His Torah with which he imbued them. That love was apparent to beis midrash talmidim as well, and continues to influence those who are privileged to learn from him.

In what clearly was an act of *hashgachah* (Divine providence) and a turning point for many talmidim, the Mashgiach was appointed *Mara D'Asra* (spiritual head) of Camp Torah Vodaath in 1969. He guided and expanded the Masmidim program in which many Torah Vodaath *bachurim* devoted a significant part of their summer day to Torah study and teaching. In the relaxed atmosphere of camp, the Mashgiach could convey more than ever the Torah outlook of his rebbi, Rav Shraga Feivel

Mendlowitz, זצ"ל, and inculcate his enormous appreciation for and effort in tefillah. Equally important, camp afforded us the unparalleled opportunity to spend Shabbos with the Mashgiach. We gained a new appreciation for the description of Shabbos as *me'ein Olam Haba,* a semblance of the World to Come.

In the mid-1970s, with the Mashgiach's blessings, a small group of talmidim founded a minyan which met on Shabbos for *Minchah* and *shalosh seudos*. Today, more than 30 years later, Beis Medrash Emunas Yisroel is a spiritual landmark in a neighborhood filled with shuls and *battei midrash*. It has gained renown as a place of impassioned tefillah, and a center of Torah learning, tzedakah, and chesed. It is a place where every Jew feels comfortable and welcome. The chassid davens alongside the Lithuanian scholar and the *baal teshuvah* in unity and mutual respect.

Shabbos in Emunas Yisroel is an especially uplifting experience. In the writings of Kabbalah, *Shalosh Seudos* is referred to as *ra'ava d'ra'avin* (favor of favors), the highest point of the Shabbos, a time when the other-worldy essence of the day is at its peak. After soul-stirring *zemiros*, with the shul enveloped in physical darkness but illuminated by spiritual light, the Mashgiach delivers his hour-long talk on the weekly *parashah*. His discourses weave together all branches of Torah interpretation in a unique way. The total is greater than the sum of its parts. The *shmuess* always concludes with a message that uplifts, a call to strive for greater heights in Torah, tefillah, strengthening of *emunah* and *ahavas Yisrael*, and other crucial concepts.

Many of the Mashgiach's *shmuessen* have been published in his *Sefer Emunas Itecha* on the Torah and festivals. Over the years, talmidim have published collections of his *shmuessen* on *Chumash* and specific topics. *Sefer Tzion V'Areha*, from which some essays in this work's third section are drawn, is devoted to his teachings regarding Eretz Yisrael and its holy cities.[1]

---

1. In 2002 a *talmid*, Rabbi Yehoshua Fieldsteel of Jerusalem, authored *Wellsprings of Faith,* a collection of the Mashgiach's *shmuessen* on *emunah* (faith), published by Feldheim.

The idea to publish the Mashgiach's thoughts on tefillah resulted from the publication of *Sefer VaAni Tefillah*, a collection of the Mashgiach's teachings on prayer published several years ago by Rabbi Moshe Licht, currently of Beitar. A number of the essays in this volume are adapted from that work. Others are based on pieces in *Sefer Emunas Itecha*, *Sefer Tzion V'Areha*, and recordings of *shmuessen* delivered at Mesivta Torah Vodaath and during the Mashgiach's visits to Eretz Yisrael.[2]

It is my sincere hope that this work will inspire its readers to strengthen their own tefillah and, in so doing, strengthen their bond with *Hashem Yisbarach*.

In addition, I hope that the section on Elul and the *Yamim Nora'im* will inspire readers during the season of *teshuvah* and throughout the year as well.

I am deeply grateful to the Mashgiach for granting his blessing to this project and for guiding me as it progressed. In the name of his many talmidim, I thank him for all that he has done for us since our youth, for his guidance, inspiration, and personal example. And I offer a tefillah that Hashem grant him and his rebbetzin, תחי', many years of good health. Many we merit that the Mashgiach continue to teach and inspire until the coming of Mashiach.

I am deeply grateful to many of the Mashgiach's talmidim for their help with this project.

R' Berel Weiss of Los Angeles, R' Yonah and R' Yisroel Blumenfrucht, and R' Hertzy Hasenfeld are the primary sponsors. May they and the other sponsors be repaid manifold for their *hachzakas haTorah* through this and other projects.

Rabbi Shlomo Lezer took time from his busy schedule to review the three sections on tefillah. His observations and contribution of additional teachings of the Mashgiach were invaluable, and I am deeply grateful to him.

Rabbi Mordechai Brown's involvement in the early stages of this project ensured that it would become a reality.

---

2. Tapes, CDs and mp3s of Rav Wolfson's discourses in Yiddish or English can be obtained by contacting Rabbi or Mrs. Vorhand at 718-438-3451 or emunas@thejnet.com.

My thanks to Rabbi Yehudah Horowitz, whose involvement and interest throughout this project was a source of *chizuk.*

My thanks also to the following, whose assistance is very much appreciated: R' Yitzchok Gottdiener, Dr. Avrohom Halle, R' Yechezkel Heimlich, R' Aharon Herzog, R' Yochanan Herzog, Dr. Yosef Gamss, R' Yaakov Goldner, R' Moshe Licht, R' Binyomin Perlman, R' Fishel Schachter, R' Sholom Schneider, and R' Shimshon Weiss.

Since my days as a talmid in Yeshivah Torah Temimah and a camper in Camp Torah Vodaath, I have been fortunate to have Rabbi Nosson Scherman as a mentor, advisor, and close family friend. In the initial stages of this project, he provided crucial guidance on the proper approach in presenting the Mashgiach's *divrei Torah* to the English readership. May the *Ribbono shel Olam* grant Rabbi and Mrs. Scherman many years of good health and much *nachas.*

I cannot adequately thank Rabbi Meir Zlotowitz for the warmth and kindness he has shown me throughout the years. May I offer a *bircas hedyot* that he be granted continued *siyata diShmaya* in his incredible *avodas hakodesh,* and together with Mrs. Zlotowitz enjoy many years of good health with much *nachas.*

My thanks to Rabbi Sheah Brander, whose artistry has enhanced the honor of Torah in our days in a unique way.

Thank you, Avrohom Biderman, for always being there when I need you; and thank you, Mendy Herzberg, for never getting impatient with my frequent questions and requests, and for coordinating the production of this book with your usual patience and professionalism.

My appreciation to Eli Kroen for the beautiful cover; to Sury Englard for her expert paginating; and to the entire staff at ArtScroll/Mesorah.

I have the privilege to teach Torah in Yeshivah Darchei Torah, a great yeshivah headed by great Torah builders. I take this opportunity to express my gratitude to our Rosh HaYeshivah, Rabbi

Yaakov Bender, and to our President, Mr. Ronald Lowinger. May they both continue to see *nachas* from the yeshivah and their families, in good health, for many years to come. Many thanks also to the menahalim of the Junior High Division, Rabbi Dovid Frischman, Rabbi Dovid Presser, and Menahel Emeritus Rabbi Raphael Skaist.

Camp Agudah truly is "Ruach Country," and I am grateful to be able to spend my summers there. I surely speak in the name of the entire camp in expressing my gratitude to *Hashem Yisbarach* that our *Mara D'Asra*, Harav Yisroel Belsky, שליט"א, is back with us this summer and has been delivering *shiurim* and inspiring us as in previous years. May Rabbi Belsky continue his *avodas hakodesh* in good health for many years to come.

My thanks to our Director, Meir Frischman, and the entire devoted head staff. My appreciation to Rabbi Simcha Kaufman, a *"mechanech's mechanech,"* for all that I have learned from him over the years.

This book's publication coincides with the first *yahrtzeit* of my dear father, ר' שמואל אביגדור בן ר' מרדכי אריה הכהן ע"ה. His appreciation for tefillah was an inspiration to all. During the shivah, a neighbor said, "When I was sitting shivah, my wife told me to make sure to unlock the front door extra early for *Shacharis*, because Mr. Finkelman was going to come early — and he did."

He was disabled for many years and walking was extremely difficult for him, but this did not prevent him from being in shul early, both in the morning and evening. Despite the difficulty, he always stood for *chazaras hashatz*. A young man once told me, "Sometimes I'm tired and I want to sit down during *chazaras hashatz*. But then I see your father standing and I say to myself: 'How I can sit when Mr. Finkelman is standing?' "

When my dear mother, מרת פריידא זעלדא רחל בת ר' משה ע"ה, would stand before her Creator in tefillah, even in her kitchen, she was transported to another world. The sight of her davening at her Shabbos candles is forever etched in our minds and hearts.

As a young growing family, we moved to Kensington because my father felt it important to be near the yeshivah where he had learned and which he always loved, Mesivta Torah Vodaath. By attending Torah Vodaath and living in its neighborhood, we were privileged to gain a great deal from the yeshivah and its illustrious rebbeim and roshei yeshivah.

May this book be a *zechus* for the *neshamos* of both my father and mother, ע"ה, and may we merit to go in their ways.

I wish to mention two other yeshivos where I was privileged to learn: Talmudical Academy of Adelphia, New Jersey, where I became a lifelong talmid of Harav Meir Hershkowitz, שליט"א (today Rosh Yeshivah of Yeshivah Bais Binyomin in Stamford); and Beth Medrash Govoha, which was headed by the Rosh Yeshivah and *manhig Yisrael* Harav Shneur Kotler זצ"ל.

My parents-in-law, Mr. and Mrs. Philip Shapiro עמו"ש, teach by example that a person should be happy with his lot and that one can always strive to be even better. May they continue to inspire us, in good health, for many years to come.

Whatever I have merited to accomplish is thanks to my wife, Tova, תחי'. May the *Ribbono shel Olam* bless us with good health and *nachas* for many years to come.

I thank the *Ribbono shel Olam* for permitting me to undertake this project and see it through to completion. May the collective tefillos of the Jewish people break all harmful decrees, silence our enemies, and bring our long-awaited salvation through the coming of Mashiach, speedily and in our time.

Shimon Finkelman
11 Menachem Av 5772

PART ONE

Perspectives *on* Tefillah

CHAPTER ONE

The Essence of Tefillah

With All Your Heart

The Torah commands us to pray every day of our lives, as it is written, וַעֲבַדְתֶּם אֵת ה' אֱלֹקֵיכֶם, *And you shall serve Hashem, your God,*[1] and וּלְעָבְדוֹ בְּכָל לְבַבְכֶם, ... *to serve Him with all your heart.*[2] On this second verse our Sages comment, "What is a 'service of the heart'? This refers to tefillah."[3]

1. *Shemos* 23:25.
2. *Devarim* 11:13.
3. *Taanis* 2a.

The Gemara teaches: The daily tefillos correspond to the daily *korbanos* (sacrifices) offered in the Beis HaMikdash.[4] *Shacharis* and *Minchah* correspond to the *Tamid* offerings; *Maariv* corresponds to the limbs and fats of offerings, which could be placed on the Altar at night.

With regard to *korbanos*, proper *kavanah*, the Kohen's intent when performing the various parts of the service, was most crucial. If while performing the main parts of the service the Kohen intended to eat its meat or burn its sacrificial parts at the wrong time or in the wrong place, the *korban* was disqualified.

With tefillah, too, proper *kavanah* is crucial. As we find in *Shulchan Aruch*:

> *Tefillah is in place of the korban. Therefore, one must be careful that it be similar to a korban with regard to kavanah. One's mind should not be occupied with foreign thoughts, just as foreign thoughts disqualified a korban.*[5]

When we pray with proper *kavanah*, we are assured that our tefillos will be accepted. As Talmud Yerushalmi comments to the verse תָּכִין לִבָּם תַּקְשִׁיב אָזְנֶךָ, *May You guide their heart, let Your ear be attentive*:[6] "If you focused your heart on your prayer, you will be informed that your prayer was accepted."[7]

According to the strict letter of the law, the Rabbinic mitzvah to daven thrice daily is fulfilled even through mere "lip service," that is, by reciting the words of the *Shemoneh Esrei* even while one's thoughts are elsewhere. And it is likely that such prayer does accomplish somewhat in Heaven. However, to fulfill the Torah's mitzvah of וּלְעָבְדוֹ בְּכָל לְבַבְכֶם, *and to serve Him with all* ***your heart****,* *kavanah* is essential, for tefillah without *kavanah* is not a "service of the heart."[8] As *Sefer Chovos Halevavos* expresses it: Tefillah

4. *Berachos* 26b.

5. *Shulchan Aruch, Orach Chaim* 98:4.

6. *Tehillim* 10:17.

7. *Yerushalmi Berachos* 5:5.

8. Therefore, our Sages teach that in order to fulfill the Torah's mitzvah, one must focus

without *kavanah* is like a body without a soul.[9]

We, the generation of *Ikvesa D'Meshicha*, the period preceding Mashiach's arrival,[10] possess lowly *neshamos* (souls) in comparison to earlier generations. Hashem loves us very much and He judges us according to our limited abilities and understanding. Some 500 ago the Arizal told his prime *talmid*, R' Chaim Vital, "Your [comparatively] minor service of Hashem is more precious to Him than the service of the Sages of the Mishnah. They possessed exceedingly great *neshamos*, but what more can be expected of us?" Thus it is possible that in our generation, we are accomplishing more in Heaven than the spiritually awesome generations of the past.

Nevertheless, if we wish to fulfill the great mitzvah of וּלְעָבְדוֹ בְּכָל לְבַבְכֶם, we must make tefillah a true service of the heart, not mere lip service.

A Time for Dveikus

When a Jew prays with *kavanah,* he is, in essence, saying to Hashem: "You are the God of my salvation; You and only You can grant me that which I need." In this way, one has not only fulfilled the mitzvah of tefillah, he has also made his tefillah a vehicle for *dveikus*, attachment to Hashem. In fact, the root of the word *tefillah* means *attachment*, as we find in the Gemara.[11] When

---

on the meaning of the words for at least the first blessing of *Shemoneh Esrei;* otherwise he must repeat *Shemoneh Esrei.* However, as *Rema* writes, already in his time the custom was not to repeat *Shemoneh Esrei,* for it is quite possible that the second time the person will again not have proper *kavanah*, and his repetition will have been for naught.

9. *Shaar Cheshbon HaNefesh* ch. 3.

10. The term *"Ikvesa D'Meshicha"* (lit. *The Footsteps of Mashiach*) is taken from the final mishnah in *Masechta Sotah.*

As Rav Wolfson has mentioned on various occasions, the Chofetz Chaim stated that *Ikvesa D'Meshicha* had already begun in his time. How long this period will last is not known. As we say in the twelfth *Ani Maamin* (the Thirteen Principles of Jewish Faith): "... and even though he (Mashiach) may delay (in coming), nevertheless, I anticipate every day that he will come."

11. See *Kesubos* 62b, רוצה אשה בקב ותפלות.

one stands before Hashem and pours out his heart in tefillah, he merits to draw closer to Him, thereby fulfilling the mitzvah of וּבוֹ תִדְבָּק, *and to Him you shall cleave.*[12]

Zohar teaches that the 613 mitzvos are actually 613 *eitzos*, methods, through which we can fulfill וּבוֹ תִדְבָּק and achieve *dveikus baShem*. Through proper tefillah, a Jew merits the ultimate purpose of all 613 mitzvos.

Drawing closer to Hashem should be our primary goal when we daven. Yes, we have our personal and communal needs, and these needs motivate us to stand before Hashem in tefillah in the hope that our requests will be accepted and our prayers answered. But attaining these needs should not be our primary goal. If this *is* our primary goal, then we are like "servants who serve their Master for the purpose of gaining reward," which is not the ideal way of serving Hashem.[13]

The fact that we have needs provides us with an opportunity to speak to our Creator. And Hashem, from His lofty place on High, turns His attention to us as we turn our hearts towards Him and pray. When we daven, we should bear in mind the words of Dovid HaMelech: וַאֲנִי קִרְבַת אֱלֹהִים לִי טוֹב, *But as for me, closeness to God is for me good.*[14]

What we have said is hinted to in the words of *Hallel*, where Dovid says:

> אָהַבְתִּי, *I love to pray. Why?*
> כִּי יִשְׁמַע ה' אֶת קוֹלִי תַּחֲנוּנָי, *for Hashem hears my voice, my supplications.*
> *Furthermore . . .*
> כִּי הִטָּה אָזְנוֹ לִי, *for He has inclined His ear to me, He turns to hear my personal tefillah and give it His undivided attention.*
> *This alone gives me sufficient reason to love to pray.*

12. *Devarim* 10:20.
13. See *Avos* 1:3.
14. *Tehillim* 73:28.

Dovid declares: יִשְׂמַח לֵב מְבַקְשֵׁי ה׳, *Those who seek Hashem will be happy of heart.*[15] Some interpret: Those who seek Hashem through tefillah are happy because of the closeness to Hashem that this brings them. Prayer brings joy to their hearts more than anything else in the world.

In a similar vein, Dovid said, כִּי טוֹב חַסְדְּךָ מֵחַיִּים שְׂפָתַי יְשַׁבְּחוּנְךָ, which literally means, *For Your kindness is better than life, my lips shall praise You.*[16] *Binah L'Itim* interprets it this way: כִּי טוֹב חַסְדְּךָ מֵחַיִּים — *What is the greatest kindness of all that You, Hashem, have granted me in my life?* שְׂפָתַי יְשַׁבְּחוּנְךָ — *the fact that You allow me to praise You as I turn my heart to You in prayer.*

An Inestimable *Zechus*

Maharal writes:

> *With tefillah, a person demonstrates that he is dependent upon Hashem, Blessed is He ... the whole concept of tefillah is an expression of man's utter dependency upon Him, that he has no means of existence on his own but only through Him, and this is why he prays to Him. When a person expresses this dependency [through tefillah], it is as if he is drawing close to Him, for whenever one is dependent upon another, he is given over and drawn close to him.*[17]

It is a great *zechus* (source of merit) to be able to come close to Hashem, to speak to Him and to beseech Him.

Consider: If someone had the opportunity to speak with a head of state, a king or a president, would he not be gripped by excitement and emotion? How infinitely greater is our opportunity three times each day to speak to the King of kings. And not only can we speak with Him during these fixed times; rather, *every time we lack something*, no matter how small — for example, if

15. *Tehillim* 105:3.

16. Ibid. 63:4.

17. *Nesivos Olam, Nesiv HaAvodah*, ch. 3.

one reaches into his pocket and cannot find his keys — we have the opportunity and the *zechus* to speak to and pray to Hashem. No words can adequately describe this opportunity that Hashem has granted us.

Unique Among Creations

The Torah states: כִּי מִי גוֹי גָּדוֹל אֲשֶׁר לוֹ אֱלֹהִים קְרֹבִים אֵלָיו כַּה' אֱלֹהֵינוּ בְּכָל קָרְאֵנוּ אֵלָיו.[18] R' Samson Raphael Hirsch translates: *Which is a great nation? One to whom God is close, like Hashem, our God, whenever we call to Him.*[19] This is the greatness of the Jewish people, that we can call to Hashem in prayer whenever we desire, and Hashem always listens. Hashem is always close to us, watching over us and providing us with our needs.

If prior to tefillah we would give serious thought to the incredible *zechus* of being able to stand before our Father in Heaven in prayer, then we would daven with genuine הִשְׁתַּפְּכוּת הַנֶּפֶשׁ, *outpouring of emotion,* and would truly fulfill the mitzvah of וּבוֹ תִדְבָּק, *and to Him you shall cleave.*

Is there anything sweeter than this? There is no physical pleasure on this earth than can compare to the pleasure of standing before Hashem in heartfelt tefillah.

As R' Eliezer Azikri says in his *Yedid Nefesh*:

> יֶעֱרַב לוֹ יְדִידוֹתֶיךָ מִנֹּפֶת צוּף וְכָל טָעַם.
> *To him [the Jew] Your friendship will be sweeter than the dripping of honeycomb and any taste.*

A Jew must tell himself: "My intimate connection with Hashem is sweeter than any pleasure that this world has to offer. Even if the request for which I have prayed is not granted to me, I still derive enormous pleasure from the relationship that I have forged with Him through my tefillah."

---

18. *Devarim* 4:7.

19. The standard translation is: *For which is a great nation that has a God Who is close to it, as is Hashem, our God, whenever we call to Him?*

In *Akdamus,* which we recite on Shavuos morning, we distinguish between the song of the Heavenly angels and that of the Jewish people. There are angels who are permitted to sing *shirah* but once in their lifetime, while a Jew can sing whenever he so desires.

In *Perek Shirah* we learn that every creature in the universe sings its own unique song to its Creator. Animals, beasts, birds, and vegetation; the oceans, the heavens, the luminaries and constellations all praise the One Above. But their song, too, is restricted to a specific time. Not so the song of the Jewish people. Whenever we wish, we can call out to Hashem with any of ten variations of prayer,[20] and ask for whatever our hearts desire.

In the *zemiros* of Shabbos eve, we sing: שְׁבָחִין אֲסַדֵּר צַפְרָא וְרַמְשָׁא, *Praise shall I prepare morning and evening.* The word צַפְרָא, *morning,* is related to the word צִפּוֹר, *bird*, for bird life awakens in the morning and its chirping is its way of singing *shirah* to Hashem. The word רַמְשָׁא, *evening,* is related to רֶמֶשׂ, *crawling creature,* for many crawling creatures creep out of their crevices in the evening, and that is when they sing their *shirah.* And so on Shabbos we sing: We, the Jewish people, are not bound by specific times in our praise of our Creator; rather, *praise I shall prepare both morning and evening.* We, as opposed to other creations, can call out to Hashem whenever we so desire.

The Heart and the Fruit

Sefer HaKuzari refers to the three times each day when we recite *Shemoneh Esrei* as "the heart of one's day and its fruit." Tefillah is the "heart" of one's day, for it is through tefillah that the remaining hours of our day are energized and granted meaning. And it is the "fruit" of one's day, because the ultimate purpose of our service of Hashem is to attach ourselves to Him, and we accomplish this when we stand before Him in heartfelt prayer.

---

20. *Midrash Rabbah* (*Parashas Va'eschanan*) lists ten different words in *Tanach* that represent ten variations of tefillah.

In a letter, the eighteenth-century luminary R' Yonason Eibeschutz wrote:

> *Most of the time, the congregation is reciting [the concluding] Kaddish following Aleinu while I am still praying the Shemoneh Esrei. Though the younger people laugh and scorn me, I am willing to bear insult, for this — the hour when I stand with my mind properly focused before the One Who listens to prayer — is my reward for all my endeavors.*

These words are cause for thought. R' Yonason authored a classic work on *Shulchan Aruch* and other scholarly works. He was an outstanding *gaon* in a generation of great scholars, he disseminated Torah to scores of *talmidim,* and guided the masses. Yet, he described the time he set aside for tefillah as חֶלְקִי מִכָּל עֲמָלִי, *my reward for all my endeavors.*

Incomparable

A chassid once came to the Beis Aharon of Karlin and reported something unusual. The local *poritz* (gentile landowner) had been gripped by a desire to go sledding. The problem was that this happened in July, when there was no snow on the ground.

No matter. The *poritz's* servants knew that "what the *poritz* wants, the *poritz* gets," or else they would suffer the consequences. The only "snow substitute" that they could find was sugar, which was so prohibitively expensive at the time that most people could not afford to put a teaspoonful in their tea.

The *poritz's* men purchased hundreds of sacks of sugar, spread the precious grains out across a large area, hitched a sled to two white stallions, and the *poritz* went sledding on that sugar. "Isn't it something?" the chassid asked the Beis Aharon. "The *poritz* can get whatever earthly pleasure he desires."

The Beis Aharon was not impressed. "You call that pleasure? I assure you that whatever pleasure the *poritz* had from his sledding does not in any way compare to the pleasure I derive from reciting *Nishmas* on Shabbos morning!"

The holy *tzaddik* R' Moshe Leib Sassover devoted himself to the mitzvah of *pidyon shevuyim* (redeeming captives). Once, R' Moshe Leib was in the midst of a three-day fast when he visited a *poritz* in the hope of redeeming a Jewish captive. At the time, the *poritz* and his friends were enjoying a lavish feast; a non-kosher delicacy, valued at some 800 *reinush,* was brought out which emitted a most delicious aroma. The aroma awakened a craving in R' Moshe Leib which, coupled with his fasting, endangered his very life. The halachah would have permitted the tzaddik to partake of the food rather than die.

However, moments later R' Moshe Leib had quelled his craving and the danger passed. He later said that as he felt himself being overcome by the aroma, he pictured himself standing in shul on Shabbos morning, reciting *Nishmas* with an outpouring of emotion. This pleasure far surpassed any earthly enjoyment and caused his craving for the food to dissipate.

A Crucial Battle

The Gemara states: "Whoever is greater than his fellow, his *yetzer hara* (evil inclination) is greater than his fellow's as well."[21] The Vilna Gaon teaches that the same applies to mitzvos; the greater the mitzvah, the greater the *yetzer hara* to not perform that mitzvah properly. As we have stated above, through tefillah, one merits to attach himself to his Creator in a most profound way, thereby fulfilling the mitzvah of וּבוֹ תִדְבָּק, which is the essential purpose of all mitzvos. Therefore, the Satan expends enormous effort in an attempt to prevent us from praying properly.

21. *Succah* 52a.

On the verse כְּרוּם זֻלּוּת לִבְנֵי אָדָם our Sages comment, "These are the things that stand at the pinnacle *(rum)* of the world, but which people treat lightly *(mezalzelin)*."[22] *Rashi* states that this refers to tefillah.

We all know how true this is. It is astounding to observe certain people's reactions when observing other Jews dedicating themselves to a particular area of *avodas Hashem*. They extol the virtues of the great *talmid chacham* who devotes himself to Torah study with great diligence. They have the highest praise for the great philanthropist who dispenses *tzedakah* with an open hand. And yet, when someone davens with genuine devotion, enunciating each word slowly and carefully, he is sometimes derided as a "*frumak*" (excessively pious one), though tefillah is one of those activities that "stand at the pinnacle of the world."

The Gemara states: "Whoever disgraces garments will ultimately not benefit from them."[23] Dovid HaMelech cut off the corner of Shaul HaMelech's garment; therefore, in Dovid's old age, garments could not provide his body with warmth.[24] As stated in holy writings, the same applies to tefillah. Those who take a light approach to tefillah will not merit to experience the immense pleasure that can be derived from it.

Developing a Taste

Everyone has within himself the ability to derive genuine pleasure from tefillah. One must approach the daily tefillos of *Shacharis, Minchah,* and *Maariv* with seriousness, investing them with all his spiritual strength. And he must not rush through the davening. If he will do this consistently and not give in to despair, then little by little he will begin to experience the immense sweetness of tefillah.

22. *Berachos* 6b.
23. Ibid. 62b.
24. *Melachim I* 1:1.

This can be likened to someone who is given a taste of a superior-quality wine. Being unfamiliar with good wine, he spits it out; to his inexperienced palate, the taste is bitter. He is offered another sample and then another, and little by little, he develops a taste for it.

The same holds true for tefillah. If one is persistent in praying slowly and with feeling, then little by little, he will develop a genuine taste for it.

Requirements

It is vital that one prays with a *minyan* that accords proper respect for tefillah, whose members pray with feeling and do not engage in conversation or other disruptions during prayers. It is also important to set aside time to ponder and learn about the greatness of tefillah and to study the meaning of the various tefillos.

In summation: Tefillah has to be of major importance in one's life. We need to view it as something crucial to our very existence, as something that shields us from all harm, both physical and spiritual, as something that brings us before the very Throne of Hashem. As *Rambam* writes: "What is the proper *kavanah* one should have [during tefillah]? He should purge his heart of all foreign thoughts and picture himself as if he were standing before the *Shechinah*."[1]

---

1. *Hilchos Tefillah* 4:16.

CHAPER TWO

Tefillah: An Expression of Faith

Of the ten *nisyonos* (spiritual tests) with which Hashem tested Avraham Avinu, the final and greatest one was the *Akeidah*. Avraham was asked to take his precious son Yitzchak and offer him as a sacrifice. This test challenged Avraham's faith in Hashem, for had not Hashem promised him "*... for through Yitzchak will offspring be considered yours*"?[1]

Similarly, in *Ikvesa D'Meshicha,* the period leading to Mashiach's arrival, the primary test is the challenge to our *emunah,* our faith.

1. *Bereishis* 21:12.

The Gemara informs us[2] that as the spiritual level of the Jewish people declined, the prophets instructed the people to focus on a few specific mitzvos as a springboard to proper observance of the entire Torah. Yeshayahu focused on 11 mitzvos, then Michah focused on three, until the prophet Chavakuk came along and taught that one mitzvah is the foundation of the entire Torah: *"And a tzaddik lives by his faith."*[3] And the very same Chavakuk teaches us the importance of prayer: *"A tefillah of Chavakuk HaNavi for erroneous utterance."*[4] *Radak* notes that in a number of ways, Chavakuk's tefillah parallels the style of Dovid's psalms in *Sefer Tehillim* — the only place in all of *Tanach* where such parallels are found. Chavakuk teaches us to have faith, and to give expression to our faith through sincere, heartfelt tefillah.

A Declaration of Faith

Rabbeinu Yonah writes[5] that sincere tefillah, as opposed to mere "lip service," is an expression of one's faith in Hashem. Tefillah is a testimony that He and only He has the all-encompassing power to fulfill our needs. Only Hashem can grant us our requests, only He can bestow upon us a flow of blessing and success, only He can grant us life and healing. This is the essence of *emunah.* When one prays as he should, he is declaring, "I believe with perfect faith that the Creator is all-powerful and that only He can fulfill my every need."

In a famous piece, *Ramban* writes that every time a Jew performs a mitzvah, he is in essence declaring his faith in the One Who commanded that mitzvah. *Ramban* then makes a statement regarding tefillah:

> *And the purpose of raising one's voice in tefillah and the purpose of battei knessios (synagogues) and communal*

2. *Makkos* 23b.

3. *Chavakuk* 2:4.

4. Ibid 3:2.

5. *Berachos* 4b ד"ה איזהו.

prayer is this: that people should have a place where they can gather and acknowledge to God that He created them and caused them to be, and where they can publicize this and declare, "We are Your creations!"[6]

Doing Battle With Amalek

In the Torah, the Tribe of Don appears to be most inferior. While Don led one of the *degalim* (the tribal formations in the Wilderness), its division brought up the rear as the Jews marched from one encampment to another: דֶּגֶל מַחֲנֵה דָן ... לָאַחֲרֹנָה יִסְעוּ לְדִגְלֵיהֶם, *The division of the camp of Don ... they shall be the last to journey according to their divisions.*[7] The Midrash relates that members of Don were expelled by the Clouds of Glory because of their sins, and it was these Jews whom Amalek was able to attack soon after the Jews left Egypt. The city of Don in Eretz Yisrael was a place of idol worship from the days of the wicked king Yeravam ben Nevat.

If all the generations since the giving of the Torah are likened to *shevatim* (tribes), then we, the generation of *Ikvesa D'Meshicha,* are the *shevet Don* of Jewish history. We are spiritually impoverished, consumed by our troubles and by distractions which we bring upon ourselves, wittingly and unwittingly. We find it very hard to express a word of tefillah with proper intent, to comprehend a passage of Gemara with our minds fully focused.

And just as Don was attacked by Amalek early in our people's history, so it is in our times.

The primary goal of Amalek is to weaken our *emunah,* our faith in Hashem. The first war with Amalek was preceded by the Jews asking, הֲיֵשׁ ה' בְּקִרְבֵּנוּ אִם אָיִן, *"Is Hashem in our midst or not?"*[8] It has been noted in holy writings that the word עֲמָלֵק has the same *gematria* as סָפֵק (*doubt* — 240).

6. *Ramban, Shemos* 13:16.

7. *Bamidbar* 2:25,31.

8. *Shemos* 17:7.

In a Torah scroll, there are a few letters which according to our tradition should be written oversized. The Chasam Sofer teaches that in the world of *gematria,* an oversized letter is equal to four times that letter's standard *gematria.* In the verse שְׁמַע יִשְׂרָאֵל ה' אֱלֹהֵינוּ ה' אֶחָד, the letters ע and ד are oversized. Thus, the *gematria* of this verse, a Jew's declaration of faith, is equal to וַיָּבֹא עֲמָלֵק וַיִּלָּחֶם עִם יִשְׂרָאֵל בִּרְפִידִם, *And Amalek came and did battle with Yisrael at Rephidim* (1,340).[9] For Amalek's goal is to place doubts in a Jew's heart, to cloud his *emunah* and weaken his belief in the One and Only God.

In our days, the world at large is steeped in heresy, with widespread denial of Hashem's existence, ר"ל, and of His involvement in our affairs. It is a world of immorality, a sin which, more than others, clouds one's *emunah* and erects a barrier between one's *neshamah* and Hashem. Truly, our generation is facing an onslaught by Amalek of epic proportions.

The happenings in the physical world often mirror that which transpires in the spiritual world. The modern world is concerned as never before with air pollution and other forms of damage to the atmosphere. This is reflective of the spiritual pollution that permeates the atmosphere of today's sinful world. It is a primary reason why so many today are beset by *sfeikos be'emunah*, doubts in matters of faith.

The unique mission of our generation is to repel these attacks and vanquish our spiritual foe. *Shevet Don* is referred to in the Torah as מְאַסֵּף לְכָל הַמַּחֲנֹת, *the gatherer for all the camps.*[10] These words have the same *gematria* as וְיָצָא חֹטֶר מִגֶּזַע יִשָׁי, *A staff will emerge from the stump of Yishai* (764)[11] — a reference to Mashiach. It is our lowly generation, the *Shevet Don* of Jewish history, that will ultimately prevail against the Satan's onslaughts, and in so doing merit the Final Redemption.

---

9. *Shemos* 17:8.

10. *Bamidbar* 10:25. They traveled in the rear and gathered all lost objects (*Rashi*).

11. *Yeshayahu* 11:1.

Illuminate Your Words

Hashem commanded Noach, צֹהַר תַּעֲשֶׂה לַתֵּיבָה, *A window shall you make for the Ark.*[12] The word תֵּיבָה, *ark,* can also mean *word.* The Baal Shem Tov interprets these words to mean: *Illuminate your words of prayer.* He interprets the verse בֹּא אַתָּה וְכָל בֵּיתְךָ אֶל הַתֵּיבָה[13] in a similar way: *Enter the words of prayer with every fiber of your being.* Gather in all your spiritual strength, concentrate on the meaning of the words, and pray with feeling. In this way one can overcome the impurity of Amalek and be saved from the deluge of sin and heresy that fills the world in our days.

The verse וַיָּבֹא עֲמָלֵק וַיִּלָּחֶם עִם יִשְׂרָאֵל בִּרְפִידִם[14] is also numerically equal to בֹּא אַתָּה וְכָל בֵּיתְךָ אֶל הַתֵּיבָה, for it is through heartfelt tefillah that we can preserve our *emunah* and overcome Amalek's onslaught.

The Little Things in Life

Tefillah need not be limited to the daily prayers established by our Sages. One can communicate with his Creator any time of day; doing so is a powerful declaration of faith that everything in life is in Hashem's hands.

The chassidic master R' Nachum of Chernobyl was renowned for his greatness in Torah and piety. He was in a constant state of *dveikus,* intense attachment to Hashem.

Once, his *talmidim* found him at prayer in a corner of his study. They approached him stealthily, and without his realizing it, bent their ears to hear what he was saying. "Master of the Universe," he pleaded, "the maid who assists my rebbetzin wishes to leave. We need her to remain at her post. Please, Hashem, instill within her a change of heart so that she does not leave."

12. *Bereishis* 6:16.

13. Lit., *Come, you and your entire household, to the Ark.*

14. Above, we noted that the *gematria* of this verse is equal to that of שְׁמַע יִשְׂרָאֵל ה' אֱלֹהֵינוּ ה' אֶחָד.

R' Nachum's *talmidim* were stunned. Later they asked him, "*Rebbi*, you, whose mind and heart are totally preoccupied with Torah and *dveikus* — how can you approach *HaKadosh Baruch Hu* with such a mundane request?"

R' Nachum's response was honest and simple: "To whom else should I turn if not the One Above?"

To ask something small and comparatively insignificant of Hashem is in fact the very pinnacle of *emunah*. To demonstrate that one believes that Hashem is not only All-Powerful, but also the One Who accomplishes anything and everything, is to show that one's faith in Hashem is complete.

It is possible that R' Nachum's primary purpose in uttering that tefillah was not that the maid should stay at her post. Rather, he saw the problem with the maid as an opportunity to express his faith in Hashem and he seized the moment. It was as if he were saying: "Master of the Universe: You are All-Powerful, and You are the One Who accomplishes everything that happens in this world. You direct every occurrence both big and small, and sustain all creatures from the largest to the smallest — even a tiny ant crawling underneath a stone benefits from Your watchful Eye. And I know that, ultimately, whether or not our maid will leave is in Your hands."

Destroy the "Serpent"

Tikkunei Zohar states:

> *A [Heavenly] announcement issues forth every day: "Whoever will kill that serpent will receive as a reward the king's daughter" — a reference to tefillah.*[15]

The "serpent" is a reference to the *yetzer hara*. Heaven will not permit someone who is enslaved to his *yetzer hara,* who pursues the physical pleasures of this world, to experience a proper, uplifting tefillah. "You are far removed from this experience," Heaven

15. *Tikkunei Zohar, Tikun* 13, p. 29b.

tells such a person, "and you are not deserving of this. You bring with you the 'serpent' and it does not permit you to enter [the world of *dveikus* that proper tefillah engenders]. First, destroy the serpent, minimize your attachment to earthly passions, do not be consumed by all that this lowly world has to offer — then you will be fit to attain proper tefillah."

This is especially true regarding the sin of פְּגַם הַבְּרִית, when one's mind is occupied with immoral thoughts, ר"ל. One who allows himself to be afflicted with this sin will lose any desire he may have had for tefillah; his davening will be devoid of feeling, of *dveikus*, and will not be accepted in Heaven.

This sin clouds one's *emunah* and can cause him to be afflicted with *sfeikos,* doubts, in matters of faith, for בִּלְבּוּל הַמַּחְשָׁבָה, intellectual confusion, is often caused by פְּגַם הַבְּרִית.

By contrast, the greatest reward for שְׁמִירַת הַבְּרִית, keeping one's eyes pure and mind free of immoral thoughts, is clarity of *emunah*. And Zohar teaches that one who vanquishes his *yetzer hara* in this all-important area is granted the ability to pray warm, heartfelt tefillos and to experience a true, spiritual pleasure when he prays.

A Pure Mouth

Another condition needed for proper tefillah is that one's mouth be spiritually pure. When one merits proper tefillah, he enters the Heavenly *Kodesh HaKodashim* and comes directly before Hashem. A mouth that speaks *lashon hara*, that discusses *machlokes*, or that speaks disrespectfully of *talmidei chachamim* will be prevented from entering the spiritual chambers of tefillah in Gan Eden. One who is in the habit of speaking *lashon hara* is in essence a *metzora*[16], who must leave his place of residence and remain in isolation until he repents and is cured of his *tzaraas*.[17]

16. Someone stricken with the Divine punishment of *tzaraas*, a skin disease, often due to the sin of *lashon hara*. See *Vayikra* ch. 13.

17. The Chofetz Chaim writes that the Torah and tefillah of a *baal lashon hara* are enveloped by a *ruach hatumah* that prevent them from ascending to Heaven. He further

Some claim that it has always been the way of chassidim to poke fun and tease one another. Nothing could be further from the truth. The early generations of chassidim enjoyed true brotherly love and mutual respect for one another. They would never have dreamed of saying something that might have hurt another's feelings.

It is not only tefillah that suffers when one is a *baal lashon hara.* One cannot merit a true attachment to Torah if his speech is not pure. For the Oral Torah is inscribed upon the lips of those who utter it, provided that those lips are pure. Doeg HaAdomi, who slandered Dovid before Shaul HaMelech,[18] is a tragic example of someone whose corrupt speech neutralized the power of his vast Torah knowledge. This is why our Sages refer to Doeg's Torah as being מִשָּׂפָה וּלְחוּץ, *from the lips and outward.*[19] His Torah knowledge was *not* inscribed upon his lips; it remained in his intellect, like any secular wisdom.

Two Covenants

Holy writings, citing *Sefer HaYetzirah*, see a deep connection between פְּגַם הַבְּרִית, immoral behavior and thought, and פְּגַם הַלָּשׁוֹן, corruption of one's power of speech. There is a form of improper speech which our Sages refer to as אֲבַק לָשׁוֹן הָרַע (lit. *the dust of lashon hara*).[20] The word אֲבַק is an acronym for **אוֹת בְּרִית קוֹדֶשׁ** *(a sign of the holy covenant)*, a reference to *bris milah.* Purity of speech along with *shemiras habris*, protecting the purity of one's eyes, ears, and intellect, are crucial for proper *emunah* and tefillah.

The connection between these two "covenants" can be seen from Yosef HaTaddik. When Yosef revealed himself to his

---

writes that even though after the *Churban Beis HaMikdash, baalei lashon hara* are no longer stricken with *tzaraas*, this only applies to the body. The *baal lashon hara's* soul is tainted with *tzaaras* even today.

18. See *Shmuel I,* ch. 22.

19. *Sanhedrin* 106b.

20. This refers to statements that either imply *lashon hara* or can lead to *lashon hara.*

brothers, they wondered in what merit he had risen to become leader of Egypt and sustainer of the entire world.[21]

He gave them two answers. The first was that despite being alone in Egypt for 22 years, he never compromised his high moral standards.[22]

His second answer was, "כִּי פִי הַמְדַבֵּר אֲלֵיכֶם, *that it is my mouth that is speaking to you,*"[23] which our Sages interpret to mean that Yosef spoke to them in *Lashon Hakodesh.* This does not mean that Yosef spoke to them in Hebrew. As *Ramban* points out, there were others outside of the family of Yaakov who knew Hebrew in those days. Yosef meant that his manner of speech was *kodesh*, sacred. It was the manner of speech used by *tzaddikim*, a manner of speech from which Pharaoh and his Egyptian populace were far removed. Yosef, in his lonely years as a slave and then a monarch in Egypt, zealously upheld the twin covenants of morality and speech, and through this he merited *malchus*, monarchy.

The level of spiritual purity we maintain has a profound effect on the quality of our tefillah. At times, a person may experience a wonderful, uplifting davening, a moment when he perceives וַאֲנִי קִרְבַת אֱלֹהִים לִי טוֹב, *But as for me, closeness to Hashem is for me good.*[24] And he wonders: "What did I do to merit this?" The holy *sefarim* write: It may be that on that day, or those that preceded it, he experienced a *nisayon* (spiritual test) in *shemiras einayim* (protecting one's eyes), *shemiras habris,* or *lashon hara*, and he prevailed. He destroyed the serpent, and received the King's daughter as a reward.

Our generation, with the difficult spiritual tests it faces, is very beloved to Hashem.[25] The generation that left the Egyptian exile

---

21. See Zohar, *Bereishis* 93b.

22. This is what *Rashi* means in stating that Yosef showed them he was circumcised (*Bereishis* 45:4). It cannot be taken literally, for many gentiles, including all descendants of Yishmael and Keturah, were circumcised.

23. *Bereishis* 45:12.

24. *Tehillim* 73:28.

25. See "A Unique Generation in Unique Times" (Appendix A) in this volume.

experienced great, open miracles. Of them, the Torah proclaims: וַיּוֹשַׁע ה' בַּיּוֹם הַהוּא אֶת יִשְׂרָאֵל..., *On that day, Hashem saved Yisrael...*[26] We live in a time when Hashem conceals Himself, yet we have faith that every day He performs hidden miracles, for ourselves individually and for our people collectively. We, too, merit the proclamation ... וַיּוֹשַׁע ה' בַּיּוֹם הַהוּא אֶת יִשְׂרָאֵל ..., though in a hidden sense.

There is another place where Scripture uses the term בַּיּוֹם הַהוּא, *on that day. "He shall say* ***on that day****, 'Behold! — this is our God, we hoped to Him and He saved us; this is Hashem to Whom we hoped, let us exult and be glad in His salvation.'* "[27] When Mashiach comes, we will exult as God reveals Himself to all, and we will be able to say that He is the One to Whom we turned our hearts with faith as we prayed, even in the darkest of times.

26. *Shemos* 14:30.
27. *Yeshayahu* 25:9.

CHAPTER THREE

Toiling in Tefillah

כָּל עַצְמוֹתַי תֹּאמַרְנָה ה׳ מִי כָמוֹךָ.

All my limbs will say, "Hashem, who is like You?"[1]

As we have already mentioned, the mitzvah of tefillah is derived from the verses וַעֲבַדְתֶּם אֵת ה׳ אֱלֹהֵיכֶם, *And you shall serve Hashem, your God,*[2] and וּלְעָבְדוֹ בְּכָל לְבַבְכֶם, *... to serve Him with all your heart.*[3] The term עֲבוֹדָה, which we have translated as *service*, also means *work*. To truly derive from tefillah the great benefits it has to offer, one must be prepared to work, to toil and invest much physical and mental effort in his davening.

1. *Tehillim* 35:10.
2. *Shemos* 23:25.
3. *Devarim* 11:13.

It is well known that the Chazon Ish toiled in Torah to the very limits of his physical strength. His close *talmid*, R' Shlomo Kohen, said of him, "As was his Torah study, so was his tefillah. His prayers pierced the Heavens. The strength and intensity with which he prayed was superhuman."[4]

Another *talmid* of the Chazon Ish, R' Meir Greineman, recalled, "His *Pesukei D'Zimrah* was said in a sweet tone, with intense feeling. Praiseworthy are the eyes that witnessed this!"

Every Tefillah a *Ne'ilah*

When we think of *Ne'ilah*, the concluding prayer of Yom Kippur, we think of the most intense, heartfelt prayers of the year. At that auspicious time, everyone, despite weakness from a day of fasting and prayer, cries out in a raised voice from the depths of his heart.

On the morning of *Shabbos Shirah*, many shuls observe the custom of reciting *Az Yashir* verse by verse, in unison. It is a joyous, uplifting experience.

However, we should not relegate impassioned tefillah to special occasions such as *Ne'ilah* or *Shabbos Shirah*. Every tefillah can be an emotional, uplifting experience. One's goal should be to make every tefillah, every day, a semblance of his Yom Kippur *Ne'ilah*, and his daily *Az Yashir* in *Shacharis* like that of *Shabbos Shirah*.

In the chassidic court of R' Menachem Mendel of Kotzk,[5] mundane matters had virtually no importance. Serving Hashem was all that mattered. On a Yom Kippur eve, a visitor overheard one of the Rebbe's disciples ask another, "What time is *Maariv*?"

The visitor was upset. "What do you mean, '*Maariv*'?" he demanded. "You should say, 'What time is *Kol Nidrei*'? Tonight is not just any *Maariv*!"

4. The Chazon Ish wrote in a letter: "How wondrous it is that a person has the ability to speak his concerns to the Master of the Universe, Blessed is His Name, as when one person speaks to another ..." (*Kovetz Igros Chazon Ish*, II:#2).

5. 1787-1859.

The disciple responded, "Here, a *Maariv* on a regular weekday is like *Kol Nidrei* on Yom Kippur eve."

True, we are not on the spiritual level of the Kotzker and his disciples; nor do we approach the greatness of the Chazon Ish. Nevertheless, we should strive to make every tefillah an intense, uplifting experience.

Daven Slowly

To pray properly, it is necessary to prepare oneself mentally beforehand. It is also vital that one set aside sufficient time for his prayers so that he can concentrate properly, and hopefully merit to pray with הִשְׁתַּפְּכוּת הַנֶּפֶשׁ, *outpouring of emotion.*

Rokeach[6] writes that one should enunciate the words of tefillah as carefully as one would count money, concentrating intently and being careful not to rush his words. Certainly, one should not treat tefillah with any less care and concern than he would accord his money! Anyone who truly derives pleasure from tefillah will not rush through it. To the contrary, he will tell himself, "I am still being warmed by the sweetness of this word; why should I hurry on to the next one?"

In his *Kuntres Acharon*, Baal HaTanya writes:

> *I have heard a report that is not good and it has caused my innards to tremble: that our people have removed as shliach tzibbur someone who seeks to lengthen the lives of those who belong to our mikdash me'at (miniature sanctuary).*[7] *As our Sages teach, three things lengthen a person's life; one of them is davening at a slow pace.*[8] *Even if someone is extremely pressed for time and [if the davening will be slow] he will not be able to remain for the Kedushah of Chazaras HaShatz, it would be far, far better that he*

6. Rabbi Elazar Rokeach of Worms (1160-1238), quoted by later commentators.

7. Lit. *miniature Beis HaMikdash,* a reference to a *beis haknesses* or *beis midrash.*

8. *Berachos* 54b.

[not be chazzan and] miss Kedushah and Borchu rather than affect the lives of those who seek to live long . . .

The Chasam Sofer's Insight

Already in his youth, the Chasam Sofer invested great effort in his tefillah; he would still be davening *Shemoneh Esrei* long after others had finished. It is told that a friend once criticized him for this, saying, "While you were still davening *Shemoneh Esrei*, I learned an entire *siman* (chapter) in *Shulchan Aruch* with the [commentary of] *Magen Avraham*!"

Young Moshe Sofer replied, "The Gemara says that one who davens slowly will have his years and days lengthened, so I will actually *gain* time by davening this way. And besides, a good davening brings greater *siyata diShmaya* in one's learning."

The Role of the *Baal Tefillah*

Dovid Hamelech says: הֵיטִיבוּ נַגֵּן בִּתְרוּעָה, *Be very musical [when you praise Hashem, sing] with deep emotion.*[9] Tefillah needs to be sweet and pleasant, uplifting to those praying and a *nachas ruach* (source of satisfaction) to Hashem.

A *baal tefillah* [i.e. *chazzan*] has a responsibility to uplift the congregation to pray with greater *kavanah*. In the words of R' Aharon Roth,[10] a *baal tefillah* has in his power to either uplift the minyan in the way of Dovid HaMelech, or, God forbid, to bring the minyan down in the way of Yeravam ben Nevat.[11]

The custom is for someone who is observing the year of mourning or a *yahrtzeit* (for a parent) to lead the tefillos. However, one must realize that this is only a benefit for the *neshamah* if the son leads the prayers in a manner that, at the very least, does not lower

---

9. *Tehillim* 33:3.

10. Author of *Sefer Shomer Emunim* and founder of the Toldos Aharon *chassidus* in Jerusalem.

11. First king of the Ten Tribes, whom our Sages label a חוֹטֵא וּמַחֲטִיא אֶת הָרַבִּים, *one who sins and causes others to sin.*

the normal standard of the congregation's *davening*. If, however, the son has a quiet voice and even his weekday service lowers the standard, or if the *yahrtzeit* falls on Shabbos and his voice is not melodious and will not inspire the minyan, of what benefit to the *neshamah* of the deceased is his serving as *baal tefillah*? To the contrary, his leading the tefillah and leaving everyone uninspired might awaken a *kitrug* (Heavenly accusation) against the deceased, God forbid.[12]

Everyone knows that a *baal tefillah* who prays halfheartedly affects the minyan in a negative way, while a *baal tefillah* who prays with emotion uplifts them.

Our Sages tell us that Navos HaYizra'eli was punished because he had a beautiful voice but did not sing when he ascended to the Beis HaMikdash for *shalosh regalim* (the Three Festivals).[13] When someone *is* a good *baal tefillah* and is asked to lead the davening, he should not refuse unless he has a compelling reason.

Don't Give Up

Some have a natural feeling for tefillah and do not find it difficult to daven slowly and with emotion. Others find that they can do this on some days, but not on others. And there are those who seem to always find a lengthy *Shacharis* difficult to endure.

The same is with Torah study. There are some who can sit with a Gemara and learn with true enjoyment for hours on end, and there are those who find this exceedingly difficult.

Those who do find it difficult should know that the more effort one invests in a mitzvah, the more he comes to enjoy it. One who forces himself day after day to learn Torah for a few uninterrupted hours will eventually derive true pleasure from learning. The same applies to tefillah. The more effort one invests in tefillah, the more one strives to concentrate on each tefillah as he enunciates each word slowly and carefully, the more he will come to enjoy it.

12. For the *neshamah* indirectly caused the standard of the davening to be lowered.

13. See *Yalkut Shimoni, Parashas Ki Sisa*, #404.

The Best Burden

When the Redemption from Egypt was about to begin, Hashem told Moshe: וְהוֹצֵאתִי אֶתְכֶם מִתַּחַת סִבְלֹת מִצְרַיִם, *And I will take you out from beneath the burdens of Egypt.*[14] *Ohr HaChaim* explains that Hashem said to the Jewish people: "I am taking you out of the sufferings that you have endured in Egypt, and these burdens will be replaced by 'burdens' of a different sort — the עֹול הַתּוֹרָה, to be a servant of Hashem and fulfill His commands."

Similarly, every person is destined to experience difficulties on this world. Better that his difficulties be his finding it hard to study Torah for hours on end or to daven for an extended period of time, rather than experiencing physical suffering, ר״ל. There is no better suffering than יִסוּרֵי מִצְוָה, *suffering for a mitzvah.* As the Gemara states regarding the words כִּי אָדָם לְעָמָל יוּלָּד, *But man is born for toil:*[15] "All bodies are created for toil; fortunate are those who merit to be toilers in Torah." And most important, the difficulties one experiences from a long learning session or davening will eventually be replaced by a feeling of intense spiritual pleasure and satisfaction that no physical pleasure can equal.

Self-Sacrifice

Moreover, R' Aharon of Belz, quoting his saintly father R' Yissocher Ber, would say that true spiritual accomplishment comes only through *mesiras nefesh*, self-sacrifice.[16] This term is commonly associated with giving one's life *al kiddush Hashem.* But the term *nefesh* can also mean "desire."[17] When a Jew overcomes his physical desires and instead channels his energy toward intense Torah study, that is *mesiras nefesh.* And when he over-

14. *Shemos* 6:6.

15. *Iyov* 5:7.

16. The Imrei Emes of Ger is quoted as saying something similar.

17. See *Rashi* to *Bereishis* 23:8.

comes the temptation to join a minyan for *Shacharis* that recites the prayers quickly, and instead attaches himself to a *kehillah* (congregation) that prays slowly and with feeling, that too is *mesiras nefesh.* The cumulative effect of such daily *mesiras nefesh* can equal that of a great act of self-sacrifice that has the power to atone for all of one's sins.

Until the feeling of pleasure for tefillah comes, one should bear in mind that what he is doing is a great source of *tikkun hanefesh* (perfection of the soul). To learn, pray, or perform any mitzvah when one derives little or no pleasure from it, to do it simply because this is what Hashem wants us to do, is a great source of merit.

Fulfill Your Mission

Moreover, every person has his own unique mission in this world and his own *tikkunim* (spiritual rectifications) to accomplish. Just as our faces are not the same, so too our *neshamos* are not the same; the fact that we appear different externally indicates that our essence is different as well. Since Adam, there have not been two individuals whose spiritual missions were identical. Every moment, there are *tikkunim* that need to be effected at that specific time to bring the world closer to the Final Redemption, and each *neshamah* must bring about the *tikkunim* with which only it has been entrusted.

With their great wisdom and Divine Inspiration, the *Anshei Knesses HaGedolah* arranged the words of the tefillos in such a way that makes it possible for each *neshamah* to accomplish on any given day that which it needs to accomplish in the realm of prayer.

It is in this vein that the Chiddushei HaRim[18] of Ger explains Hillel's words: וְאִם לֹא עַכְשָׁיו אֵימָתַי, *And if it now, then when?*[19] When you arise in the morning with awe of Hashem, ready for

18. R' Yitzchak Meir of Ger, grandfather of the Sfas Emes.
19. *Avos* 1:14.

another day of mitzvos, realize that on this day you must rectify that which, on this specific day, requires *tikkun*. Hashem has allotted you a specific number of years on this world, with a specific number of days, hours, and seconds, for that which must be accomplished at each specific moment.

Therefore, one should never say, "I don't feel like learning today, or putting effort into my *davening* today; tomorrow will be a better day." No! Tomorrow has its own mission, just as today has its own mission. What needs to be accomplished today cannot be postponed for tomorrow.

וְאִם לֹא עַכְשָׁיו אֵימָתַי, *And if it now, then when?* For tomorrow will be an עַכְשָׁיו all its own.

On Time

An important aspect of proper tefillah is arriving on time for davening. Our Sages teach that the first ten adult males who form the minyan receive reward equivalent to that of the entire congregation.[20] If one cannot be among the first ten, he should at least make sure to arrive at shul before the prayers commence. To do so benefits one's *neshamah* in a profound way.

As we have mentioned, every *neshamah* descends to this world to achieve its *tikkun*, the spiritual rectification that is uniquely its own. Some *neshamos* need to descend to this world many times until they achieve their *tikkun*. This can be a process of many centuries. However, we know that Hashem's way of dealing with humanity is *middah k'neged middah* (measure for measure). "Hashem is your shadow";[21] just as a person's shadow moves according to his movements, so does Hashem act towards us in the way that we ourselves act.

When a Jew approaches Torah study, tefillah, and other mitzvos with *zerizus*, alacrity, Hashem responds in kind. A person

---

20. *Berachos* 47b.

21. *Tehillim* 121:5.

who arises swiftly to be on time for *Shacharis*, who puts aside his activities in the middle of the day and evening to be on time for *Minchah* and *Maariv,* can merit that Hashem will speed his *tikkun*, bringing his *neshamah* to its desired state of perfection sooner than would otherwise have been possible.

People have a variety of excuses for coming late to tefillah. One should bear in mind that the mitzvos we perform on this world provide us with spiritual "sustenance" and "clothing" for our souls in the Next World. As we say in the prayer prior to donning the *tallis* in the morning: "Just as I cover myself with a *tallis* in this world, so may I merit the rabbinical garb and a beautiful cloak in the World to Come in Gan Eden."

Torah is the soul's sustenance, while mitzvos form its garments. Each mitzvah is a thread; from many threads a garment is woven. The quality of this spiritual garment will reflect the quality of the mitzvos performed. Someone who is a habitual latecomer to shul, thus offering prayers of inferior quality, will find himself in the Next World with a garment that is torn and patched. Is this what we want for ourselves?

A Delicacy Without Taste

The writings of Kabbalah state that it is auspicious to recite the verse הָבִיאָה לִּי צַיִד וַעֲשֵׂה לִי מַטְעַמִּים וְאֹכֵלָה (*Bring me some game and make for me delicacies to eat*)[22] prior to davening. *Tikkunei Zohar* states that the *Shechinah*, as it were, says to the Jewish people, "*Make delicacies for Me such as I love.*"[23]

The taste of food depends very much on how it is prepared. If it is prepared in haste and as a result is not seasoned properly, it will taste bland and will bring no pleasure to the palate.

The same is true of tefillah. If someone rushes into shul late, whips on his *tallis* and *tefillin*, skips *Korbanos* and rushes through

22. *Bereishis* 27:7.

23. Ibid. v. 4; see *Sefer HaTanya* ch. 27.

Pesukei D'Zimrah so that he can catch up to the minyan for *Shemoneh Esrei*, his davening will be like a delicacy that could have been delicious but was not, due to poor preparation.

The Implications of Tardiness

When the Beis HaMikdash stood, the Kohanim were divided into 24 *mishmaros* (watches), with each *mishmar* performing the service one week at a time. The Mishnah states that the *mishmar* of the family of Bilgah was penalized by having their "window sealed."[24] Each *mishmar* had its own window built into a wall in the Temple Courtyard where its slaughtering knives were stored. Bilgah's window was sealed, and thus its members needed to use the windows of the other Kohanim.

According to one opinion in the Gemara, Bilgah was penalized because of its tardiness. It happened that the new week ushering in Bilgah's service had begun, and the Kohanim of this family had not yet arrived to begin their service! *Rashi* explains that their tardiness indicated that the Kohanim's service in the Beis HaMikdash was not beloved to them. For this, they deserved to be penalized.

Why did our Sages choose to penalize them by sealing their window? For a Kohen's service to achieve its desired purpose, it is necessary that his efforts be endowed with a *shefa*, a flow of spiritual energy from Above. Bilgah's lack of regard for the Divine service caused this Divine flow to cease. The sealing of their window on earth paralleled the sealing of their Heavenly window. Now, to perform the service, they would need to tap in to the *shefa* of the other families of Kohanim.

Coming late for tefillah is an indication that tefillah is not something precious to the person. This in itself can cause one's prayers to lose their effectiveness so that they do not achieve their desired purpose in Heaven.

---

24. *Succah* 56a.

As mentioned earlier,[25] it was *Shevet Don* whom Amalek attacked soon after the Jews departed Egypt. The Torah refers to Amalek's victims as נֶחֱשָׁלִים, which *Targum Onkelos* translates as מִתְאַחֲרִין, *tardy ones.* Don was slow in moving on as the Jews traveled through the Wilderness. This is why they found themselves outside of the Clouds of Glory, which made it possible for Amalek to attack them. It was fitting that they should be attacked by the nation of אֲשֶׁר קָרְךָ[26], who sought to inflict a קְרִירוּת, *coldness,* in the Jews' service of Hashem, cooling their flame of excitement and zeal in serving their Creator.

We, the *Shevet Don* of Jewish history (see ch. 2), must correct this spiritual blemish by striving with all our might to be on time for daily tefillah. If one finds this difficult, he should understand that, as stated in holy writings, that which is one's *tikkun* is not achieved easily.

Measure for Measure

On Erev Shabbos the Chiddushei HaRim would involve himself with *tikkun neshamos,* helping *neshamos* from the Next World to achieve their spiritual remedy so that they could merit their place in *Gan Eden.* Late one Erev Shabbos a *neshamah* came for its *tikkun.* "I'm sorry," said the Chiddushei HaRim, "but the Rebbetzin already lit the Shabbos candles. I cannot help you now."[27]

Consider: This *neshamah* had merited to come to the Chiddushei HaRim, and yet the *tzaddik* could not assist it. It seems that this *neshamah,* during its lifetime on this world, was in the habit of coming late for tefillah and other mitzvos. Tardiness had become a part of its spiritual essence, so when it needed the *tzaddik's* help, it could not get there on time.

25. See "Tefillah: An Expression of Faith" (ch. 2).

26. From *Devarim* 25:18.

27. From *Me'ir Einei HaGolah.*

Our Sages relate that Shlomo HaMelech overslept on the morning of the *chanukas haMikdash,* the Temple's dedication — and this led to its destruction. It follows, then, that the way to speed the coming of Mashiach, when the Beis HaMikdash will be rebuilt, is by being on time for tefillah, especially in the morning.

Furthermore, when a Jew hurries to fulfill a mitzvah, then measure for measure he awakens a desire in Heaven to "hurry" the process that leads to the Final Redemption.

The Poor Man's Offering

There are those who feel inadequate when standing before their Creator in prayer, echoing the words of the *Megillah,* "*... for it is forbidden to enter the king's gate in a garment of sackcloth.*"[28] One can get discouraged despite his best efforts to daven well. "Who am I to expect Hashem to answer my requests? And who am I to offer praise of Him? I know my own self-worth, and I know that as hard as I try, I do not daven with proper *kavanah.*"

To the words קוֹל ה' בַּכֹּחַ, *The voice of Hashem is in power,*[29] *Yalkut Shimoni* comments, "in accordance with each individual's power." Hashem does not demand of us more than we are capable of.

This is the concept of the *Korban Oleh V'Yored,* the sin offering whose composition is dependent on the sinner's financial standing. A man of means brought an animal; a poor man brought two birds; a destitute man brought a simple meal offering. The meal offering is called a *minchah,* which literally means *gift.* This is the term used for a gift to royalty, as it is written, מַלְכֵי תַרְשִׁישׁ וְאִיִּים מִנְחָה יָשִׁיבוּ, *The kings of Tarshish and the isles will return the gift.*[30] Similarly, the gift that Yaakov sent to Esav, which included precious gems and pearls,[31] was called a *minchah.*[32]

---

28. *Esther* 4:2.

29. *Tehillim* 29:4.

30. Ibid. 72:10.

31. *Bereishis* 32:14; see *Rashi.*

32. Ibid.

The destitute man's *minchah* offering is especially beloved to Hashem because it was the best he could offer, and paying for it was not easy for him.

Someone who can concentrate on the words of tefillah and can pray in the desired manner with proper preparation is expected to do so. Someone of lower spiritual standing is expected to try his utmost to make his davening the best it can be. If he does so, then Hashem will see to it that the tefillah he has offered will reach its intended place in Heaven.

Minchah

The Gemara teaches, "A person should always be careful regarding *Tefillas Minchah*, for Eliyahu was answered only through *Tefillas Minchah*."[33] *Shacharis*, which contains *Pesukei D'Zimrah, Birchos Shema,* and the tefillos that follow *Shemoneh Esrei* can be likened to a rich man's *korban*. *Maariv,* which is comprised of *Shema* and its accompanying blessings and *Shemoneh Esrei,* is like the poor man's offering. *Minchah,* which has neither *Pesukei D'Zimrah* nor the *Shema,* is like the *korban* of the destitute man.

But there is something unique about *Minchah*. It must be recited in the middle of the day, when often a person is occupied with some important matter but must interrupt it so that he can daven with a minyan before the end of the designated time. This makes *Minchah* especially beloved to Hashem despite its brevity.

Maariv

Maariv also requires a renewed effort because so often we are tired and worn out after a long day. This is why *Nusach Sefard* begins *Maariv* with verses that inspire such effort: "... *Behold, bless Hashem, all you servants of Hashem, who stand in the house of*

33. *Berachos* 6b. This refers to Eliyahu's tefillah on Mount Carmel. See *Melachim I,* ch. 18.

Hashem in the nights."[34] The term הָעֹמְדִים, *who stand,* alludes to those who stand resolutely at night and do not succumb to weariness as they daven.

"Hashem, Master of Legions, is with us."[35] Those who stand erect at night, davening *Maariv* with passion and *kavanah,* are the "legion" of which Dovid HaMelech speaks.

It is truly unfortunate that some utilize the time when these verse are recited to finish a conversation or engage in other mundane activities. What kind of "legion" is it that serves its Master in this way?

We have already cited our Sages' statement regarding tefillah: "These are the things that stand at the pinnacle *(rum)* of the world, but which people treat lightly *(mezalzelin).*"[36] Fortunate are those who appreciate the primacy of tefillah in a Jew's life and invest great effort, day after day, in maximizing the power of their davening.

---

34. *Tehillim* 134:1.
35. Ibid. 46:8.
36. *Berachos* 6b.

CHAPTER FOUR

Adding Power to Your Tefillah

Our previous essay, "Toiling in Tefillah," discussed how one can make his davening a true *avodah sheb'lev*, service of the heart. Now we will turn our attention to other mitzvos that can have a powerful impact on the power and quality of our tefillah.

The study of Torah purifies the heart and fills it with joy,[1] causing one's inner love of Hashem to be revealed. Studying Torah before *Shacharis* helps to make the davening a more uplifting experience. If one normally finds tefillah somewhat of a burden, the joy and *ahavas Hashem* he feels as a result of his Torah learning will change that. The effect one's learning has on the

1. See *Tehillim* 19:9.

tefillah that follows it is in direct proportion to the time and effort he invests in his learning.

Quality Time

Dovid HaMelech says, "At midnight I will arise to thank You, because of Your righteous judgments."[2] The Midrash relates:

> *A harp was suspended over Dovid's bed. Precisely at midnight, the northern wind would blow through the harp, causing its strings to vibrate and play . . . As soon as Dovid heard it, he would arise and study Torah. When the Jewish people heard Dovid's voice as he studied, they said, "If Dovid, King of Israel, is studying Torah, then we should certainly be doing so!"*[3] *Immediately, they would begin to study as well.*[4]

For generations, it was customary for Jews to arise at midnight, reciting the *Tikkun Chatzos* prayers to mourn the *Churban Beis HaMikdash,*[5] study Torah until daybreak, then immerse in a *mikveh* and daven *Shacharis*. They were able to maintain such a schedule by davening *Maariv* soon after dark and, after a small meal and brief learning session, immediately retire for the night. After a few hours of sleep, they were ready to begin the next day at midnight.

One of the Torah giants of nineteenth-century Hungary is reported to have said, "When a Jew arises at midnight to learn Torah until daybreak and then, after a cup of coffee to refresh himself, immerses himself in tefillah, he experiences a spiritual pleasure to which no earthly pleasure can compare."

This was in earlier generations. Later generations were physically weaker. This is why the *Geonim*[6] added the blessing of

2. *Tehillim* 119:62.

3. It is the way of kings to arise late, not early.

4. *Eichah Rabbah* 2:23; see also *Berachos* 3b.

5. See *Shulchan Aruch, Orach Chaim* 1:2.

6. The *Geonim* were the leaders of the yeshivos in Bavel in the period shortly after the

הַנּוֹתֵן לַיָּעֵף כֹּחַ (*Blessed are You, Hashem ... Who gives strength to the weary*) to *Birchos HaShachar.*[7] For us, arising at midnight is something we can do only on occasion, if at all. However, it is important to strive to be in shul early enough to have some sort of learning session before *Shacharis.* The *dveikus* and *ahavas Hashem* that will result from this will have a dramatic effect on one's davening. And it will help him to have proper *kavanah* for the crucial first blessing of *Shemoneh Esrei.*

A Spiral of *Dveikus*

The famed *tzaddik* Rav Yehudah ("Reb Yidel'e") Horowitz of Dzhikov witnessed something that left a lifelong impression upon him. At the Knessiah Gedolah,[8] he watched the Imrei Emes of Ger learning Torah with a level of *dveikus* that was plainly obvious and quite unusual. It is far easier for one to feel an intense attachment to Hashem as he davens than when he learns. Nevertheless, such a feeling during learning *is* possible, and whatever level we achieve through our learning will impact our davening.

The converse is true as well. The *dveikus* achieved during tefillah will impact the learning that follows it. When one feels the closeness to Hashem that comes from an impassioned *Nishmas* on Shabbos or Yom Yov; from an ecstatic *Hallel* on Yom Yov or Rosh Chodesh; or even from a weekday *Shemoneh Esrei,* his Torah study is of an altogether different sort. It is with greater joy, with a higher sense of purpose, and of course, with a higher degree of *dveikus.*

As an analogy, let us imagine the attitude towards mitzvos of a *navi* (prophet) who merited to have Hashem speak directly to him. Does anyone doubt that this will profoundly impact his

---

completion of the writing of the Talmud. Their period of leadership lasted some 400 years.

7. See *Beis Yosef* to *Orach Chaim* ch. 46.

8. World Conference of Agudath Israel held in Vienna in 1923.

entire approach to mitzvos? Is it possible to hear the voice of Hashem and *not* improve the manner in which one learns, davens, eats matzah on Pesach, or gives *tzedakah*? How can a person remain on the same spiritual level after hearing Hashem's voice?

Similarly, how can one's approach to Torah study or any other mitzvah not be affected by the intense *dveikus* that can result from heartfelt tefillah?

Teshuvah Before Tefillah

Contemplating thoughts of *teshuvah* (repentance) prior to tefillah is another great means of empowering one's davening. The mishnah states: "Repent one day before your death."[9] As *Rabbeinu Yonah* explains, one should engage in *teshuvah* every day of his life, for one can never be sure how long he will live. This was Shlomo HaMelech's intent in saying, "Let your garments always be white."[10] Even a brief thought of *teshuvah,* such as "I know that my ways are not good, and I sincerely want to improve," has great value in Heaven. Far better, however, is when a person finds a place where he can meditate in private, give serious thought to his spiritual state, and contemplate ways to improve. If in such a moment he can, with Hashem's help, find it within himself to shed a tear, then it is a true *eis ratzon* (auspicious time).

Unfortunately, the *Satan* uses every means at his disposal to prevent us from engaging in such soul-searching. People are so busy with their daily routine that often they give not a thought to their spiritual standing.

Every day of one's life, one must ask himself a one-word question, a question that Hashem posed to Adam after he ate from the Tree of Knowledge: אַיֶּכָּה, *Where are you?*[11] Hashem was asking,

---

9. *Avos* 2:10.

10. *Koheles* 9:8.

11. *Bereishis* 3:9. In the plain meaning of the word, Hashem was drawing Adam into conversation by asking where he was after he hid in fear following his sin. See "Rosh Hashanah: A New Breath of Life" (ch. 33).

"What is your spiritual standing? Are you meeting the challenges that the yetzer hara has sent your way?"

The Satan tries to deny us peace of mind so that we will never ponder such thoughts. How wonderful it is to ask oneself this question every morning before turning one's heart towards Hashem in tefillah.

Tzedakah

Another way to add power to tefillah is by giving *tzedakah* prior to davening. The mitzvah of *tzedakah* is a great *tikkun* for the *neshamah,* even more than fasting and other forms of physical affliction. This is because, as stated in *Sefer HaTanya,*[12] *tzedakah* is one of the mitzvos that correspond to all 613 mitzvos. We know that this is true of *mitzvas tzitzis*, as stated by *Rashi.*[13] The uniqueness of *tzitzis* has to do with its being a garment that clothes the body. The 248 positive commandments and the 365 negative commandments correspond to the 248 limbs and 365 sinews of the human body. A mitzvah such as *tzitzis*, which adorn a garment that clothes not one limb but a significant portion of the body, represents in a certain sense all 613 mitzvos.

The mitzvah of *tzedakah,* as well, is referred to as a garment, as Yeshayahu HaNavi says: וַיִּלְבַּשׁ צְדָקָה כַּשִּׁרְיָן, *He clothed himself with tzedakah as armor.*[14] Our Sages derive from here: Just as small scales of armor combine to make a large coat of mail, so do small coins of *tzedakah* add up to a large amount.[15] *Tzedakah,* like *tzitzis*, represents the 613 mitzvos and is a great source of atonement for one's sins. When it is given prior to tefillah, it elevates the soul and empowers one's davening.

Furthermore, giving *tzedakah* removes *timtum halev*, the spiritual defilement caused by sin that prevents a person from feeling

12. Chapter 17.
13. *Bamidbar* 15:39.
14. *Yeshayahu* 59:17.
15. *Bava Basra* 9b.

a connection to Hashem and joy in performing His mitzvos. Regarding *tzedakah* the Torah states, "You shall not harden your heart or close your hand against your destitute brother."[16] "Opening the hand" to give *tzedakah* opens the heart. Our Sages also teach that when one gives a coin for *tzedakah*, he merits to greet the *Shechinah*.[17]

Regarding *korbanos* we are taught: "Whether one gives a lot or a little, as long as his intention is for the sake of Heaven [it is pleasing to Hashem]."[18] Hashem derives as much, if not more, satisfaction (as it were) from the poor man's simple sacrifice as from the rich man's lavish one. The same is true of *tzedakah*. A yeshivah student's dollar, which may represent a significant amount of his spending money, is as precious to Hashem as the wealthy man's large donation. What matters more than the sum is the intent and personal sacrifice that the *tzedakah* represents.

The Arizal teaches that one should give three coins to *tzedakah* during *Pesukei D'Zimrah* when saying the words וְאַתָּה מוֹשֵׁל בַּכֹּל *(and You rule everything)*,[19] because in the realm of Kabbalah, the word בַּכֹּל alludes to the *Shechinah*.[20] Perhaps this act of *tzedakah* is considered "before tefillah" since it precedes both *Shema* and *Shemoneh Esrei*. Nevertheless, it is preferable to give *tzedakah* before the very start of *Shacharis*. And if one's pockets are empty, he should say, or at least have in mind, "It is my desire to give *tzedakah;* however, I am presently unable to do so." Yearning to do the mitzvah also serves to open one's heart so that his davening will be more effective.

---

16. *Devarim* 15:7.

17. *Bava Basra* 10a.

18. *Menachos* 110a.

19. In the piece that opens with וַיְבָרֶךְ דָּוִיד.

20. See *Ramban* to *Bereishis* 24:1. In another *shmuess*, Rav Wolfson, citing the *Ben Ish Chai*, said that it is a *segulah* for the healing of the sick to give *tzedakah* when saying words that are found later in that same verse: [וְאַתָּה מוֹשֵׁל בַּכֹּל וּבְיָדְךָ כֹּחַ וּגְבוּרָה וּבְיָדְךָ לְגַדֵּל וּלְחַזֵּק לַכֹּל], *and it is in Your hand to make anyone great and strong.* When giving the *tzedakah*, one should have in mind the name of the *choleh*.

CHAPTER FIVE

Ahavas Yisrael and Tefillah

The Arizal teaches that prior to *Shacharis,* one should accept upon himself the mitzvah of *ahavas Yisrael,* to love every Jew with an unconditional love. The reason for this is that there is a vast difference between tefillos that are uttered by an individual and those uttered by a *tzibbur* (congregation). As it is written, הֵן אֵל כַּבִּיר לֹא יִמְאָס, *Behold, God does not despise the numerous.*[1] One can consider himself to truly be part of a *tzibbur* only if he has accepted upon himself to love every Jew like himself. Then he can declare, בְּתוֹךְ עַמִּי אָנֹכִי יֹשָׁבֶת, *I dwell among my people.*[2]

1. *Iyov* 36:5. See *Berachos* 8a.
2. *Melachim II* 4:13.

Tefillah is an expression of *ahavas Hashem,* of which the Torah states, וְאָהַבְתָּ אֵת ה' אֱלֹהֶיךָ, *And you shall love Hashem, your God.*[3] These words have the same *gematria* as וְאָהַבְתָּ לְרֵעֲךָ כָּמוֹךָ אֲנִי י־ה־ו־ה, *And you shall love your fellow as yourself, I am Hashem* (907).[4] Without true *ahavas Yisrael,* it is impossible to attain *ahavas Hashem.*

R' Aharon HaGadol of Karlin said that if one wishes to know what sort of portion is in store for him in the World to Come, he should ponder how much spiritual pleasure and feeling of *kedushah* (sanctity) he experiences on the holy day of Shabbos. And if he desires to know his own level of *ahavas Hashem,* he should take stock of his true measure of *ahavas Yisrael.*

This is why in both *Shacharis* and *Maariv, ahavas Yisrael* precedes *ahavas Hashem.* Before reciting *Shema* which contains the verse וְאָהַבְתָּ אֵת ה' אֱלֹהֶיךָ, we first recite the blessing of "Who chooses His people Israel with love" (in *Shacharis*) and "Who loves His people Israel" (in *Maariv*). While these blessings speak not of the love of Jews for one another, but of the love of Hashem for the Jewish people, they do relate to *ahavas Yisrael.* Hashem's unconditional love for every Jewish *neshamah* is predicated on the inherent goodness and inextinguishable spark of *kedushah* in every Jewish soul. And it is these very qualities that should inspire us to feel a boundless, unconditional love for our fellow Jew.

Love Your Antagonists

In his *Sefer Shomer Emunim,* R' Aharon Roth, one of the great chassidic leaders of recent times, addresses his followers:

> *The most important thing of all, that with which I constantly begin my talks to you, is to be bonded together by bonds of love, without any discord, Heaven forfend. This was always my goal, and with the help of Hashem, it will*

3. *Devarim* 6:5.

4. *Vayikra* 19:18.

continue to be my desire forever. For through this, we unite ourselves with Hashem Yisborach, Who dwells in His people's midst.

Now, as we near the arrival of Mashiach, the Satan is investing all his power to sow seeds of discord among us, so that we will grow distant from Hashem and our redemption will be delayed. For Zohar teaches that even one kehillah (congregation) that engages in teshuvah with all its heart can bring forth the sprouting of redemption.[5]

I beg of you: Do not be among those who speak lashon hara about any sect or group of chassidim — God forbid to follow this path of fools! Do you think that this is my desire, that Jews should be separated from one another? Why, the very goal of the Baal Shem Tov was only to bring genuine unity among Jews, that Jews should be truly close with one another!

Even if one sees his fellow Jew conducting himself in an improper way, it is useless to speak about this to others — what is the point of causing Heavenly indictment against the Jewish people?[6] *Rather, one should humble himself in following the way of tzaddikim and not feel animosity even towards those who disdain our path. We should strive to draw them close and love them, to seek merit for them and to pray that they should not incur Divine wrath, God forbid.*

For Jews are a holy people, and in essence they want to avoid evil. However, the yetzer hara confuses and blinds them ... In this last generation (before Mashiach), when it is bitter and dark and the world is filled with heresy ... if a Jew merely believes in our Creator, this is significant in Heaven, and all the more so if he lives a life of Torah and mitzvos.

---

5. *Zohar Chadash, Midrash HaNe'elam, Parashas Noach.*

6. In *Sefer Shemiras HaLashon* (*Shaar HaZechirah* ch. 2), the Chofetz Chaim, citing Zohar, writes that when Jews speak against one another, this gives the Satan power to indict the Jewish people before Hashem.

Therefore, if a Jew has spoken against you, do not reject him because of this . . . rather, our goal must be to love every Jew and to draw close every person who comes our way.[7]

A Letter in the Torah

The name יִשְׂרָאֵל forms the initial letters of יֵשׁ שִׁשִּׁים רִבּוֹא אוֹתִיּוֹת לַתּוֹרָה, *There are 600,000 letters in the Torah.*[8] Every Jewish soul is rooted in a particular letter of the Torah. And just as a *sefer Torah* is rendered *pasul* (invalid) if even one letter is slightly defective, so too are the Jewish people "incomplete" and not fulfilling their destiny as God's chosen people if even one Jew is lacking in his commitment to Torah and mitzvos.

Every letter of the Torah is unique; no two letters convey the same teaching. In a similar sense, no two souls are alike, and like the crowns on the letters in a Torah scroll, every Jewish soul is crowned with some special quality that makes it unique.

Chiddushei HaRim teaches that every *neshamah* has its own unique *chein*, grace, through which it finds favor in Hashem's eyes. The quality that earns it this favor is hidden from everyone. If one recognizes that he is blessed with a particular quality and decides that it is *that* quality which makes him unique and favorable before Hashem, he can be certain that such is not the case. For each *neshamah's* uniqueness is hidden, and no human being can perceive it.

The totality of Torah thought can be divided into four branches: פְּשַׁט, the literal or evident meaning of the text; רֶמֶז, hints or allegorical illustrations of Scripture; דְרוּשׁ, halachic and aggadic derivations; and סוֹד, secrets, the esoteric aspects of Torah *[Kabbalah]*.[9] We can apply this to the way we perceive the Jewish soul which the Torah's letters represent.

7. *Shomer Emunim,* Introduction, chapter 14.

8. *Zohar Chadash* to *Shir HaShirim.*

9. The initial letters of these four terms spell פַּרְדֵס, *orchard.*

Often, we are quick to pass judgment on others based on what we see before our eyes, without contemplating what may lie beneath the surface. In other words, we judge the person by his פְּשַׁט, plain appearance. Other times, we do give thought to analyzing another's actions and in this way better understand who he is and why he acts as he does. Then, we have understood the person according to his רֶמֶז and דְּרוּשׁ.

But even this is insufficient to truly comprehend the essence of a *neshamah*. To do this, we would have to know his סוֹד, the deepest secrets that lie within his soul, the quality that makes him beloved to his Creator. This we cannot know — and so, we can never truly perceive the essential greatness of a Jew.

Opportune Times

There is a particular week of the year when it is most opportune to strengthen our love and respect for our fellow Jew.

The term *sefirah*, as in *Sefiras HaOmer*, refers to the *counting* of the 49 days between the Exodus from Egypt and the giving of the Torah at Sinai. In the writings of Kabbalah the term also refers to the *Sefiros HaElyonos*, the Heavenly Emanations, attributes of Hashem through which He conducts the affairs of this world.

There are seven *Sefiros*, corresponding to the seven days of the week. They represent *middos* of Hashem, as it were, attributes that we must strive to emulate and incorporate into our lives to be used in the appropriate way. Each week of *Sefiras HaOmer* corresponds to one of these *Sefiros-middos*, and each day corresponds to a specific combination of *sefiros*. In many communities a beautiful tefillah is said following the nightly counting of the *Omer* in which we pray that in the merit of our counting, we should rectify our failings with regard to that *sefirah*. It is our sacred task to place special emphasis on perfecting ourselves regarding the *sefirah* of that week.

The order of the seven *sefiros* are:

חֶסֶד, *kindness*
גְבוּרָה, *power*
תִּפְאֶרֶת, *splendor*
נֶצַח, *eternity*
הוֹד, *glory*
יְסוֹד, *foundation*
מַלְכוּת, *kingship*

The translations of these terms refer to how these *Sefiros* relate to Hashem. As they relate to us and our efforts at *tikkun hamiddos*, refining our character traits, חֶסֶד means to develop within ourselves the attribute of reaching out to others with kindness and to feel love towards Hashem. גְבוּרָה means to exercise inner strength and self-control, and to develop our awe of Hashem. תִּפְאֶרֶת is a harmonious blend of the first two *middos*.

נֶצַח relates to נִצָּחוֹן, *victory* or *perseverance*, while הוֹד relates to הוֹדָאָה, *admission* or *subordination*. In *Tikkunei Zohar*, each of the seven *middos* corresponds to a part of the human anatomy. נֶצַח and הוֹד are the two legs upon which the body stands.

In life, different situations may require opposite approaches. When one faces danger, it may be necessary to fight that danger head on and vanquish it. At other times, one is best off with a "soft" approach, avoiding a confrontation. As *Rashi* says regarding the Plague of Hailstones in Egypt: The soft wheat and spelt survived the powerful attack of hailstones because their flexibility enabled them to bend, while the stiff flax and barley were destroyed.[10] Sometimes, it is softness and submission that are the key to our survival.

In our relationship with Hashem, הוֹד represents *thanks* and recognition of the endless kindness that He performs for us — as we mention thrice daily in the *Modim* blessing. It represents submission to His will and recognition that we are helpless without Him.

10. *Shemos* 9:31-32 with *Rashi.*

In our relationship with our fellow Jew, הוד means to feel subordinate to others by recognizing their inherent worth and qualities. It means treating others with respect and recognizing that though we may be superior to someone intellectually, professionally, or due to our accomplishments in the community, he may possess some hidden quality that makes him spiritually greater than us.

A Day of Revelation

The week of הוד reaches its climax on the Yom Tov of Lag BaOmer, the day of *Sefiras HaOmer* that corresponds to the *middah* of הוֹד שֶׁבְּהוֹד. That day is the *yahrtzeit* of the great Tannaic sage Rabi Shimon bar Yochai, who on the last day of his life revealed to his disciples the deepest secrets of the Torah. According to *Bnei Yissoschor*, it was on Lag BaOmer that Rabi Shimon instructed a disciple to record the holy Zohar, the prime source of Kabbalistic thought based on his teachings.

The Gemara relates how, after emerging from the cave in which he and his son R' Elazar had been living an other-worldly existence for 13 years, Rabi Shimon pointed out a simple Jew's devotion to the mitzvos of Hashem.[11] Just as Rabi Shimon revealed the secrets of the Torah, so did he reveal the secret greatness that is hidden within every Jew's soul.

Thus, the week of הוד and especially the day of Lag BaOmer are most auspicious for focusing on the qualities of one's fellow Jew and in this way strengthening *ahavas Yisrael.*[12]

Purim Connection

Shulchan Aruch makes note of the fact that Purim and Lag BaOmer always fall on the same day of the week,[13] indicating

---

11. *Shabbos* 33b.

12. Lag BaOmer is also a most auspicious time for tefillah. Great chassidic leaders said that one's *avodas Hashem* on Lag BaOmer can accomplish as much as can be achieved on Yom Kippur.

13. *Orach Chaim* 428:1 offers the word פְּל"ג as an acronym for פּוּרִים - ל"ג בָּעוֹמֶר.

a connection between the two. Purim is a day of *ahavas Yisrael,* when we exchange *mishloach manos* with others and extend charity to any poor man we meet. It is also a day that represents the indestructible spark of holiness that shines in the soul of every Jew.

The story of the Megillah opens with the feast of Achashverosh, a feast the Jews attended despite Mordechai's warning not to do so. It was this sin that made them deserve Haman's decree of annihilation. Yet, this very feast ultimately brought about their salvation, for it resulted in Vashti's execution, which paved the way for Esther's ascension to the throne as queen. This, says *Chasam Sofer,* was because despite their grievous sin, the Jews' essential greatness was still intact and they were still beloved in Hashem's eyes.

When we recognize how much Hashem loves every one of us, we realize how much we need to love one another.

The Rebbe of Komarna said that on Purim the tefillos of the Jewish people ascend without any interference of destructive forces that normally stand in their way. He added that on this day, a simple Jew can gain access to Heavenly chambers that are normally accessible only to *tzaddikim.*

Purim and Lag BaOmer — days when a Jew's hidden greatness is revealed. Days of *ahavas Yisrael.* Days when our tefillos possess a heightened spiritual power.

CHAPTER SIX

Destroying the Edifice

"*How good are your tents, Yaakov, your dwelling places, Yisrael!*"[1] The "tents" and "dwelling places" are our *battei knessios* and *battei midrashos* (synagogues and study halls). In his prophetic vision, the wicked Bilaam exclaims, "How good . . ." like someone who is so awed by what he sees that he is at a loss for words.

Dovid HaMelech makes a similar exclamation: *"How beloved are Your dwelling places, Hashem, Master of Legions!"*[2]

Elsewhere, Dovid says, *"Hashem loves the gates of Zion more than all the dwelling places of Yaakov. The most glorious things are spoken*

1. *Bamidbar* 24:5.
2. *Tehillim* 84:2.

of you, O city of God . . ."[3] The Gemara comments regarding "the gates of Zion" that since the time of the *Churban* (Destruction), Hashem's Presence is most manifest where Torah is studied with the intent of determining the Halachah.[4] The Gemara does not distinguish between Torah studied in Eretz Yisrael and Torah studied in the Diaspora. Hashem's Presence is there as the students plumb the depths of Halachah.

But how does this fit with the words עִיר הָאֱלֹהִים, *city of God,* in the next verse? What connection can there be between a *beis midrash* in Bavel and the holy city of Jerusalem?

The Gemara provides the answer. "The *battei knessios* and *battei midrashos* of Bavel are destined to be transplanted in Eretz Yisrael."[5] When Mashiach arrives, our places of Torah and tefillah, anywhere in the world, will be transported to our Holy Land.

But there is one condition, for the entire verse reads: נִכְבָּדוֹת מְדֻבָּר בָּךְ, עִיר הָאֱלֹקִים ..., which can be translated, *The most glorious things are spoken **in** you, O city of God . . .* Only if we show proper reverence for our places of Torah and tefillah, by avoiding mundane conversation inside them, can we hope to have them relocated to Eretz Yisrael at the time of Redemption.

A Miniature Mikdash

The Torah states: וּמִקְדָּשִׁי תִּירָאוּ, *Revere My sanctuary.*[6] These words require us to not only have proper reverence for the Beis HaMikdash, but also for the *mikdash me'at,* the miniature Beis HaMikdash — that is, the *beis hamidrash* and *beis haknesses.* One of the worst disgraces to such holy places is when people use them as gathering places for *devarim beteilim* (mindless chatter). In the words of the Chofetz Chaim, this sin transforms the *beis haknesses*

3. Ibid. 87:2.
4. *Berachos* 8a.
5. *Megillah* 29a.
6. *Vayikra* 26:2.

into "a place of idol worship."[7]

Zohar states:

> *Regarding one who converses in a beis haknesses: Woe unto him, for he lacks faith [in Hashem]; woe unto him, for he has no portion in the God of Israel, for he demonstrates that he [believes that he] has no God and that He is not present there [in the beis haknesses], and he has no fear of Him . . .*[8]

The Chasam Sofer discusses the respect that the sanctity of a *beis haknesses* or *beis hamidrash* demands:

> *For HaKadosh Baruch Hu, in His mercy and kindness, left over for us a miniature mikdash — the beis haknesses and beis hamidrash. If we treat them as sacred places, then they will be transported to Eretz Yisrael; they presently have the sanctity of Eretz Yisrael; and the tefillos uttered in them will ascend to the gateway of heaven.*
>
> *However, if, God forbid, we treat these holy places in a shameful way and speak idle chatter in them, then the vapor of this idle chatter is present there and the "prince of the diaspora" (i.e. the Satan) clothes himself in it. He becomes the "master of this beis haknesses," Heaven forfend; he accepts the tefillos and deposits them with the external forces . . .*[9]

---

7. *Mishnah Berurah* 151:1 citing *Semak.* To speak *lashon hara* or other forms of forbidden speech in shul is a particularly grave sin, says the Chofetz Chaim, "for in doing so, one shows lack of regard for the *Shechinah*; [furthermore,] there is no comparison between one who sins in private and one who does so in the palace of the King, in the King's Presence. This evil is compounded when one causes others to join in his sin . . . so that from a few individuals come many groups that engage in strife with one another — until the shul becomes like one huge torch . . . and who is the cause of all this if not the one with whom it all started? Surely, that individual will be 'rewarded' for all that he caused.

"Therefore, one who is truly God-fearing should always be careful not to engage in idle talk, not in the *beis haknesses* and not in the *beis hamidrash*. Rather, these places will be used by him strictly for Torah and tefillah" (ibid, 151:2).

8. *Zohar,* vol. II, p. 131b.

9. *Derashos Chasam Sofer,* vol. II, p. 309.

During Tefillah

While a shul should never be a place for mindless chatter and frivolity, it is proper to greet one's friend and inquire as to his well-being — but not during davening. *Shulchan Aruch* states:

> *One should not engage in conversation when the shaliach tzibbur (i.e. chazzan) is repeating Shemoneh Esrei (chazaras hashatz). If he does speak, he is a sinner; his sin is too great to bear, and we rebuke him.*[10]

The words גָדוֹל עֲוֹנוֹ מִנְשׁוֹא, *his sin is too great to bear,* are adapted from the words of Kayin after he murdered Hevel: גָדוֹל עֲוֹנִי מִנְשׂוֹא, *Is my sin too great to bear?*[11] *Shulchan Aruch* does not apply these words to any other sin. This is sufficient proof of the severity of conversing during *chazaras hashatz.*

Picture the following: Your shul, having outgrown its quarters, has moved into a new, beautiful building. Every member has contributed beyond his means to make this dream a reality.

One day, a stranger comes in with a sledgehammer and without provocation begins pounding away at the shul's new walls. How would you react? Would you stand by indifferently? Certainly not.

This is how one should view someone who engages in conversation during davening. He is destroying the shul and corrupting the congregation's power of tefillah.[12]

In many chassidic courts, the rebbe davens in a small room adjoining the shul.[13] In a certain court, the shul suffered serious damage as a result of two fires. Both times, the rebbe's private room was untouched. When someone mentioned this to the

10. *Orach Chaim* 124:7. Rav Wolfson once commented that, especially in our generation, it is important that rebuke be given in a way that does not cause embarrassment, and preserves the person's dignity.

11. *Bereishis* 4:13.

12. *Eliyahu Rabbah,* citing *Kol Bo,* writes: "Woe to those who engage in conversation during tefillah, for we have seen many *battei knessios* destroyed because of this sin. Men of distinction should be designated to stand guard regarding this" (*Mishnah Berurah* 124:27).

13. The room has openings in the wall so that the rebbe can hear the *baal tefillah.*

rebbe and suggested that the rebbe's spiritual powers had saved his room from damage, he replied, "No, it was no *mofeis* (miracle) at all. In my room, no one talks during davening, so the fire could not damage it."

It is certain that those shuls where, tragically, people regularly engage in conversation during davening will remain where they are when the dawn of redemption arrives.

A Public *Kiddush Hashem*

One who joins a minyan that accords tefillah the respect it demands is counted as a *mekadesh Shemo b'rabbim*, one who has sanctified Hashem's Name in public. In the words of *Shulchan Aruch HaRav*:

> *Though tefillah b'tzibbur (praying as part of a minyan) is a Rabbinic mitzvah, it is in fact greater than a positive Torah commandment, for it is a public kiddush Hashem. [Proof of this is that] one may transgress a positive mitzvah and free his Canaanite slave so that he can thereby complete the quorum of ten [the number required for a minyan].*[14]

Rabbeinu Yonah writes that the sin of *chillul Hashem* is more serious than other sins, to the point that even Yom Kippur accompanied by *teshuvah* and suffering do not atone for it. Conversely, *kiddush Hashem* is greater than other mitzvos and it does atone for *chillul Hashem.*[15] Thus, one who is careful to daven with a *minyan* and shows respect for the tefillah by scrupulously avoiding idle chatter fulfills the mitzvah of וְנִקְדַּשְׁתִּי בְּתוֹךְ בְּנֵי יִשְׂרָאֵל, *And I will be sanctified among Bnei Yisrael.*[16] This can atone for a *chillul Hashem* he may have caused, and for other sins as well.

14. *Shulchan Aruch HaRav, Orach Chaim* 90:17.
15. *Shaarei Teshuvah* 4:5,16.
16. *Vayikra* 22:32.

The Tosafos Yom Tov's Tefillah

Conversing during davening is not only a *chillul Hashem*; it can bring untold harm upon the Jewish people, ר"ל. In the years 1648-1649, the Cossack massacres brought death and destruction to the Jewish communities of Poland. R' Yom Tov Lipman Heller, author of *Tosafos Yom Tov*, knew through Divine Inspiration that the primary cause of this terrible Heavenly decree was the lack of respect for *kedushas beis haknesses* and the talking that was all too common during davening. He therefore composed a special tefillah to be recited in shul every Shabbos morning, which confers blessing upon those who sanctify Hashem's Name through their conduct during tefillah:

> מִי שֶׁבֵּרַךְ אֲבוֹתֵינוּ אַבְרָהָם יִצְחָק וְיַעֲקֹב מֹשֶׁה אַהֲרֹן דָּוִד וּשְׁלֹמֹה, הוּא יְבָרֵךְ אֶת כָּל מִי שֶׁשּׁוֹמֵר פִּיו וּלְשׁוֹנוֹ שֶׁלֹּא לְדַבֵּר בְּעֵת הַתְּפִלָּה. הַקָּדוֹשׁ בָּרוּךְ הוּא יִשְׁמְרֵהוּ מִכָּל צָרָה וְצוּקָה וּמִכָּל נֶגַע וּמַחֲלָה, וְיָחוּלוּ עָלָיו כָּל הַבְּרָכוֹת הַכְּתוּבוֹת בְּסֵפֶר תּוֹרַת מֹשֶׁה רַבֵּינוּ וּבְכָל סִפְרֵי הַנְּבִיאִים וְהַכְּתוּבִים, וְיִזְכֶּה לִרְאוֹת בָּנִים חַיִּים וְקַיָּמִים, וִיגַדְּלֵם לְתוֹרָה וּלְחוּפָּה וּלְמַעֲשִׂים טוֹבִים, וְיַעֲבוֹד אֶת ה' אֱלֹהֵינוּ תָּמִיד בֶּאֱמֶת וּבְתָמִים, וְנֹאמַר אָמֵן.
>
> *He Who blessed our forefathers, Avraham, Yitzchak, and Yaakov, Moshe, Aharon, Dovid, and Shlomo — may He bless everyone who guards his mouth and tongue from speaking during tefillah. May HaKadosh Baruch Hu protect him from every trouble and distress, from every plague and illness; may all the blessings written in the Torah transmitted by Moshe Rabbeinu and in the books of the Prophets and Writings come to rest upon him; may he merit to see offspring who will live and endure, and may he raise them to Torah, marriage, and good deeds; and may he serve Hashem, our God, always, in truth and perfection. Now let us respond: Amen.*

May we merit to be included in this blessing.

CHAPTER SEVEN

Striving for Greater Heights

As mentioned in the Preface, Beis Medrash Emunas Yisroel, where Rav Wolfson serves as Rav, is a landmark of avodas hatefillah. The following essay is based on addresses given by Rav Wolfson to his kehillah many years after its establishment.

One needs to guard against the tendency, as one grows older, to lose some of the enthusiasm of youth and grow complacent in spiritual matters. Also, one always can use *chizuk* (encouragement) in *avodas Hashem*. With this in mind, I would like to review some important insights that I shared with you a number of years ago.

Our *kehillah* was founded by a group of *bachurim* from our yeshivah (Mesivta Torah Vodaath) who felt that this would lead to the strengthening of tefillah. The author of *Shomer Emunim*[1] would say that he is not overly impressed with the fire for *avodas Hashem* that *bachurim* exhibit. The real test of their spiritual standing comes after marriage. In this vein, commentators explain Dovid HaMelech's words: *"Who may ascend the mountain of Hashem, and who may stand in the place of His sanctity?"*[2] Ascending to the heights of spirituality is not sufficient; one must be able to "stand" and remain at the level that he has attained.

Raising One's Voice

The following is excerpted from a famous piece by *Ramban*:

> *And the purpose of raising one's voice in tefillah and the purpose of battei knessios (synagogues) and communal prayer is this: that people should have a place where they can gather and acknowledge to God that He created them and caused them to be, and where they can publicize this and declare, "We are Your creations!" This is the intent [of our Sages] of blessed memory, in [their explanation of the verse]* וַיִּקְרְאוּ אֶל אֱלֹהִים בְּחָזְקָה*, And they called out mightily to God.*[3] *"From here [i.e the word* בְּחָזְקָה*, mightily] you learn that prayer requires a loud voice, for boldness can overcome evil."*[4]

Note that *Ramban* stresses "raising one's voice in tefillah." R' Aharon of Karlin said that while great people can have proper *kavanah* even when praying quietly, the average person needs to raise his voice to accomplish this (except during *Shemoneh Esrei*).[5]

---

1. R' Aharon Roth, founder of the Toldos Aharon *chassidus* in Jerusalem a generation ago.

2. *Tehillim* 24:3.

3. *Yonah* 3:8.

4. *Ramban, Shemos* 13:16.

5. It should be noted, however, that this does not mean to scream in a wild, unbecoming way. Dovid HaMelech declares: *"Bow before Hashem with the beauty of holiness"* (*Tehillim* 29:2). Service of Hashem must be performed with הִדּוּר, in a manner that is dignified and proper. One should pray with emotion, warmth, and energy, in a raised voice that will aid in concentration, in a way that will bring glory to Hashem and inspire others to do the same.

In *Sefer Chareidim*[6] R' Elazar Azkari[7] writes:

> *As tefillah is referred to as* עֲבוֹדָה*, (service) and the Jewish people are called* עֲבָדִים *(servants), it is proper to serve [Hashem] in a loud voice in tefillah, with all one's limbs in motion and with kavanah in one's heart, to the point that one is left exhausted from exertion; and so too with Torah study.*[8]

The Baal Shem Tov said of himself that his purpose in descending to this world was to strengthen the concept of tefillah among the Jewish people.[9] All of the Baal Shem's disciples made tefillah a primary focus of their life's mission. This was especially true of R' Aharon HaGadol of Karlin and his disciples.[10] It was their custom to pray energetically and with warmth.

The story is told of rabbanim in the city of Karlin who as opponents of *Chassidus* were unhappy with the style of davening in the beis midrash of R' Aharon HaGadol. These rabbanim summoned R' Aharon to a meeting at which they voiced their complaints.

R' Aharon responded by turning to one of the rabbanim and saying, "*Shalom aleichem*, Avremal! How are you?"

The rav became incensed at this show of disrespect and shouted, "How dare you speak to me this way? I'm not your friend that you should refer to me as 'Avremal'!"

R' Aharon spoke calmly. "I understand your point, but why do you have to shout?"

The rav replied, "I'm shouting because you've said something that affected me in a very personal way, and so I became excited."

---

6. Ch. 31.

7. 1533-1600.

8. That raising one's voice in tefillah aids one's *kavanah* is stated in Halachah. In the laws of Rosh Hashanah we find: "While throughout the year we pray [*Shemoneh Esrei*] in a whisper, on Rosh Hashanah and Yom Kippur it is customary to pray in a raised voice" (*Orach Chaim* 582:9). The reason for this, says the Chofetz Chaim (*Mishnah Berurah* #24), is so that one will pray with added *kavanah*.

9. See *Sefer Meor VaShemesh*.

10. Among those who strove to emulate R' Aharon's approach to tefillah were the chassidic courts of Stolin, Lechovitch, Strelisk, Slonim, and Stretin.

"Listen to what you yourself have just said," R' Aharon responded. "When something affects you in a very personal way, you become emotional and this causes you to shout. This is how we chassidim approach tefillah. The opportunity to stand before the *Ribbono shel Olam* in prayer touches the very essence of our *neshamos* and we become excited. We find it impossible to pray quietly; we simply must cry out in a loud voice."

In the Book of *Eichah* the prophet laments: *"They [the Jews' enemies] raised a clamor in the House of Hashem like on a festival day."*[11] *Targum* explains that when the Babylonians entered the Beis HaMikdash to destroy it, their shouts matched those of the Jewish people when they prayed on Pesach. And the Talmud states[12] that the recitation of *Hallel* in Jerusalem on the *Seder* night was so loud that it seemed as if the roofs were cracking![13] Once again, we see the importance of praying in a raised voice.

The tefillah of *Ne'ilah* at the conclusion of Yom Kippur is the climax of the season of *teshuvah* that begins with Rosh Chodesh Elul. *Tzaddikim* who davened in a quiet manner all year would not deviate from their custom during *Ne'ilah*. However, the average person simply davens better when he raises his voice, and during *Ne'ilah* every Jew strives his utmost to pray with *kavanah*. This is why it is common in virtually all communities for people to raise their voices during *Ne'ilah*.

Daven Slowly

In *Iggeres HaKodesh*[14] the *Baal HaTanya* writes:

> *And now I will, once again, put forth my very important, heartfelt request before the members of our brotherhood, both near and far, to uphold the following:*

11. *Eichah* 2:7.

12. *Pesachim* 85b as elucidated by *Rashi*.

13. Chassidic *sefarim* derive from these sources that the Yom Tov of Pesach is a time for special emphasis on tefillah.

14. Page 103.

Throughout the weekdays, businessmen who are in a hurry should not serve as the shliach tzibbur [i.e. chazzan]. Only rebbeim or those who eat at their father-in-law's table should lead the davening. Shacharis should last a minimum of one and a half hours. The shliach tzibbur should be chosen by lots or by majority preference, and he should be surrounded by those who likewise have the time to daven slowly and with feeling ...

To daven properly, it is necessary to first prepare oneself mentally for the privilege of meriting a private audience with one's Creator. It is also vital that one set aside sufficient time for his davening so that he can concentrate properly, and hopefully merit to pray with הִשְׁתַּפְּכוּת הַנֶּפֶשׁ, *outpouring of emotion.*

What is considered a sufficient amount of time? In his letter, the *Baal HaTanya* writes that a weekday *Shacharis* should last an average of 1-1/2 hours. We find the following halachah in *Shulchan Aruch*: If one is forced to interrupt his *Pesukei D'Zimrah* because of a situation that makes prayer halachically impossible,[15] then if the interruption lasts as long as it takes to recite the entire *Pesukei D'Zimrah,* one must return to the beginning of *Baruch She'amar*. How long should it take the average person to recite the entire *Pesukei D'Zimrah*, from the beginning of *Baruch She'amar* until the conclusion of *Yishtabach*? *Magen Avraham* rules that it is one half-hour.[16] Apparently, this is the amount of time that the average person is expected to invest in reciting the praises composed by Dovid HaMelech, *Shiras HaYam,* and the rest of *Pesukei D'Zimrah.*

There were *tzaddikim* whose *Shacharis* lasted many hours. I knew a precious Chabad chassid in Williamsburg, R' Avrohom Ziskind, ז"ל. When we arrived in shul for *Shacharis* on Shabbos morning, R' Avraham was already in the midst of his prayers. And

15. As when one must take care of his bodily needs.

16. *Magen Avraham* 53:5. In Beis Medrash Emunas Yisroel, led by Rav Wolfson, a weekday *Pesukei D'Zimrah* lasts approximately 25 minutes.

when others would return for *Minchah* on a short winter Shabbos day, they would find him still in the midst of his morning tefillos.

It was not that he simply said the words very slowly. He prayed with heartfelt emotion, tears flowing from his eyes the entire time. These were not tears of sorrow; this is forbidden on Shabbos. They were tears of joy, from the joy of drawing close to Hashem through tefillah. This is how *tzaddikim* davened; they experienced a true sweetness in their tefillos, to the point that they found it hard to pull themselves away from one word and begin the next.

True, there were *tzaddikim* who would daven quickly, also out of love of tefillah. They took such pleasure from each word of tefillah that they could not wait to reach the next word. And there were *tzaddikim* who davened quickly for a very different reason. They feared that if they davened slowly, the Satan would gain access to their intellect and damage their tefillah with foreign thoughts and distractions.

However, such an approach worked only in earlier generations. As a Jerusalem *tzaddik* once told me, in the court of Kotzk and other such places the Satan had no power of entry before tefillah, so the fast pace of tefillah worked to keep him out. However, in our generation, the Satan is already present in our thoughts before the davening has begun. By davening slowly, it is possible for us to drive him out of our thoughts for at least part of the time.

In Unison

Further in *Kuntres Acharon*, the *Baal HaTanya* writes:

> *One is obligated to reprove his fellow Jew even 100 times. Therefore, I will not restrain myself from crying out in pain. I beg of you with an abundance of mercy: Have pity upon yourselves, safeguard, and be exceedingly careful regarding Torah and the "service of the heart" which is tefillah, to pray with kavanah, and that everyone should begin the*

davening in unison word by word, not this one at his own pace and the other one at his own pace, this one silent and the other one involved in idle chatter, God forbid.

The primary cause [of tefillah that is rushed and not in unison] is that the selection of the shliach tzibbur is without rhyme or reason, either because anyone that wants can go up and claim the amud (chazzan's place) or because no one qualified wants to step forward.

The remedy to this situation is to establish a rule to which everyone must adhere, to select a group of qualified shluchei tzibbur ... They shall lead the tefillah word by word in a loud voice, and they shall daven neither too long nor too short, חס ושלום. *Each one will be obligated to ascend to the amud on his appointed day and he should gather around him all who raise their voices at least somewhat in tefillah and who do not rush their words, as is the established rule in many communities. My purpose now is to renew and strengthen these rules, so that they remain in place forever.*

Gevald! How long will the current situation remain a pitfall for us? Aren't all the sufferings and Divine warnings that we have already received sufficient? May Hashem protect us and console us twofold, and may He purify our hearts so that we may serve Him in truth. "Strengthen yourselves and He will give courage, all who await Hashem."[17]

Years ago, I often davened in Beis Midrash Karlin-Stolin in Williamsburg. There, uplifted souls who davened with a burning passion would encircle the *shliach tzibbur* and, in unison, raise their voices aloud in tefillah. When this is done, each person inspires his neighbor. This is how the Jewish people sang *shirah* after walking through the Yam Suf, as we say in *Shacharis*: יַחַד כֻּלָּם הוֹדוּ, *all of them* ***in unison*** *gave thanks.* And this is the way of the Heavenly angels, as we say each morning: ... וּמַשְׁמִיעִים בְּיִרְאָה יַחַד בְּקוֹל..., *... they proclaim with awe,* ***together****, loudly ...*

17. *Tehillim* 31:25.

With Love

There is another important ingredient in the *shirah* of the Heavenly angels. As we say in davening: כּוּלָּם אֲהוּבִים, *they are all beloved.* The angels are joined together with pure love; therefore, their singing is in unison and with unity.

This factor was present when the Jews sang *Shiras HaYam* after the Splitting of the Sea. As we say each morning, *"For this the beloved offered praise and exultation to God; the friends offered hymns, songs, blessings, and thanksgivings."* With these bonds of love they burst forth יַחַד, *in unison,* with their prophetic song.

The Arizal and later the Baal Shem Tov placed great emphasis on the need for genuine love among their disciples. Genuine *ahavas Yisrael* among members of a congregation grants enormous power to their tefillos when they pray together.

Garments of Royalty

In *Megillas Esther* we read כִּי אֵין לָבוֹא אֶל שַׁעַר הַמֶּלֶךְ בִּלְבוּשׁ שָׂק, *For one may not come before the gate of the king in sackcloth.*[18]

Zohar states that to be fit to stand before the King of kings in tefillah, one must be dressed properly. *Shulchan Aruch* states that one should be dressed nicely when reciting *Shemoneh Esrei.*[19]

However, for *Shacharis,* which is the main tefillah of the day, we need more than clean, honorable clothing. *Tallis* and *tefillin,* for those to whom these mitzvos apply, are essential for tefillah; they uplift the *neshamah* and bring us to a more lofty spiritual level. A *tallis gadol* (full-size *tallis*) has a greater *kedushah* than a *tallis kattan* (worn by most under their shirt), and this is why the custom for Sephardim and German Jews is that even *bachurim* wear a *tallis gadol.* But the *tallis kattan* also endows us with sanctity and serves to empower our tefillah.

---

18. *Esther* 4:2.

19. *Orach Chaim* 98:4.

Zohar and other holy *sefarim* teach that when one dons *tzitzis*, he makes himself a "throne" (receptacle) for the *Shechinah's* Presence, and when he dons *tefillin*, he draws the *Shechinah* upon himself.[20] As the Torah states: וְרָאוּ כָּל עַמֵּי הָאָרֶץ כִּי שֵׁם ה' נִקְרָא עָלֶיךָ וְיָרְאוּ מִמֶּךָּ, *And all the people of the earth will see that the Name of Hashem is proclaimed upon you and they will revere you,*[21] to which our Sages comment, "This refers to the *tefillin shel rosh* (of the head)."[22]

The more *mehudar* (beautiful within the context of Halachah) are one's *tzitzis* and *tefillin*, the greater their *kedushah*. It is of utmost importance that one have *tzitzis* and *tefillin* that not only are kosher, but are also *mehudar*. If a *ben Torah*, whose *neshamah* is uplifted by his immersion in Torah, tefillah, and spiritual development, does not give attention to the quality of his *tzitzis* and *tefillin,* Heaven will hold him accountable.

One should purchase these items only from a God-fearing Jew who he knows can be trusted. One should not purchase inexpensive *tzitzis* threads made by machine. From the spinning of the threads and on, the *tzitzis* need to be made *lishmah* (for the sake of the mitzvah), and some are stringent regarding earlier steps in the production process as well. *Tzitzis* made with these *hiddurim* (enhancements) can be expensive, but are well worth the investment.

Tefillin must be purchased from a *sofer* who is known to be a *yerei Shamayim* and also should be *mehudar*. The word תְּפִילִין is related to the word טָפֵל, that which is attached to something greater than itself. By wearing *tefillin*, one's *dveikus*, spiritual attachment to *Hashem Yisborach*, becomes strengthened — and that, as we have said previously, is a primary goal of tefillah.

---

20. See *Biur HaGra* to *Orach Chaim* 25:1.

21. *Devarim* 28:10.

22. *Menachos* 35b.

PART TWO

Expositions on the Siddur

CHAPTER EIGHT

Pesukei D'Zimrah: Breaking Through the Barriers

The ultimate goal of *Tefillas Shacharis*, beginning with *Birchos HaShachar* and *Pesukei D'Zimrah*, is to pray the *Shemoneh Esrei,* when we enter the inner chambers Above and stand directly before Hashem.[1]

To gain entry into a king's inner chamber, to stand before his royal majesty, one must first pass through various hallways and anterooms. And so it is with tefillah. As we proceed through *Shacharis*, our tefillos must ascend through four spiritual worlds, each one representing a higher level of *kedushah*.

1. See *Berachos* 30b and *Sanhedrin* 22a; and *Rambam*, *Hilchos Tefillah* 4:16.

- *Birchos Hashachar* and *Korbanos* correspond to our physical world, the עוֹלָם הָעֲשִׂיָּה.
- When we begin *Baruch She'amar*, we ascend to the next world, the עוֹלָם הַיְצִירָה, where the Heavenly angels are found.
- *Birchos Krias Shema*, beginning with *[Baruch Atah . . .] Yotzer Ohr*, bring us into the עוֹלָם הַבְּרִיאָה, the world of the כִּסֵּא הַכָּבוֹד, God's Throne of Glory, and where certain select angels are granted entrance. It is customary to sit during *Birchos Shema* because at this point we become a מֶרְכָּבָה (lit. *chariot*), a bearer of God's Presence, though our recitation of this portion of tefillah.
- *Shemoneh Esrei* ushers us in to the highest world, the עוֹלָם הָאֲצִילוּת, when we merit to stand directly before Hashem.

Breaking Through the Barriers

In *Sefer Shaarei Orah*[2] we find: It is well known that the atmosphere is filled with Heavenly angels, both good and evil. There are good angels who bring our tefillos to Heaven, and evil angels who prevent certain tefillos from ascending. As stated in the holy writings, there are tefillos that are not worthy of ascending; angels of destruction snatch them and cast them away in the place of "disqualified sacrifices" (פְּסוּלֵי הַמּוּקְדָשִׁים).

Also, the atmosphere is filled with angels of destruction created by our sins, and it is necessary to break through this spiritual barrier for our tefillos to ascend to their intended place. How do we accomplish this?

---

2. A kabbalistic work written centuries ago that is based on the traditions passed down by *Ramban* and other early commentators.

Three Dimensions of Tefillah

In *Sefer Tehillim*, a number of chapters are introduced with the word תְּפִלָּה: There is תְּפִלָּה לְמֹשֶׁה, *A prayer of Moshe*;[3] תְּפִלָּה לְדָוִד, *A prayer of Dovid*;[4] and תְּפִלָּה לְעָנִי, *A prayer of a poor man.*[5] Zohar[6] writes that these represent three dimensions of prayer. *A prayer of Moshe* is one that is rooted in a deep understanding of God's greatness and the workings in the Heavenly worlds. *A prayer of Dovid* is the sort of tefillah that fills many chapters of *Sefer Tehillim*: Dovid's ecstatic, lilting praises of Hashem, pulsating with love and awe of his Creator. *A prayer of a poor man* is the pleading before Hashem for one's needs, as a poor man begs for what he lacks.

In *Shacharis* we find all three of these prayers. After reciting *Birchos HaShachar*, we "clear the air" by reciting *Korbanos* and the *Ketores*. This can be likened to an aerial bombing to "soften up" the enemy before the ground troops move in. The "scents" of the *Korbanos* and *Ketores* rise Heavenward and destroy many of the spiritual barriers that threaten to impede our tefillos.

Then, the task of destroying the most formidable barriers begins with *Pesukei D'Zimrah,* which for the most part is *a prayer of Dovid.* This is followed by the first of the blessings preceding *Shema,* a *prayer of Moshe*, in which we relate how the Heavenly retinue, the various groups of angels, join in unison to offer their praises of Hashem. Finally, we come to *Shemoneh Esrei*, when each of us offers *a prayer of a poor man,* as we plead to Hashem for our needs and the needs of our fellow Jews.

These three components of *Shacharis* are alluded to in the verse from which we derive that Avraham established *tefillas Shacharis*:

---

3. Chapter 90.
4. Chapters 17 and 86.
5. Chapter 102.
6. *Parashas Balak,* 195a.

וַיַּשְׁכֵּם אַבְרָהָם בַּבֹּקֶר אֶל הַמָּקוֹם אֲשֶׁר עָמַד שָׁם אֶת פְּנֵי ה׳.
Avraham arose early in the morning to the place where he had stood before Hashem.[7]

The Gemara states that עָמַד, *stood,* is a reference to tefillah.[8] The word עָמַד is an acronym for **עָ**נִי, **מ**ֹשֶׁה, **ד**ָּוִד.

Pesukei D'Zimrah's Power

While the plain meaning of פְּסוּקֵי דְ׳זִמְרָה is *verses of song,* it can also be interpreted as *verses that cut away,* as in וְכַרְמְךָ לֹא תִזְמֹר, *And your vineyard you shall not prune.*[9] Dovid HaMelech says, זַמְּרוּ אֱלֹהִים זַמֵּרוּ, זַמְּרוּ לְמַלְכֵּנוּ זַמֵּרוּ, which is commonly translated as *Sing unto God, sing; sing unto our King, sing.*[10] These words can also be interpreted as *Sing unto God, and this will cut away [the barriers that impede our tefillah]*. This is the power of *Pesukei D'Zimrah.*

With Dovid at Our Side

In *Baruch She'amar,* with which *Pesukei D'Zimrah* begins, we say, וּבְשִׁירֵי דָוִד עַבְדֶּךָ נְהַלֶּלְךָ ה׳ אֱלֹהֵינוּ, *and through the songs of Dovid, Your servant, we shall praise You, Hashem, our God.* Most of *Pesukei D'Zimrah* is comprised of verses and entire chapters from Dovid HaMelech's *Sefer Tehillim.*

The Gemara tells us that when the teachings of a deceased scholar are quoted in this world, his "lips move in the grave"; meaning, his soul in the Next World connects to this thought.[11] When we recite the chapters of *Tehillim* that form the bulk of *Pesukei D'Zimrah,* Dovid HaMelech, the "sweet singer of Israel," sings along with us. How fortunate are we to have Dovid as part of our minyan!

---

7. *Bereishis* 19:27.
8. *Berachos* 26b.
9. *Vayikra* 25:4.
10. *Tehillim* 47:7.
11. *Yevamos* 97a and *Bechoros* 31b.

Many of the opening verses of Dovid's psalms contain his name. To understand the significance of this, let us imagine a king's palace surrounded by sword-bearing guards. No one dares to even approach the palace gates without authorization.

One day, a peasant dressed in rags walks confidently toward the gate. He has been sent from the battlefield by the commander of the king's forces with an urgent message for the king. As proof, he shows the guard a document sealed with the commander's official seal. Immediately, the gates open and the peasant is ushered inside.

When we mention Dovid's name as we recite *Tehillim*, and when we begin *Pesukei D'Zimrah* with the words וּבְשִׁירֵי דָוִד עַבְדֶּךָ נְהַלֶּלְךָ, we are invoking the merit of the one whom Scriptures describes as גִּבּוֹר חַיִל וְאִישׁ מִלְחָמָה, *a might man of valor and a man of war.*[12] Dovid's merit opens the gates of Heaven and destroys the spiritual forces that seek to prevent our prayers from ascending Heavenward.

Sefer Tehillim is a fountain of hope and salvation, for the individual Jew and the Jewish people as a whole. Each psalm is invested with enormous spiritual power. This is certainly true of the psalms that form the bulk of *Pesukei D'Zimrah.*

A Humble, Praying Soul

Dovid describes his essence by saying וַאֲנִי תְפִלָּה, *But I am prayer,*[13] meaning that his primary quality was his power of prayer.[14] *Sfas Emes* explains that this is one reason why the holy day of Hoshana Rabbah[15] is known as יוֹם הָעֲרָבָה, *the Day of the Willow.*[16] Willow

12. *Shmuel I* 16:18.

13. *Tehillim* 109:4.

14. *Rashi* interprets: "And I constantly pray to You."

15. The seventh day of the Succos festival.

16. The basic reason for this name is that in the Temple era, it was on this day that the Kohanim encircled the Altar seven times as tall *aravah* branches rested against the sides of the Altar. Also, the prophets instituted the custom of taking a bundle of five *aravah*

leaves are shaped like human lips; this, says the Midrash, is what the *aravah* represents. Zohar teaches us that on each day of Succos the succah is visited by the seven *Ushpizin*, Exalted Guests.[17] On Hoshana Rabbah, the *Ushpizin* are led by Dovid HaMelech, whose lips poured forth prayer in time of distress, yearning, salvation, and hope. Therefore, Hoshana Rabbah, the day of Dovid, is the "Day of the Lips."

In describing the terrible punishments that may be visited upon the Jewish people should they stray from the proper path, the Torah promises that ultimately, the dawn of salvation will appear:

> וְזָכַרְתִּי אֶת בְּרִיתִי יַעֲקוֹב וְאַף אֶת בְּרִיתִי יִצְחָק וְאַף אֶת בְּרִיתִי אַבְרָהָם אֶזְכֹּר וְהָאָרֶץ אֶזְכֹּר.
>
> *I will remember My covenant with Yaakov and also My covenant with Yitzchak and also My covenant with Avraham will I remember, and I will remember the Land.*[18]

According to Zohar, the word וְהָאָרֶץ, *and the Land,* in this verse alludes to Dovid, whose humility likened him to the earth upon which everyone treads.[19] Dovid's humility allows him to connect to the most lowly *neshamos* and lift them up from the spiritual morass in which they are mired.[20] Our lowly generation, the generation of *Ikvesa D'Meshicha* (the period that precedes Mashiach's arrival), can uplift itself by connecting with Dovid as we recite his *Pesukei D'Zimrah* with *kavanah* and genuine humility before Hashem.

---

branches in hand on this day, a practice that we still follow.

17. Avraham, Yitzchak, Yaakov, Moshe, Aharon, Yosef, and Dovid.

18. *Vayikra* 26:42.

19. On another occasion, Rav Wolfson said that just as the earth has in it the potential for growth, so too from Dovid will sprout forth Mashiach and the end of this *galus*. This is why in *Shemoneh Esrei* and other places Mashiach's arrival is referred to as צְמִיחָה, *sprouting*, a term associated with plant life.

20. Dovid says of himself, "But I am a worm, not a man" (*Tehillim* 22:7) and "For I am poor and needy" (86:1).

Chiddushei HaRim writes that the very name דָּוִד represents his humility. Dovid began as a דַּל, a poor, humble shepherd. Then he rose straight and tall like a ו as he became king of the Jewish people. Yet, despite his rise to prominence, he remained the same דַּל, humble man, as before.

His Essence Cries Out

R' Yechezkel of Kuzhmir interprets וַאֲנִי תְפִלָּה, *but I am prayer*, by way of a parable. If a wealthy man loses his fortune but still dresses as a man of wealth, he must explain his situation to any potential benefactor from whom he seeks assistance. After all, he still wears his silken garments and carries his silver walking stick. Externally, he appears to be the same rich man he once was. Therefore, an explanation is in order for why he needs financial help.

Such is the not the case with the beggar who knocks on someone's door wearing tattered rags, torn shoes, holding a wooden stick. His very appearance cries out, "I am destitute — help me! Give me clothing, give me shoes!"

Dovid said to Hashem, "There is no need for me to enunciate my troubles and needs. My situation cries out for help — my essence is my prayer."

Our essence, too, cries out for help.

The *Tiferes Shlomo* of Radomsk taught that when one attaches himself to the ways of a *tzaddik,* his soul merits to receive a *nitzotz,* holy spark, of that *tzaddik's* soul. By reciting *Pesukei D'Zimrah* with true humility, we can merit a *nitzotz* of Dovid and then our very essence will cry out to Hashem — "וַאֲנִי תְפִלָּה!"

Together

It is unfortunate that some do not accord *Pesukei D'Zimrah* the importance it deserves. They are content to come late to shul and recite *Pesukei D'Zimrah* quickly, even skipping parts.[21] The chassidic master R' Levi Yitzchak of Berditchev[22] would speak of how crucial *Pesukei D'Zimrah* is to the effectiveness of one's *Tefillas Shacharis.*

21. *Shulchan Aruch* does inform us which parts a latecomer may skip so that he will be able to pray *Shemoneh Esrei* together with the minyan. However, this is after the fact, and certainly not ideal.

22. As quoted in *Sippurei Ramach.*

Dovid did not write *Sefer Tehillim* in a day. It was the work of a lifetime. Each chapter corresponds to a *heichal,* a spiritual edifice in Heaven; each chapter provides the "key" to opening that edifice. When a minyan begins a particular chapter in unison, its collective merit allows its tefillos to enter that *heichal* with great power and it can accomplish a great deal. This is not the case when each person prays at his own pace, with one person reciting *Ashrei* while the other is up to *Mizmor L'Sodah*. Then, each one's prayer stands on its own, and its power is much weaker.

That praying in unison is crucial for a truly powerful tefillah experience is hinted at in the opening words of *Pesukei D'Zimra* (according to *Nusach Ashkenaz),* for the initial letters of **בָּרוּךְ שֶׁאָמַר וְהָיָה הָעוֹלָם** spell בְּשָׁוֶה, *in unison*. In *Nusach Sefard*, the opening words are **הוֹדוּ לַה׳ קִרְאוּ בִשְׁמוֹ**, whose initial letters (when rearranged) spell בְּקָהָל, *with the congregation,* an allusion that one should make sure to begin his davening together with the minyan.

Those who follow these guidelines and pour out their hearts before Hashem in the desired way know that no earthly pleasure can compare to it. And when one's *Shacharis* is as it should be, he merits success the entire day, both in spiritual and material pursuits.

In the Way of Moshe

When we precede the requests that form most of *Shemoneh Esrei* with the praises of *Pesukei D'Zimrah*, we are going in the ways of Moshe Rabbeinu. As the Gemara states:[23]

> *R' Simlai expounded: A person should always [first] arrange his praises of HaKadosh Baruch Hu and only then should he pray. From where do we derive this? From Moshe, for it is written, "And I prayed to Hashem at that time ... Hashem Elokim, You have begun to show Your servant Your greatness and Your strong hand, for what power on*

23. *Berachos* 32a.

earth can perform according to Your deeds and mighty acts?"[24] *And only afterwards does it say, "Let me now cross and see the good Land [of Eretz Yisrael] ..."*[25]

Baal HaTurim notes that the *gematria* of the word וָאֶתְחַנַּן, *And I prayed,* with which Moshe opened his words at that time, is equal to שִׁירָה, *song.*[26] Moshe preceded his request to enter Eretz Yisrael with songs of praises of Hashem in the hope that through this his tefillah would be accepted.

Shabbos — A Day of Song

The Beis Avraham of Slonim offers a homiletic interpretation of the verse וָאֶתְחַנַּן אֶל ה' בָּעֵת הַהִוא לֵאמֹר:

ו' אֶתְחַנַּן אֶל ה', *During the six workdays I pray to Hashem*
בָּעֵת הַהִוא, *that when that special time — the day of Shabbos — arrives*
לֵאמֹר, *I should merit to properly utter sacred words of tefillah as is befitting this holy day.*

In *Shacharis* of Shabbos morning we say, *"And the day of Shabbos gives praise, saying, 'A psalm, a song for the day of Shabbos. It is good to praise Hashem ...'"*[27] The very essence of Shabbos is *shirah,* songs of praise of Hashem. The sanctity and exalted spirit that permeate Shabbos give our tefillos added spiritual power. As much as our weekday tefillos can accomplish, our Shabbos tefillos can accomplish much more.[28] This is why the *Pesukei D'Zimrah* portion of Shabbos morning is greatly expanded.[29]

---

24. *Devarim* 3:23-24.

25. Ibid. v. 25.

26. 515.

27. *Tehillim*: 92:1-2.

28. It is well known that the Chazon Ish would say the same regarding Torah study on Shabbos.

29. There are other proofs of the *shirah* aspect of Shabbos, among them the expanded *Bircas Yotzer* with its *Kel Adon* arranged according to the *Aleph-Beis.*

The Great *Hallel*

One of the special Shabbos additions is Psalm 136, which our Sages refer to as הַלֵּל הַגָּדוֹל, *The Great Hallel.*[30] It contains 26 verses, corresponding to the numerical value of י־ה־ו־ה, which outline the prime elements in Creation and the major events in our nation's exodus from Egypt and conquest of Eretz Yisrael.

In some *siddurim* each verse of this psalm has alongside it the name of a specific angel who sings that verse in Heaven. For example, one angel is assigned the verse וּלְעוֹג מֶלֶךְ הַבָּשָׁן כִּי לְעוֹלָם חַסְדּוֹ. No two angels recite the same praise. Only through the collective songs of the countless legions of angels is the Heavenly song complete and fit to be presented as a "crown" to Hashem.

Yet, we earthly beings, descendants of Avraham Avinu, merit to recite *all* 26 praises of this psalm. And though our numbers are minuscule compared to the myriad angels, the crown that our tefillos form is on a par with theirs. As we say in the *Nusach Sefard* version of the *Mussaf Kedushah* of Shabbos and Yom Tov:

> *A crown they will give You, O Hashem, our God — the angels of the multitude above, together with Your people, Israel, who are assembled below.*

Nishmas

The beautiful, soul-stirring *Nishmas* prayer, recited Shabbos and Yom Tov morning after *Shiras HaYam,* is an outpouring of gratitude and praise to Hashem. It depicts our utter dependency on His mercy, our total inadequacy to properly praise Him, and our enthusiastic resolve to dedicate ourselves to His service. The Mishnah[31] refers to *Nishmas* as בִּרְכַּת הַשִּׁיר, *the Blessing of the Song,* because, as *Tosafos* explains, it is the conclusion of *Pesukei D'Zimrah.*[32]

30. See *Pesachim* 118a.

31. Ibid.

32. *Tur* (*Orach Chaim* ch. 281) writes that it is recited only on Shabbos and Yom Tov

Nishmas occupied a special place in the hearts of the Baal Shem Tov's *talmidim.* All week long they would eagerly anticipate the moment on Shabbos morning when they could burst forth, with raised voices and an outpouring of emotion, as they began *"Nishmas kol chai ..."* — this, despite the fact that they recited all of *Pesukei D'Zimrah*, every day, with great concentration and emotion.

Aside from its essential uplifting message, there is a deeper reason why *tzaddikim* would recite *Nishmas* with flaming passion. We know that on Shabbos every Jew is blessed with a *neshamah yeseirah*, additional soul. The soul is comprised of three parts: *nefesh, ruach,* and *neshamah.*[33] Each of the three parts of the *neshamah yeseirah* are bestowed upon us in two stages; the first on Friday night and the second on Shabbos morning, when the sanctity of Shabbos intensifies.[34]

On Friday night, upon reciting בּוֹאִי בְשָׁלוֹם we receive the first part of the additional *nefesh*; at *Barechu*, we receive the *ruach*; and upon reciting the blessing of הַפּוֹרֵס סוּכַּת שָׁלוֹם, we receive the *neshamah*. On Shabbos morning, upon reciting *Nishmas* we receive the second part of the additional *nefesh*; during the *Shemoneh Esrei* of *Shacharis* we are endowed with the *ruach*; and at the *kedushah* of *Mussaf* we receive the *neshamah*. Thus, *Nishmas* signals a greater *neshamah yeseirah* and hence a greater passion for the spirituality of the moment.

Tzaddikim have taught that our Shabbos experience gives spiritual energy to the forthcoming week. On the other hand, the more spiritual effort we expend during the six workdays, the

---

because the absence of work on these days affords us the time to focus on the prayer's message and recite it with proper *kavanah.*

33. *Nefesh* is the soul's life-giving force; *ruach* is the seat of its emotions; and *neshamah* is the place of its intellect.

34. There is a steady increase of *kedushas Shabbos* as the day progresses, until late Shabbos afternoon, which in Kabbalistic literature is known as רַעֲוָא דְרַעֲוִין, *[the time of] favor of favors*. It is because of the additional aspect of the *neshamah yeseirah* on Shabbbos morning that, according to the Arizal, one should immerse himself in a *mikveh* on Shabbos morning even if he has already done so on Erev Shabbos.

more prepared we are to absorb the blessings of Shabbos. The effort we expend in reciting *Pesukei D'Zimrah*, every day of the week and especially on Shabbos, has a profound impact on all our endeavors, that day, that week, and in a true sense for the rest of our lives.

CHAPTER NINE

Baruch She'amar

Tur states:

> *Baruch She'amar* should be recited in a sweet melody, for it is a beautiful, precious song [to Hashem]. As stated in *Sefer Heichalos,* it contains פ"ז (87) words, as in רֹאשׁוֹ כֶּתֶם פָּז, *His head is* ***fine gold.***[1]

One can merit that his davening becomes a "crown of fine gold" for the King of kings.

The commentators cite the ancient tradition that *Baruch She'amar* was incorporated into the daily tefillah by the *Anshei Knesses HaGedolah* some 2,400 years ago when a script with its text fell from Heaven. Each word therefore has special significance.

1. *Shir HaShirim* 5:11.

Tzaddikim invested enormous effort in their recitation of *Baruch She'amar.* They hung onto each word, reciting it with love and ecstasy. R' Asher of Karlin would say the words יָחִיד חֵי הָעוֹלָמִים *(O unique One, life-giver of all the worlds)* with great power and melody. After his passing, a grandchild said, "The יָחִיד חֵי הָעוֹלָמִים [i.e. Hashem] will be forever, but the way my grandfather would say יָחִיד חֵי הָעוֹלָמִים is gone forever." We should strive to understand the sacred words of *Baruch She'amar* on our level and recite them with proper *kavanah.*

Foundations of Faith

Baruch She'amar's opening phrases encapsulate the very foundations of our *emunah.*

בָּרוּךְ שֶׁאָמַר וְהָיָה הָעוֹלָם, בָּרוּךְ הוּא.

Blessed is He Who spoke and the world came into being, blessed is He.

Hashem created the world יֵשׁ מֵאַיִן, out of nothingness, by way of the עֲשָׂרָה מַאֲמָרוֹת, the Ten Utterances with which *Sefer Bereishis* opens. And He did not, God forbid, abandon His world after its creation, as the next phrase indicates:

בָּרוּךְ אוֹמֵר וְעֹשֶׂה, *Blessed is He Who speaks and does.* Note that the first phrase is past tense, שֶׁאָמַר, *Who* ***spoke,*** while the second is in the present, אוֹמֵר, *Who* ***speaks.*** Creation is an ongoing process; as we say every morning in the first of the *Birchos Shema, "... and in His goodness renews daily, perpetually, the work of creation."* The world exists at any given moment only because Hashem wills it to be.

We can liken this to the difference between placing a cup on a table and holding it in one's hand. In the former case, the cup can remain on the table indefinitely because it was once placed there. In the latter, each second that the cup does not fall to the ground is only due to the person's grip at that moment.

לְעוֹלָם ה׳ דְּבָרְךָ נִצָּב בַּשָּׁמָיִם, *Forever, Hashem, Your word stands firm in Heaven.*[2] Hashem's constant renewal of Creation indicates His *hashgachah pratis*, His exacting guidance of all that transpires in our lives.

Who Upholds His Decrees

בָּרוּךְ גּוֹזֵר וּמְקַיֵּם.
Blessed is He Who decrees and upholds.

In this lowly world, heads of state and aspiring politicians make empty promises which they cannot fulfill and have no intention of fulfilling. Of the *Ribbono shel Olam*, however, the Torah states: *God is not a man that He should be deceitful, nor a human being that He should relent. Would He say and not do, or speak and not confirm?*[3]

There is another aspect of Hashem's absolute faithfulness in upholding His utterances. One of the Thirteen Principles of Faith is: *I believe with perfect faith that this Torah will not be exchanged nor will there be another Torah from the Creator, Blessed is His Name.* Judaism is distinguished from other religions by the fact that our entire nation — over one million men, women, and children — stood at the foot of Mount Sinai as Hashem revealed the Ten Commandments to His people. Hashem, to Whom past, present, and future are one and the same, used His Torah as the "blueprint" for this universe, and it will remain the purpose and design of Creation forever. The Torah, like its Author, is eternal.

The holy Skulener Rebbe, R' Eliezer Zusha Portugal, of blessed memory, offered an original interpretation of בָּרוּךְ גּוֹזֵר וּמְקַיֵּם. The Rebbe suffered terrible persecution and imprisonment at the hands of the Romanian government because of his *mesiras*

2. *Tehillim* 119:89.
3. *Bamidbar* 23:19.

nefesh for Torah observance. As he languished in prison, the Rebbe found himself with more time than usual to focus on the meaning of his daily prayers. One morning, while reciting *Baruch She'amar,* he was bothered by a question. The term גּוֹזֵר, *decree,* when associated with the workings of Heaven, usually refers to a decree that is unpleasant, often a form of punishment. The rest of *Baruch She'amar,* however, speaks only of blessing and compassion.

The Rebbe wondered, what does בָּרוּךְ גּוֹזֵר וּמְקַיֵּם mean?

A thought struck him: The word גּוֹזֵר refers to the suffering that Hashem decrees upon a person. The word מְקַיֵּם in this context means *to sustain,* to give one the ability *to endure. Blessed is He Who decrees* suffering upon a person, *and sustains* that person so that no matter how broken his body is, it *endures* and he is able to survive and remain among the living.

The Rebbe became filled with joy and hope, for he felt that this interpretation related to him personally. Hashem had decreed that the enemies of Torah should be allowed to imprison him and Hashem would ensure that no matter what his captors did to him, he would remain alive and ultimately would be freed.[4]

A Torah World

בָּרוּךְ עֹשֶׂה בְרֵאשִׁית.

Blessed is He Who maintains creation.

These words can also be interpreted as *Blessed is He Who effects happenings in His creations in accordance with the Torah, which begins with the word* בְּרֵאשִׁית. The Torah insights and rulings of the luminaries in any given generation can literally effect changes in the workings of this world. This is illustrated by the following story:

4. Every year, on the anniversary of his release from prison, the Skulener Rebbe would recount this episode to his chassidim.

In the city of Volozhin more than two centuries ago a Jew was stricken with a serious lung condition. When his condition did not improve he decided to move to Switzerland where, he was told, the rarified climate might help his condition. Then his deceased father appeared to him in a dream:

"My son," he said, "if you want to live, remain in Volozhin. You see, the condition from which you suffer can also affect the lungs of animals. Now, how long can an animal suffering from such a condition live? The vast majority of Ashkenazic poskim are of the opinion that such an animal is a treifah, for it would die within the year.

"However, the Shaagas Aryeh, of blessed memory,[5] *who served as Rav of Volozhin, held that such an animal can live many years, and is therefore kosher. The rabbanim of Volozhin continue to follow the Shaagas Aryeh's psak (ruling).*

"In Heaven, the Shaagas Aryeh's psak is accepted for the city of Volozhin. As long as you remain in Volozhin, you are in the domain of his psak and therefore you can live. However, if you move to Switzerland, you will then fall under the psak of the rabbanim who rule the animal to be a treifah, and you will die within the year. So do not leave Volozhin."

The man remained in Volozhin and, though his lungs never healed, he lived to a ripe old age.

The Earth's Yearning

בָּרוּךְ מְרַחֵם עַל הָאָרֶץ.

Blessed is He Who has mercy on the earth.

We commonly associate feelings and emotions with human beings and, to a lesser degree with the animal kingdom and other

5. R' Aryeh Leib Gunzberg, one of the great Torah giants of that era.

creatures. In a deeper sense, every one of Hashem's creations has a desire — to fulfill the purpose for which it was created, and in so doing draw close to the Source whence it came.

Inanimate earth is the lowest form of creation. Yet, our Sages say the word אָרֶץ, *earth,* is related to רָץ, *run*: "Why is it called אָרֶץ? Because it runs to fulfill its Creator's desire."[6] When the earth produces fruit and other forms of plant life, it has fulfilled its purpose.

But not every piece of ground is intended for plowing and sowing. When a Jew treads a path on his way to serving Hashem, it is a fulfillment of that road's "mission" and brings it to its *tikkun* (spiritual rectification). And it is for this that the earth yearns.

"The roads of Zion are in mourning, for lack of festival pilgrims."[7] The roads of Jerusalem yearn for the days when Jews will once again tread upon them on their way to the Beis HaMikdash in honor of Yom Tov. When we say the words *Blessed is He Who has mercy on the earth,* we are in essence saying, "Master of the Universe: Even if we are unworthy, please have mercy on the earth of our Holy City and return us to its soil so that we can serve You as in days gone by."

Invoking His Mercy

בָּרוּךְ מְרַחֵם עַל הַבְּרִיּוֹת.

Blessed is He Who has mercy on the creatures.

A Jew's deeds and words in this world have enormous spiritual power. We can liken this to a main switch that controls the lights of a skyscraper. A small action by a Jew on this world can effect powerful happenings in all the Upper Worlds.

6. *Bereishis Rabbah* 5:8.

7. *Eichah* 1:4.

Ramchal[8] writes that when a Jew washes his hands upon arising in the prescribed manner of *negel vasser,*[9] he does far more than remove the spiritual impurity that descended upon his body as he slept. He effects a *tikkun* in all of creation.[10] The same applies to his other actions as well.

We are the ones who initiate Hashem's compassion towards animals and other creatures. Heaven is merciful upon animal life when man is merciful towards it. And once the Divine mercy begins to flow, man benefits from it as well. To the verse *Both man and beast You save, O Hashem,*[11] the Midrash states: "Man, in the animals' merit, is saved by Hashem."[12] At times there are *kitrugim,* Heavenly indictments, which threaten to deny mankind the mercy that it needs. However, if it is decreed that animal life be the beneficiary of Hashem's mercy, then once the Divine compassion begins to flow, it can benefit mankind as well.

However, when man is not compassionate towards animals, Heaven acts towards him in the same way.

The Gemara relates:

> *There was once a calf being led to slaughter. It went and hung its head among the folds of Rebbi's [R' Yehudah HaNasi's] garments and it cried. Rebbi told it, "Go; for this you were created!"*[13]
>
> *They said in Heaven, "Since he did not show mercy, let suffering come upon him." (Rebbi endured physical suffering for 13 years.)*
>
> *And they [the suffering] left [Rebbi] as a result of an incident. One day, Rebbi's maidservant was cleaning the house. There was a litter of baby weasels that was cased*

8. R' Moshe Chaim Luzzatto, author of *Mesilas Yesharim* and other classic works.

9. Three times on each hand, alternately; see *Shulchan Aruch, Orach Chaim* 4:2.

10. *Derech Hashem,* part IV, chapter 6.

11. *Tehillim* 36:7.

12. *Vayikra Rabbah* 27:1.

13. Rebbi was correct that the animal would achieve its purpose by being slaughtered. Nevertheless, he should have shown compassion for its plight.

upon the floor and she was sweeping them out. Rebbi told her, "Let them be; it is written, 'and His mercy is upon all His creations.'"[14]

They said in Heaven, "Since he shows mercy, let us show mercy to him."[15]

We should emulate Hashem and demonstrate mercy towards every creature.

Blessed is He Who has mercy on the creatures.

His Kindness Is Forever

בָּרוּךְ מְשַׁלֵּם שָׂכָר טוֹב לִירֵאָיו.

Blessed is He Who gives a goodly reward to those who fear Him.

Sefer Chovos HaLevavos discusses at great length the constant wonders and acts of kindness with which Hashem blesses a human being from the moment he enters this world. As we say in the prayer of *Nishmas:*

> *Were our mouth as full of song as the sea, and our tongue as full of joyous song as its multitude of waves, and our lips as full of praise as the breadth of the heavens, and our eyes as brilliant as the sun and the moon, and our hands as outspread as eagles of the sky, and our feet as swift as hinds — we could still not thank You sufficiently, Hashem, our God and God of our forefathers, and to bless Your Name for even one of the thousand thousand, thousands and thousands and myriad myriad of favors that You performed for our ancestors and for us.*

Were we to spend a lifetime thanking Hashem for even one of His infinite kindnesses, it would not be sufficient. And yet,

14. *Tehillim* 145:9.

15. *Bava Metzia* 85a.

Hashem acts towards us as if we owe Him nothing. He rewards us for every good deed, word, and thought.

And He even grants reward לִירֵאָיו, *to those who fear Him.* Imagine someone approaching a policeman and requesting reward for stopping at a red light. The officer would consider the man insane, and rightfully so! Still, Hashem rewards us even for refraining from committing a sin. When we succeed in overcoming the temptation to eat food of questionable kashrus, or restrain ourselves from speaking *lashon hara*, we have earned Divine reward.

People of Redemption

בָּרוּךְ פּוֹדֶה וּמַצִּיל — *Blessed is He Who redeems and rescues.*

In Chapter 34 of *Sefer Tehillim,* the verses' initial letters (with the exception of the first and last verse) follow the order of the *aleph-beis.* The last of these 22 verses speaks of the punishment that is meted out to the wicked: תְּמוֹתֵת רָשָׁע רָעָה וְשֹׂנְאֵי צַדִּיק יֶאְשָׁמוּ, *The death blow of the wicked is evil, and the haters of the righteous will be condemned.*[16] The chapter's concluding verse is: פּוֹדֶה ה׳ נֶפֶשׁ עֲבָדָיו וְלֹא יֶאְשְׁמוּ כָּל הַחֹסִים בּוֹ, *Hashem redeems the soul of His servants, and all who take refuge in Him will not be condemned.*

R' Tzadok HaKohen of Lublin explains: Hashem has two different ways through which He judges man and guides his life. At times the method is *din,* strict justice, whereby man is rewarded or punished in accordance with his deeds. Other times, through some merit, either individually or collectively, we are beneficiaries of Hashem's compassion and He "redeems" us from our travails despite the fact that we have not earned it. This method is known as *pidyon* (redemption).[17]

---

16. *Tehillim* 34:22.

17. Rav Wolfson notes that chapter 25 of *Tehillim* also follows the order of the *Aleph-*

The last verse of chapter 34, which begins with the word פּוֹדֶה, *redeem,* and does not follow the systematic order of the other verses, teaches that the Heavenly conduct of *pidyon* goes beyond the order of reward and punishment. It is an expression of Hashem's love for His beloved children, which is unconditional and eternal. It brings about salvation at times when we are unworthy.

It was through *pidyon* that the Jewish people were rescued at the Sea of Reeds following the exodus from Egypt, when the Angel of the Sea argued, "These (the Egyptians) are idol worshippers and these (the Jews) are idol worshippers!" Thus does the *Maariv* blessing that speaks of the Exodus conclude with the verse, *"For Hashem has* **redeemed** [פָּדָה] *Yaakov, and delivered him from the hand of one mightier than he."*[18] The "mighty one" is the Satan, who sought to prevent our redemption by way of indictment, but Hashem cast his arguments aside and redeemed us.

Blessed is He Who redeems and rescues.

Merciful Father

בָּרוּךְ אַתָּה ה׳ ... הָאֵל הָאָב הָרַחֲמָן.
Blessed are You, Hashem ... the God, the merciful Father.

Hashem is *God* of the entire universe, and *Father* to the Jewish People, His beloved Chosen Nation, as it is written, *"You are children to Hashem."*[19] He is our *merciful Father* Who grants us mercy and compassion through His Thirteen Attributes of Mercy even when we are undeserving.

Beis and concludes with a verse that is not part of the order and which speaks of *pidyon.*

18. *Yirmiyahu* 31:10.

19. *Devarim* 14:1.

הַמְהֻלָּל בְּפֶה עַמּוֹ.

Who is lauded by the mouth of His people.

Grammatically, it should read בְּפִי עַמּוֹ, *by the* ***mouths*** *of His people.* The Arizal explains that the singular is used here because the *gematria* of בְּפֶה is 87, alluding to the 87 words of *Baruch She'amar* that were sent to us from Heaven, as elaborated upon above.

מְשֻׁבָּח וּמְפֹאָר בִּלְשׁוֹן חֲסִידָיו וַעֲבָדָיו.

Praised and glorified by the tongue of His devout ones and His servants.

His devout ones are those who serve Hashem out of love; *His servants* serve Hashem out of awe, a lower level. Because of their essential difference, these two groups praise Hashem through tefillah in very different ways. For *His devout ones,* tefillah is a joyous, exhilarating experience; for *His servants*, it is an obligation that they faithfully fulfill.

A *Shacharis* Synopsis

נְהַלֶּלְךָ ה׳ אֱלֹהֵינוּ בִּשְׁבָחוֹת וּבִזְמִרוֹת.

We shall laud You, Hashem, our God, with praises and songs.

Praises refers to *Mizmor L'Sodah*[20] which we recite soon after *Baruch She'amar. Beis Yosef*[21] writes that because of this psalm's singular quality, it should be recited slowly and melodiously. *Songs* refers to *Ashrei* and the *Hallelukas.*[22]

20. *Tehillim* ch. 100.
21. *Orach Chaim* ch. 51.
22. *Tehillim,* chs. 146-150.

וּנְגַדֶּלְךָ. — We shall declare Your greatness.

This refers to *Az Yashir* (the Song of the Sea), which is introduced with the words וַיַּרְא יִשְׂרָאֵל אֶת הַיָּד **הַגְּדֹלָה**, *And Yisrael saw* ***the great*** *hand [of Hashem].*[23]

וּנְשַׁבֵּחֲךָ. — And we shall praise You.

This refers to the *berachah* of יִשְׁתַּבַּח שִׁמְךָ *([May Your Name] be praised)* with which *Pesukei D'Zimrah* concludes.

וּנְפָאֶרְךָ. — And we shall glorify You.

This refers to the opening blessing of *Bircas Shema,* in which we declare, וְעַל מְאוֹרֵי אוֹר שֶׁיָּצַרְתָּ, הֵמָּה **יְפָאֲרוּךָ** סֶּלָה, *and for the luminaries of light that You have formed, may they* ***glorify You*** *forever.*

וְנַמְלִיכְךָ וְנַזְכִּיר שִׁמְךָ.
And we shall proclaim Your reign and mention Your Name.

This refers to *kabbalas ol malchus Shamayim,* acceptance of the sovereignty of Heaven, when we recite the *Shema.*

מַלְכֵּנוּ אֱלֹהֵינוּ יָחִיד חֵי הָעוֹלָמִים.
Our King, our God, O Unique One, Live-giver of the worlds.

The word חֵי, *Life-giver,* whose *gematria* is 18, alludes to the 18 blessings of *Shemoneh Esrei.*[24]

23. *Shemos* 14:31.

24. *Shemoneh Esrei* means *eighteen,* the number of blessings that the *Anshei Knesses HaGedolah* composed for this prayer. Later, a 19th blessing, *V'lamalshinim,* was added.

מֶלֶךְ מְשֻׁבָּח וּמְפֹאָר עֲדֵי עַד שְׁמוֹ הַגָּדוֹל.

King Whose great Name is eternally praised and glorified.

Praised and glorified allude to the praises included in *Ashrei* and *Uva L'Tzion* which follow *Shemoneh Esrei.*

When addressing an earthly king, we dare not refer to him by his name, for this would be disrespectful; his position is his praise. Regarding Hashem, however, there is no greater praise than *His great Name*, which represents His sublime attributes.

בָּרוּךְ אַתָּה ה׳, מֶלֶךְ מְהֻלָּל בַּתִּשְׁבָּחוֹת.

Blessed are You, Hashem, the King Who is lauded with praises.

When we say these words, we should contemplate how utterly fortunate we are to have the privilege every day of our lives to stand before our Creator in prayer and declare His praises.

CHAPTER TEN

Mizmor L'Sodah

In *Pesukei D'Zimrah* on weekdays,[1] immediately following *Baruch She'amar*[2] we recite Psalm 100, מִזְמוֹר לְתוֹדָה, *A Song of Thanksgiving. Baruch She'amar* can be likened to *Birchos HaNehenin,* the blessings we recite before enjoying the pleasures of food, drink, or fragrance. We recite *Baruch She'amar* prior to singing the praises of our Creator, an incomparable privilege and pleasure. We begin our praises with *Mizmor L'Sodah* because *hakaras hatov,* gratitude, is a fundamental concept in *avodas Hashem.* This is obvious from many laws that are basic to Jewish living.

1. *Mizmor L'Sodah* is not recited on Shabbos and Yom Tov because it is in place of the קָרְבַּן תּוֹדָה, the thanksgiving offering, which, as a private sacrifice, could be brought only on a weekday. On Shabbos, Rav Wolfson noted, immediately following *Baruch She'amar* (according to *Nusach Sefard*) we recite *Mizmor Shir L'Yom HaShabbos* (Psalm 92), in which we say: "It is good to thank Hashem, and to say praise to Your Name."
2. According to *Nusach Sefard.*

We begin our day with *Modeh Ani*: *"I gratefully thank You, O living and eternal King, for You have returned my soul within me with compassion ..."*

A Jew is required to recite 100 blessings a day,[3] each blessing an expression of praise of Hashem. That *Mizmor L'Sodah* is the 100th psalm in *Sefer Tehillim* alludes to this enactment of Dovid HaMelech.[4]

In the Temple era, a farmer in Eretz Yisrael would apportion *bikkurim* from his first ripened crops, as an expression of thanks for the bountiful blessings that Hashem had bestowed upon him.

Shulchan Aruch states that *Mizmor L'Sodah* should be recited melodiously, for at the time of the Final Redemption all songs will be set aside except for this song of thanksgiving;[5] *hakaras hatov* is a fundamental concept and is not subject to change. When a Jew expresses his gratitude to Hashem, he opens the Divine gates of thanksgiving. This initiates a flow of blessing so that he will have yet more reasons to express his thanks.[6]

Furthermore, when we express our gratitude to Hashem, we effect a *tikkun* for the sin of Adam who in his very first conversation with Hashem expressed ingratitude.[7]

A *Tzaddik's* Legacy

Rabbi Alexander Ziskind of Horodna, author of *Yesod V'Shoresh HaAvodah,* was a Lithuanian *tzaddik* whose soul was aflame with love of Hashem and joy in serving Him. The Chozeh of Lublin, a chassidic giant whose insight was known to be supernatural, said that R' Alexander Ziskind's path of *avodas Hashem* was beloved in Heaven.

3. *Shulchan Aruch, Orach Chaim* 46:3.
4. See *Tur, Orach Chaim* ch. 46.
5. *Shulchan Aruch* 51:9.
6. The topic of thanksgiving is further discussed in "*Modim*" (ch. 21).
7. When Hashem confronted Adam concerning his eating from the Tree of Knowledge, he responded by placing the blame on the "woman whom You gave to be with me" (*Bereishis* 3:12; see *Rashi*).

In his ethical will, this *tzaddik* enumerated various situations in his lifetime in which he found cause to thank Hashem. It is not a simple task to write about oneself. There is often a danger that one's thoughts might be influenced by *ga'avah* (pride). However, R' Alexander Ziskind was a pure *neshamah*. He was distant from any hint of pride, and therefore his words leave a deep impression upon the reader. In one section of his will he wrote:

> *I gave praise and thanks to my Creator, blessed is His Name, for the great kindness that He did for me in that from my youth, He provided me with a private room in which I could devote myself to Torah and tefillah, as you well know. Having such a room is fundamental to anyone who strives for spiritual perfection in this lowly world. Whenever I contemplated this kindness — sometimes many times in a single day — I would express my thanks to Hashem.*
>
> *Because my Shemoneh Esrei is usually quite lengthy, I rarely am able to recite Kedushah with the minyan, or the "Yehei Shemei Rabbah" that follows the Shemoneh Esrei of Maariv, and this pained me greatly. On the occasions when I was able to recite these prayers, I would offer a powerful, mental thanks to Hashem that He granted me this merit.*
>
> *. . . My beloved children: Whenever I received a letter from you, or if I was informed that all was well with you, I would express my thanks to Hashem with the following words: "I give thanks to my Creator, blessed is His Name, that He provided me with the good news of the well-being of my children and grandchildren."*
>
> *When I would don my Shabbos clothing on Friday afternoon, I would express my great thanks to Hashem and say, "I thank You, My Creator, that You have given me clothing of excellent quality to wear in honor of Shabbos — not because I am deserving of this, but because of Your abundant kindness. For I know that there are many great*

tzaddikim whose greatness I do not approach who do not have such clothing for Shabbos. And so I thought to myself that it would be sinful were I not to express my gratitude to You for this."

In the winter, I wear a woolen overcoat. Whenever I put it on, I thank Hashem for giving it to me. For I know very well that without this coat, I would suffer very much from the cold.

Whenever I possessed what I needed and did not have to borrow from others, I would express my thanks to Hashem and say, "Thank You, Hashem, for providing me with all my needs." I said this expression of thanks many times.

When I would forget to do something and then would recall it soon enough so that nothing was lost in between, I would express my thanks to Hashem for allowing me to recall it in time.

If my eyeglasses would fall and not break, I would express my thanks to Hashem. For I know with complete and genuine faith that whatever happens to a person, be it a small goodness or something painful, all is from Hashem. Everything is through His constant, exacting Providence at every moment.

Therefore, my beloved children: I beseech you very, very much that you should be meticulous in this Divine service, to find reason to express your thanks to Hashem many, many times each day.

Only With Joy

We can interpret the words מִזְמוֹר לְתוֹדָה to mean *A song for the fact that I have been granted the ability and the understanding to offer You thanksgiving.* Later in this chapter, Dovid says, עִבְדוּ אֶת ה' בְּשִׂמְחָה בֹּאוּ לְפָנָיו בִּרְנָנָה, *Serve Hashem with gladness, come before Him with joyous song.* The awareness that we are truly fortunate to be able to sing Hashem's praises in tefillah every day of our lives should be sufficient reason to recite them joyously.

Joy is a crucial component of *avodas Hashem.* In fact, Zohar states that this was the reason why the offering of *korbanos* in the Beis HaMikdash was accompanied by the Levi'im's musical renditions. When a person brought an offering as an atonement for a sin, he felt broken and dispirited by the enormity of his misdeed, and thus there was an absence of *simchah.* The joy created by the Levi'im's renditions compensated for the joy that was lacking.

In this psalm, Dovid stresses the importance of serving Hashem with joy.

When speaking with boys who had just become bar mitzvah, the Chasam Sofer would say: "Now you are an אִישׁ (*man*).[8] The word אִישׁ stands for אַהֲבָה (*love*); יִרְאָה (*awe*); and שִׂמְחָה (*gladness*)." For a mitzvah that lacks any of these three components is incomplete.

The Gemara cites a Tannaic teaching: "One should not rise to pray *[Shemoneh Esrei]* amidst sadness ... but rather amidst the joy associated with a mitzvah."[9] Another teaching states that one should rise to pray after Torah study that concludes with a clear-cut halachah (הֲלָכָה פְּסוּקָה).[10] When someone studies a topic in Gemara and clarifies it to the point that the halachah is clear, the joy he experiences is immeasurable. It is with this sort of *simchah* that one should commence davening.[11]

Dovid alludes to this in this psalm, for the words עִבְדוּ אֶת ה' בְּשִׂמְחָה are preceded by הָרִיעוּ לַה' כָּל הָאָרֶץ *(call out to Hashem, everyone on earth).* The first letters of these four words spell הֲלָכָה.

---

8. The mishnah states: "A thirteen-year-old (male attains adulthood) for (the observance of) mitzvos" (*Avos* 5:21). As a source for this, *Bartenura* cites the verse where thirteen-year-old Levi, son of Yaakov Avinu, is referred to as אִישׁ (*Bereishis* 34:25).

9. *Berachos* 31a.

10. Ibid.

11. When the *Baraisa* says "One should not rise to pray" it refers to *Shemoneh Esrei.* Rashi to *Berachos* 31a [ד"ה אלא מתוך שמחה] writes that we fulfill the dictum of preceding *Shemoneh Esrei* with *simchah shel mitzvah* by reciting verses concerning the Exodus in *Shacharis*; *Ashrei* before the *Shemoneh Esrei* of *Minchah*; and the verses that immediately precede the *Shemoneh Esrei* of *Maariv.*

The Path to Joy

R' Chaim Vital writes that his master and teacher, the Arizal, was able to attain awesome spiritual levels because of the joy with which he performed mitzvos. The way to achieve a true state of joy is by strengthening one's *emunah.*

The word שָׂמַח, *he was glad,* has the same pronunciation as סָמַךְ, *he relied upon.* The word עָצַב, *he was sad,* is similar in pronunciation to עָזַב, *he forsook.* One who is strong of faith and relies on Hashem in his personal life is a happy person, while one who feels forsaken and lost is a sad, depressed individual.

As a young man, the Chassidic master R' Shimon Yaroslaver was destitute, but this did not affect his spirit in the least. It happened that a man observed how R' Shimon studied Torah in a beis midrash for hours on end while projecting an aura of joy and serenity. When the man asked R' Shimon how he supported himself, he replied, *"Ich hob tzvei ki'in,"* which literally means, "I have two cows."[12] The man inquired and discovered that this was not so; R' Shimon did not own even one cow. Disturbed, the man confronted R' Shimon and said, "I would think that a person so devoted to God's service would never veer from the truth. Why did you tell me that you have two *'ki'in'?"*

R' Shimon replied, "You misunderstood me. My *ki'in* are not in the barn; they are in the *siddur.* Every morning we say in *Hodu*: **כִּי** בוֹ יִשְׂמַח לִבֵּנוּ, **כִּי** בְשֵׁם קָדְשׁוֹ בָטָחְנוּ, ***For*** *in Him will our hearts be glad,* ***for*** *in His Holy Name we trusted.*[13] I put my faith in Hashem, and He makes sure that I lack for nothing!"

One whose soul is pure and whose faith in Hashem is strong is truly the happiest of men.[14]

---

12. In the chassidic Yiddish pronunciation a cow is *"a ki."*

13. *Tehillim* 33:21.

14. Rav Wolfson added that this sheds additional light on the teaching that "When Adar enters, we increase our joy" (*Taanis* 29a). Adar is the month of Purim, when Hashem performed great hidden miracles in the days of Mordechai and Esther. *Megillas Esther* is an eternal lesson of how even in exile, Hashem watches over His beloved nation

The Moment of Truth

Conversely, we find in the *Tochachah* (Admonitions) that a primary reason for those punishments was *"because you did not serve Hashem, your God, with gladness and goodness of heart."*[15]

As we know, it is possible to carry out one's obligations as a Jew out of habit, without joy or feeling. However, the moment of truth comes when one is faced with a *nisayon* (spiritual test).

A century ago, when many thousands of Jewish immigrants arrived in America, the vast majority of them were Shabbos-observant. They faced difficult tests in earning a livelihood, because most businesses were open on Shabbos and would not allow workers to miss that day's work. Those who served Hashem by force of habit, without joy, could not muster the spiritual strength to withstand this test. They desecrated the Shabbos, their children abandoned virtually any sort of mitzvah observance, and their grandchildren identified themselves as Jews in name alone.[16]

However, those who served Hashem with *simchah,* whose *emunah* gave them the determination to remain strong and trusting in Hashem despite the hardships, remained observant and raised beautiful generations faithful to Hashem and His Torah.

Therefore, Dovid says: *Serve Hashem with gladness, come before Him with joyous song.* When a Jew arises in the morning, dons his *tefillin,* and begins to daven, he should be overcome with a desire to sing joyfully to Hashem, out of gratitude for this great kindness. When he opens his *gemara,* he should be ecstatic that he is

---

with incredible *hashgachah pratis,* exacting Divine Providence. This awareness should strengthen one's faith and lead to increased joy.

15. *Devarim* 28:47.

16. R' Moshe Feinstein said that some of those immigrants did continue to observe Shabbos, but without joy or feeling. Instead, they told their children, "What can we do? We are Jews, and Jews don't work on Shabbos." Their children were lost to assimilation. It was only those who told their children that keeping Shabbos is a great, immeasurable privilege, and that they would not give it up for all the money in the world, who merited generations faithful to Hashem and His Torah.

meriting to study the word of the living God. He should realize that as he studies the holy Torah, the *Ribbono shel Olam* is teaching him its meaning[17] and that it is for Torah that the world was created.

The Name "*Elohim*"

דְּעוּ כִּי ה׳ הוּא אֱלֹהִים הוּא עָשָׂנוּ וְלוֹ אֲנַחְנוּ ...
Know that Hashem, He is God, it is He Who made us and we are His ...

The name *Elohim* refers to Hashem as the One Who is all-powerful. At Mount Carmel, when Eliyahu HaNavi challenged the false prophets of Baal, a great miracle occurred as a Divine fire descended to consume the offering Eliyahu had brought. The multitudes that had gathered clearly perceived that there is no power save for the *Ribbono shel Olam*. As one they shouted: ה׳ הוּא הָאֱלֹהִים, ה׳ הוּא הָאֱלֹהִים, *Hashem, He is the God, Hashem, He is the God!*[18] In *Mizmor L'Sodah,* in which we declare the importance of serving Hashem joyously, we also declare our recognition that there is no power in the world that is independent of *Hashem Yisborach.* And we then declare our recognition that *it is He Who made us.* Whatever our station in life, whether our days are spent in the beis midrash or in the business world, everything that we have we owe to Hashem. Without His help, we cannot accomplish anything.

The American expression "making a living" should be anathema to a Torah Jew. It implies that we are the masters of our fate,

---

17. R' Chaim Volozhiner writes: "Each time one immerses himself in [Torah study] and attaches himself to it in the proper manner, it is amid a spirit of gladness as when they [the words of Torah] were given at Sinai ... The reason for this is that at the time of that sacred event, everyone present became attached, as it were, to the spoken word of *Hashem Yisborach.* So too, now, every time — literally — that one toils and delves into it, he is actually attached to it through His spoken word" (*Nefesh HaChaim* 4:14).
18. *Melachim I* 18:39.

like Pharaoh who declared, *"Mine is the River and I have made myself."*[19]

As we say in this verse, *it is He Who made us.* When a Jew goes about earning a livelihood, he makes the required *hishtadlus,* effort. Ultimately, however, it is Hashem and Hashem alone Who determines whether or not one's effort will bear fruit. We don't "make a living"; Hashem makes it for us.

In this verse, the *kri,* oral pronunciation, of the eighth word is וְלוֹ, *and we are His,* while the *ksiv,* written spelling, is וְלֹא, *[it is He Who made us] and not us.* The two spellings complement each other. If a Jew truly feels *and we are His,* that we are Hashem's beloved people and that our life's mission is to serve Him with all our heart, then he will recognize that *[it is He Who made us] and not us,* that whatever we have is only because He wills it to be.

The Sheep of His Pasture

... עַמּוֹ וְצֹאן מַרְעִיתוֹ.

... His nation and the sheep of His pasture.

In Psalm 23, Dovid says: *"Hashem is my Shepherd, I shall not lack ... Though I walk in the valley overshadowed by death, I will fear no evil, for You are with me."* In this long, difficult *galus* our nation has faced many bitter enemies, who were bent on annihilating us, ר"ל. The Hamans in every generation seek to destroy us, but Hashem, our omnipotent Shepherd, thwarts their plans. In the difficult times in which we live, the recognition that we are His nation and the sheep of His pasture infuses us with hope and faith that salvation will come, hopefully soon and in our time.

19. *Yechezkel* 29:3.

With Thanksgiving and Praise

בֹּאוּ שְׁעָרָיו בְּתוֹדָה חֲצֵרֹתָיו בִּתְהִלָּה.

Enter His gates with thanksgiving,
His courts with praise.

There are people who come to the *beis hamidrash* or *beis haknesses* with a feeling that the *Ribbono shel Olam* owes *them* a debt of gratitude for their having interrupted their busy schedules to come to daven or learn. Dovid HaMelech tells us that our attitude must be the very opposite. When we enter a place of Torah or tefillah, we must do so with a feeling of true gratitude for having been granted another opportunity to study Hashem's holy Torah or to come close to Him through tefillah.

I knew a fiery Stoliner chassid, Reb Nissim Pilchik. One gained a great deal from being in his proximity! He would sometimes say, "One must thank the *Eibershter* that one is allowed entrance into Stolin!"

Similarly, one should feel boundless gratitude to Hashem each time he merits to experience the holy day of Shabbos, and each morning that he merits to don *tallis* and *tefillin.*

The holy *Alshich* offers this interpretation: *Enter His gates with thanksgiving* — One must be overcome with thanks to Hashem even when he has merely "entered the gates" — that is, has just begun to embark on the path of *avodas Hashem.* Though he has not yet experienced the immense pleasure that can be experienced during an impassioned tefillah or when learning a *blatt Gemara,* nevertheless, he should be overcome with gratitude for having been granted the privilege to perform these mitzvos. If he will "enter the gates" with gratitude then he will merit to enter *His courts with praise,* that is, he will grow in his service of Hashem, to the point that he will merit true *dveikus* with his Creator and will have gone from one who merely stands at the outer gates to one who is granted entry into the King's court.

And when that occurs, he will experience *avodas Hashem* on an entirely new level. For he entered the gates בְּתוֹדָה, *with thanksgiving,* but upon entering the court he offers תְּהִלָּה, *praise,* which, according to Zohar, is a far greater level of prayer. This is why the greatest chapter in *Tehillim*, Psalm 145, begins with the word תְּהִלָּה (see following chapter).

Dovid begins this psalm with gratitude and concludes it in a similar way: *Give thanks to Him, bless His Name. For Hashem is good, His kindness endures forever, and from generation to generation is His faithfulness.*

CHAPTER ELEVEN

Ashrei

Tehillah L'Dovid (Psalm 145, which forms the bulk of *Ashrei*)[1] is the crown of *Sefer Tehillim*. It is the only chapter which Dovid opens with the word *Tehillah* (a praise), representing an exalted level of prayer. It is the final chapter of Dovid's personal supplication and praise before Hashem. In the remaining five chapters, Dovid invites all of creation to join him as he offers praise with an eye to the future redemption.

The Gemara teaches that whoever recites *Tehillah L'Dovid* thrice daily is assured a place in the World to Come.[2] This psalm, says the Gemara, possesses two special qualities: Its verses follow the order

1. The opening verse of *Ashrei* is from *Tehillim* 84:5. The second verse immediately precedes Psalm 145. *Ashrei's* concluding verse is from 115:18.

2. *Berachos* 4b. On weekdays we recite *Ashrei* twice in *Shacharis* and once in *Minchah*. On Shabbos and Yom Tov it is recited once in *Shacharis*, once in *Mussaf*, and once in *Minchah*.

of the *Aleph-Beis*, and it contains the verse פּוֹתֵחַ אֶת יָדֶךָ וּמַשְׂבִּיעַ לְכָל חַי רָצוֹן, *You open Your hand and satisfy the desire of every living thing.*

On the surface, these two reasons seem unrelated. As we shall explain, however, they in fact complement one another.

First, we must pose an obvious question. How can we say that Hashem satisfies the desire of *every living thing* when we know that over the course of history, many countries have been struck by famine and many impoverished souls have suffered from hunger?

This question is rooted in a total misunderstanding of the workings of this world. People tend to take for granted the ways of nature, which are in truth Hashem's constant, hidden miracles. For example, when the sun rises each morning we do not give the matter a second thought. Imagine, however, if the sun rose just once in a lifetime. Picture how excited one would be on the night before the great event. Imagine his amazement as the rays of the sun would begin to shine above the horizon. "Miraculous!" one would surely exclaim.

The Chasam Sofer describes the feelings of a Jew who was born in the Wilderness, where our nation sojourned for 40 years on the way from Egypt to Eretz Yisrael. He was born into a world where food fell from heaven each day in the form of *mann*. When this person is asked by someone, "What did you subsist on all that time?" he replies, "Why, from *mann* — how else do you think we lived?"

Then, he follows Yehoshua bin Nun across the Jordan River. The *mann* ceases to fall and this man is told, "Don't worry, we'll have food to eat. There will be plenty of food growing out of the ground and hanging from trees."

The man is incredulous. "What are you talking about? Since when does food grow from the ground?"

This man, writes the Chasam Sofer, views normal food in the way that the average person views *mann*.

However, the miracle of how Hashem provides sustenance to His creatures daily, continuously, goes much further. He provides each creature with the particular *type* of food that it requires.

Cows find it in pasture, fish find it in the sea, insects find it on the ground, and man, of course, finds an amazing variety of foods all over the world.

Famine and deprivation are facts of history, but they are the exception, not the rule, and they occur through specific Divine decree. Just as illness, ר"ל, occurs only through Divine decree and exacting *hashgachah pratis* (Divine providence), so it is with hunger.

For the most part, the billions of living creatures in this world have always had their needs provided for, day in, day out. The way in which Hashem has, for close to 6,000 years, provided His creatures with the particular sustenance that each one requires is truly miraculous and is one of the greatest expressions of His kindness. Each species finds what it needs for survival. Fish that swim near the sea's surface find their food there, while deep-sea creatures find their food down below. Birds of prey find their food, and smaller birds find theirs. *He gives bread to all His living creatures, for His kindness is forever.*[3]

A Balancing Act

There is incredible balance in Hashem's amazing world. Worms are needed to consume surplus plants, and birds are needed to consume worms that, if allowed to live, would devastate plant life. The proportion of beasts to birds and birds to insects is exactly what is needed for the smooth functioning of what is called "nature." Insects burrow holes in the ground, making it porous to facilitate plant growth.[4]

3. Ibid. 136:25. In discussing the uniqueness of *Ashrei,* the Gemara wonders why the verse beginning with פּוֹתֵחַ אֶת יָדֶךָ is recited daily, while this verse from Psalm 136 is not. The Gemara concludes that *Ashrei* has an additional quality in that it follows the order of the *Aleph-Beis.*

4. In *Sing, You Righteous,* R' Avigdor Miller writes: In 1885 the Pennsylvania legislature offered cash rewards for the killing of hawks and owls, which they regarded as an unnecessary nuisance to society. After two years, fields and orchards had been overrun by mice, rats, and insects, resulting in $2 million worth of damage. The law was repealed.

Another related miraculous facet of creation: the instincts with which Hashem has endowed each creature to ensure its survival. In *Sefer Mishlei* Shlomo HaMelech says:

> *Go to the ant, lazy one; see her ways and grow wise. Though there is neither officer nor guard nor ruler over her, she prepares her bread in the summer and gathers her food in the harvest time.*[5]

The Midrash[6] relates: In the summer months, an ant stores enough food to help it survive the winter. One ant will not touch food that belongs to another. Once, an ant dropped a grain of wheat. All the other ants realized from its scent that this grain was not theirs and none touched it until its owner retrieved it.

There are three "chambers" in an anthill. The ant stores no food in the upper hill where it might be ruined by rain. It stores nothing in the lowest chamber where underground moisture will ruin it. The ant stores food only in the middle chamber.

You open Your hand and satisfy the desire of every living thing. Hashem provides each living thing the particular sustenance that it desires. But that is not all. The *Aleph-Beis* is the order of letters of which the Torah is comprised and with which the universe was created. The verses of *Ashrei* follow the order of the *Aleph-Beis* to teach that Hashem's system for providing sustenance for all living creatures is not at all haphazard. To the contrary, it follows an incredible order, an order so complex and fine-tuned that no human mind could possibly duplicate it — or fully comprehend it.

Ashrei is an exalted song of praise to Hashem, a joyous acknowledgment of the incredible symphony that is this world. One who recites *Ashrei* thrice daily with this thought in mind, and not out of habit, devoid of feeling, is truly a *ben Olam Haba*, one who is worthy of the World to Come.

---

5. *Mishlei* 6:6-8.

6. *Devarim* 5:2.

A Time for Contemplation

The importance of praying with *kavanah* (concentration) is particularly relevant to *Ashrei. Shulchan Aruch* states that one who recites the verse ... פּוֹתֵחַ אֶת יָדֶךָ without *kavanah* should repeat it.[7] In fact, the opening words of *Ashrei* teach us how importance it is to make tefillah a true "service of the heart."

אַשְׁרֵי יוֹשְׁבֵי בֵיתֶךָ עוֹד יְהַלְלוּךָ סֶּלָה.

Happy are the dwellers of Your house; they will continue to praise You, Selah.[8]

It is from this verse that our Sages derive that before davening, one should first take ample time to meditate and focus his heart towards Hashem.[9]

In *Sefer Tehillim*, Dovid HaMelech makes use of ten forms of introductory praise,[10] corresponding to the Ten Utterances (*Asarah Maamaros*) with which the world was created.[11] Zohar states that אַשְׁרֵי is the greatest of the ten; its letters are contained within the Torah's opening word, בְּרֵאשִׁית, which is the first of the Ten Utterances.[12] The thrice-daily *"Ashrei"* opens with not one but two verses beginning with this word. The second, which immediately precedes Psalm 145 in *Sefer Tehillim,* should fill our hearts with joy: אַשְׁרֵי הָעָם שֶׁכָּכָה לּוֹ אַשְׁרֵי הָעָם שֶׁה' אֱלֹהָיו, *Praiseworthy is the people for whom this is so, praiseworthy is the people whose God is Hashem!*

---

7. *Orach Chaim* 51:7.

8. *Tehillim* 84:5.

9. *Berachos* 32b. The derivation is: One must first be among יוֹשְׁבֵי בֵיתֶךָ, those who dwell in Hashem's house and contemplate His greatness, and only then יְהַלְלוּךָ סֶּלָה, can one attain the proper frame of mind for tefillah. The Mishnah (ibid. 30b) teaches that the pious ones of earlier generations would meditate for a full hour before praying.

10. Such as מִזְמוֹר, תְּהִלָּה, and לַמְנַצֵּחַ (see *Pesachim* 117a).

11. See *Avos* 5:1.

12. *Rosh Hashanah* 32a.

My God, the King

תְּהִלָּה לְדָוִד אֲרוֹמִמְךָ אֱלוֹהַי הַמֶּלֶךְ וַאֲבָרְכָה שִׁמְךָ לְעוֹלָם וָעֶד.

A psalm of praise by Dovid: I will exalt You, My God, the King, and I will bless Your Name forever and ever.

With these words Dovid begins Psalm 145. As we mentioned in our introduction to *Pesukei D'Zimrah,* the opening verse of many chapters of *Sefer Tehillim* contains Dovid's name. As we explained, by mentioning Dovid's name we are invoking his merit, which opens the gates of Heaven and destroys spiritual forces that seek to impede our prayers.

In this opening verse, Dovid uses the word אֱלוֹהַי, *my God.* He proclaims the *Ribbono shel Olam's* greatness by declaring: "Hashem, You are *my* God, with Whom I have my own personal relationship. I can call upon You for all my needs, big and small. I can speak to You at any time of day or night. Nothing that I need is too insignificant to request of You, for all that I have is given to me through Your exacting hand of providence."

Would someone dare come before a king of flesh and blood and say, "Your Highness, I am sorry to trouble you, but I need some potatoes for tonight's supper. Perhaps you could help me?" No one would bother an earthly king with such a request.

Yet, Hashem is ready to hear our every request, big or small. And as we have explained elsewhere, one should never feel that a small request is not something for which one should pray. To the contrary, by beseeching Hashem for even the small things in life, we demonstrate our faith that everything that transpires in our life happens through *hashgachah pratis,* exacting Divine providence.

Note that here the word אֱלוֹהַי, *my God,* is spelled with a ו; generally the word is spelled without a ו. The "full" spelling alludes to Hashem's way of providing each one of us with *all* of our particular needs, whatever they might be.

At the same time that Hashem is *my God,* He is also הַמֶּלֶךְ, *the King,* who at any given moment is giving life to all of Creation as He directs and controls its workings with amazing precision.

One who makes this proclamation each day, with *kavanah* and feeling, can rest assured that he will merit the verse's conclusion: *I will bless Your Name forever and ever,* for as the Sages teach, whoever recites *Ashrei* thrice daily is assured of a place in the World to Come.

Foundations of Faith

גָּדוֹל ה׳ וּמְהֻלָּל מְאֹד וְלִגְדֻלָּתוֹ אֵין חֵקֶר.

Hashem is great and exceedingly lauded, and His greatness is beyond investigation.

Hashem's greatness, His essence, is beyond human comprehension. We can prove His existence by way of investigation and philosophical debate, but this alone will not suffice to establish the truth of His holy Torah as the purpose and blueprint of Creation. What sets the Jewish religion apart from others is expressed in the next verse:

דּוֹר לְדוֹר יְשַׁבַּח מַעֲשֶׂיךָ וּגְבוּרֹתֶיךָ יַגִּידוּ.

Each generation will praise Your deeds to the next, and of Your mighty deeds they will tell.

Regarding the mitzvah to recall the Revelation at Sinai [מַעֲמַד הַר סִינַי], *Ramban* writes:

> *The Torah commands as a positive mitzvah that we make known to our offspring from generation to generation all that transpired there, both visually and audibly. There is a very great purpose to this mitzvah. Had the words of Torah come to us through Moshe alone, though the truth of*

his prophecy was verified through signs and wonders, this would not have prevented a false prophet or dreamer from placing a doubt in the hearts of men by performing wonders and then commanding them to do that which contradicts the Torah. However, now that the Torah has reached our ears directly from the Almighty, and our own eyes have seen without any intermediary, we can refute any such imposter and declare him a liar — no sign will help him ... and when we will transmit this fact to our children, they will know that it is the truth beyond any doubt, as if every generation had witnessed it themselves. For we would not declare a falsehood to our children, nor bequeath to them that which is empty and without purpose.[13]

דּוֹר לְדוֹר יְשַׁבַּח מַעֲשֶׂיךָ וּגְבוּרֹתֶיךָ יַגִּידוּ ...

Of Mercy and Kindness

חַנּוּן וְרַחוּם ה׳ אֶרֶךְ אַפַּיִם וּגְדָל חָסֶד.

Gracious and merciful is Hashem, slow to anger and great in bestowing kindness.

A person can sin grievously and repeatedly, yet it may be years before any retribution is forthcoming, as Hashem waits for the sinner to mend his ways and return to Him. *Gracious and merciful is Hashem, slow to anger ...*

13. *Ramban* to *Devarim* 4:9. According to Zohar, the term מַעֲשֶׂיךָ in this verse, which literally means *Your deeds,* can also mean *Your tzaddikim.* A *tzaddik's* very essence sings the praise of his Creator.

Once, a *poritz* (gentile landowner) was walking with a family member when he chanced upon R' Mordechai of Lechovitz in the midst of tefillah. The *poritz* told his relative, "You know how much I love you, but I assure you that this Jew loves his God even more."

Rav Wolfson related that he had the privilege of being present when the saintly Satmar Rav, R' Yoel Teitelbaum, read the *Megillah* on Purim. The reading lasted some two hours, yet no one found it long or difficult to sit through. To the contrary, they were transported to another world; it was as if for those two hours, they were in the city of Shushan. From the nuances of the Rav's reading, it was possible to gain new insight into the Megillah's holy words. The Rav's very essence gave praise to his Creator.

But that is not all. Hashem is *great in bestowing kindness.* In his *Sefer Tomer Devorah,* R' Moshe Cordovero[14] describes how the *Ribbono shel Olam* tolerates, in a way that is beyond comprehension, those who flout His will:

> *There is not a moment that man is not nourished and sustained by the Divine force that gives him life ... No man ever sinned against God without God Himself granting him existence and the ability to move his limbs at that very moment. Yet, even though a person uses this very gift to transgress, God does not withhold it from him at all. Rather, the Holy One, Blessed is He, tolerates this insult and continues to bestow upon him the ability to move his limbs.*[15]

The gift of *teshuvah* (repentance) and the time that is allotted to us as Hashem awaits our return is one of His great expressions of mercy and kindness.

A Breeze of Life

טוֹב ה׳ לַכֹּל וְרַחֲמָיו עַל כָּל מַעֲשָׂיו.

Hashem is good to all, His mercies are on all His creations.

Once, the Baal Shem Tov and his disciples were studying together outdoors in the shade of a tree. It was a warm, windless day. Then, for a few brief moments, a gentle breeze ruffled the leaves. The Baal Shem Tov told his disciples, "Do you know what just happened? A worm on a leaf of this tree was suffering from the blazing hot sun. The *Ribbono shel Olam* therefore sent a slight breeze which was enough to cause that leaf to disconnect from its branch and fall to the ground beneath the tree, with the worm still clinging to it. Now the worm is in the shade of the tree."

14. 1522-1570. Translation from *Tomer Devorah* is from the edition published by Rav Wolfson's *talmid,* R' Berel Fink.

15. *Tomer Devorah* concludes: "This [Godly] attribute of being tolerant is one that man should emulate. Even when he is insulted to this degree, he should still not withdraw his benevolence from the recipient."

Atmospheric changes for miles around are necessary to cause a breeze. Hashem made all this happen for the sake of one minuscule worm. *Hashem is good to all, His mercies are on all His creations.* At any given moment, Hashem is ensuring the well-being of billions upon billions of His creatures, in ways that are beyond our comprehension.

This is but one aspect of His goodness. Another is the axiom that whatever Hashem does is ultimately for the good. When we view certain isolated events in Jewish history, they seem anything but good. However, that is only from our shortsighted perspective. Hashem's plan can span many generations. Many *neshamos* are in this world now as *gilgulim* (reincarnations) to atone for sins that they may have committed generations ago. And the sufferings in the present may lead to great and wonderful benefits in the future.

Hashem is good to all, His mercies are on all His creations.

Sweetening Judgments

When suffering and tribulation are visited upon an individual, it is crucial that he strive to accept it with love as an expression of Hashem's will. Through such acceptance, he can merit הַמְתָּקַת הַדִּינִים, *sweetening of judgments,* so that any further judgment that had been decreed in Heaven will be transformed into a flow of mercy and compassion. The *shefa,* spiritual emanations from Above, come down to this world by way of the letters of the *aleph-beis.* By accepting Hashem's judgments without complaint, one can merit that צָרָה will be transformed into רְצֵה (Heavenly desire on his behalf); נֶגַע, *plague,* into עֹנֶג, *delight,* and פֶּשַׁע, *willful sin,* into שֶׁפַע, *(a Divine) flow (of blessing).*[16]

16. Rav Wolfson added that proper observance of Shabbos is auspicious for *hamtakas hadinim.* The Gemara states that if someone observes Shabbos properly, even if he is a sinner as in the days of the wicked generation of Enosh, he will merit to have his sins forgiven (*Shabbos* 118b). Observing Shabbos as a day of עֹנֶג, *spiritual delight,* can eradicate נֶגַע. The passage in *Bircas Hamazon* for Shabbos opens with the word רְצֵה, symbolizing the dissipation of צָרָה by proper observance of *Shabbos Kodesh.*

In this vein, Bnei Yissoschor offers an interpretation of the verse רְאֵה עָנְיִי וַעֲמָלִי וְשָׂא לְכָל חַטֹּאותָי, *Behold my affliction and my toil and take away all my sins.*[17] When one accepts his afflictions and declares, "*Ribbono shel Olam,* I know that You are doing this for my good; it is all for the best and I accept it with love," then he merits that his sins are removed and his sufferings may end.

A Jew's Essence

יוֹדוּךָ ה' כָּל מַעֲשֶׂיךָ וַחֲסִידֶיךָ יְבָרְכוּכָה.
All Your works shall praise You, Hashem, and Your devout ones will bless You.

Generally, the term *chassidim*, devout ones, in *Tanach* and tefillah refers to exceptionally righteous individuals. In this verse, it refers to every Jewish soul.

The verse begins by saying that all of Creation sings praise to Hashem. This concept is the theme of Chapter 148 of *Sefer Tehillim*, which is also recited as part of *Pesukei D'Zimrah*: *Praise Him, sun and moon; praise Him all bright stars ... Mountains and all hills, fruitful trees and all cedars. Beasts and all cattle, crawling things and all fowl ...* When a creation carries out its Creator's will, it sings His praises. When rain waters the earth, causing vegetation to grow, when birds chirp and the sun shines, the world is singing *shirah* to Hashem.

The Jewish people, however, whose souls are bound up with Torah and mitzvos, do much more. *Your devout ones will bless You.*

Dovid HaMelech declares: תְּנוּ עֹז לֵאלֹהִים, *Grant strength to God.*[18] Divine wisdom has decreed that the way in which Hashem guides this world is a reflection of the words and deeds of His beloved

17. *Tehillim* 25:18.
18. *Tehillim* 68:35.

nation. If we are faithful to the Torah and are devoted to its calling, then we initiate a flow of compassion and blessing to the world. If our service of Hashem is wanting, then the opposite occurs.

R' Chaim Volozhiner interpreted דַּע מַה לְּמַעְלָה מִמְּךָ, *Know what is above you* (a watchful eye, an attentive ear, ...)[19] to mean: דַּע, *Know,* מַה לְּמַעְלָה, *that that which happens Above* is מִמְּךָ, *from you,* i.e., because of your actions on this world.[20]

And so we, the devout ones of this world, "bless" Hashem and grant Him strength every time we do a mitzvah, enunciate a word of Torah or tefillah, perform an act of kindness, or think a thought that is pure and spiritual.

If we were to ponder this thought three times a day when we say these words in *Ashrei,* surely we would be worthy of the World to Come.

For Each Generation

מַלְכוּתְךָ מַלְכוּת כָּל עֹלָמִים וּמֶמְשַׁלְתְּךָ בְּכָל דּוֹר וָדוֹר.

Your kingdom is a kingdom spanning all eternities, and Your rule is for all generations.

Hashem is King over all the upper and lower worlds, and will be so forever. This is an unchanging fact, as we declare each morning in the piece immediately preceding *Ashrei*: *"Hashem reigns, Hashem has reigned, Hashem shall reign for all eternity."* However, *how* He rules the world is dependent on the level and needs of each generation. Hashem does not expect of our generation what was expected of the lofty generations that preceded us. Especially in today's decadent society, every effort we make to serve Hashem with a pure mind and heart is exceedingly precious to Him.

---

19. *Avos* 2:1.

20. *Ruach Chaim* ad loc.

The Missing *"Nun"*

Though the verses of *Ashrei* follow the order of the *aleph-beis,* there is no verse for the letter נ, because, says the Gemara,[21] the נ represents the נְפִילָה, *downfall,* of the Jewish people as foretold by the prophet Amos: נָפְלָה לֹא תוֹסִיף קוּם בְּתוּלַת יִשְׂרָאֵל, *She has fallen and will no longer rise, the maiden of Israel.*[22]

Zohar offers a parable of a king whose queen fell into disfavor twice and was sent away from his palace. When the king decided it was time for a reconciliation, he sent for the queen to return. She sinned yet a third time and once again was sent into exile. Later, when the king sent for her to return, the queen said, "This time, let the king come himself and take me out of my misery." In this way, Zohar interprets Amos' words in a positive sense: *She has fallen and will no longer rise* ***on her own****.* Rather, when the day of the Redemption dawns, God Himself will come and say, *Arise, maiden of Israel!*

Dovid foresaw this as well. As the Gemara continues, though he made no mention of Israel's downfall, his *Ruach Hakodesh* inspired Dovid to declare, סוֹמֵךְ ה' לְכָל הַנֹּפְלִים, *Hashem supports all the fallen ones.* The day will come when Hashem Himself will bring us back from this long and difficult exile.

An Exercise in Faith

As mentioned at the outset of this essay, the Sages see פּוֹתֵחַ אֶת יָדֶךָ וּמַשְׂבִּיעַ לְכָל חַי רָצוֹן, *You open Your hand and satisfy the desire of every living thing,* as *Ashrei's* primary verse.

Once, an elite group of chassidim came to R' Yisrael of Rizhin for a *berachah.* These young men lived an other-worldly existence; nothing but Torah and mitzvos mattered to them. On their *kvittel,* they requested that the Rebbe bless them with

21. *Berachos* 4b.

22. 5:2.

success in their service of Hashem. The Rizhiner said to them, "And what about a *berachah* for *parnasah* (success in earning a livelihood)? The same *Shulchan Aruch* that states one must have proper *kavanah* when reciting the first blessing of *Shemoneh Esrei* also states that one must have *kavanah* when reciting פּוֹתֵחַ אֶת יָדֶךָ וּמַשְׂבִּיעַ לְכָל חַי רָצוֹן."

Rambam is of the opinion that it is a Biblical mitzvah to pray every day. *Ramban's* view is that this is a Rabbinic mitzvah, but he agrees that in an עֵת צָרָה, *time of travail,* prayer is mandated by the Torah. *Maharal* explains that the very act of prayer is a demonstration of faith that only Hashem can rescue us from our distress.

And so it is when we pray for *parnasah.* When we say the words פּוֹתֵחַ אֶת־יָדֶךָ ... with proper intent, we demonstrate our belief that what we will earn and how we will earn it is entirely in Hashem's hands. In this way, our tefillah becomes an exercise in *emunah* and even as we ask for our material requirements, we are uplifted and draw closer to the One Who provides every creature with its every need.

Unanswered Prayers

קָרוֹב ה׳ לְכָל קֹרְאָיו לְכֹל אֲשֶׁר יִקְרָאֻהוּ בֶאֱמֶת.

Hashem is close to all who call upon Him, to all who call upon Him sincerely.

When we pray sincerely, Hashem listens. No sincere tefillah goes to waste. And yet, there are times when despite our best efforts to pour out our hearts in sincere, meaningful prayer, our tefillos seems to go unanswered.

As the moment for the destruction of Sodom approached, Hashem said, *"Can I conceal from Avraham that which I am about to do?"* The Torah then goes on to relate the praises of Avraham, that his family would develop into a great nation, that Hashem cherished him because he commanded his offspring and household to go in Hashem's ways by doing charity and justice.[23]

Hashem then informed Avraham of the impending destruction, and Avraham responded with his impassioned plea that Sodom and its neighboring cities be saved if only a few *tzaddikim* would be found among their inhabitants. However, none could be found and the cities were obliterated.

What was the point of informing Avraham that Sodom would be destroyed? He prayed, yet his tefillah went unanswered.

The *Yitav Lev*[24] explains that it was not for Sodom that Hashem wanted Avraham's prayer; Sodom's fate was sealed. Hashem knew that Avraham would have worthy descendants who would follow his path of charity and justice. And Hashem knew that there would come a time when Avraham's descendants would find themselves in dire straits, in a situation when only a tefillah from as great a personage as Avraham could save them. But there would be no one in that generation who approached Avraham's greatness. So at that time, Hashem would reach into His treasure house of unanswered prayers and use the prayer Avraham had uttered on behalf of Sodom to save Avraham's own progeny.

No tefillah is said in vain. *Hashem is close to all who call upon Him, to all who call upon Him sincerely.*

---

23. *Bereishis* ch. 18:17-19.

24. Rav of Sighet, Hungary, and grandfather of the Satmar Rav, R' Yoel Teitelbaum.

CHAPTER TWELVE

Psalm 146: My Soul Praises Hashem

In *Pesukei D'Zimrah*, Psalm 146 immediately follows *Ashrei*, as it does in *Sefer Tehillim*.[1] Dovid concludes Psalm 145 with: תְּהִלַּת ה׳ יְדַבֶּר פִּי וִיבָרֵךְ כָּל בָּשָׂר שֵׁם קָדְשׁוֹ לְעוֹלָם וָעֶד, *May my mouth declare the praise of Hashem and may all flesh bless His name forever and ever.* Dovid is not satisfied to praise Hashem on his own. In the final chapters of *Sefer Tehillim*, each one beginning with הַלְלוּיָהּ, he invites all of creation to join him in expressing praise of the Creator.

1. The introductory and concluding verses in *Ashrei* are taken from other chapters.

The word הַלְלוּיָהּ combines the words הַלְלוּ *([they shall] give praise)* and יָהּ, the name of God. The combination of these two words alludes to a basic concept of Jewish prayer. When we daven and express praise of Hashem, we should do so with passion and intensity. Those who engage in הַלֵּל, *praise*, should experience such an attachment to יָהּ, the One Whom they praise, that they feel nullified in His Presence, like a small candle next to a roaring flame. And so הַלְלוּ and יָהּ become הַלְלוּיָהּ.

Dovid's Yearning

The opening verses of Psalm 146 illustrate Dovid's intense yearning to cleave to Hashem through tefillah. In the previous chapter, Dovid praised Hashem with all 22 letters of the *Aleph-Beis,* a praise that encompasses all of creation, which came into existence by way of these holy letters. Dovid has declared: *You open Your hand and satisfy the desire of every living thing;* every creature large and small is sustained through the kindness of Hashem and the amazing manner in which He provides such sustenance. And yet, Dovid, the embodiment of prayer, desires to praise Hashem further. And so he declares, הַלְלִי נַפְשִׁי אֶת ה׳ אֲהַלְלָה ה׳ בְּחַיָּי אֲזַמְּרָה לֵאלֹהַי בְּעוֹדִי, *I will praise Hashem while I live, I will make music to my God while I exist.*

> I knew a Stoliner Chassid named R' Nissim Pilchik, *z"l.* He was a soul on fire; the way he lived his Shabbos was a sight to behold, and his davening energized the entire minyan. If a second minyan would commence davening after he had completed *Shacharis,* R' Nissim would join them for *Pesukei D'Zimrah* (omitting the opening and closing blessings). He explained, "When I heard those *Yidden* saying those holy, sweet words, I simply couldn't hold myself back — I had to daven along with them! Those sacred words are so filled with life!"

Dovid ended the previous psalm by saying: *May all flesh bless His Holy Name forever.* And he begins this psalm by implying: *And if others will heed my call and bless His Holy Name, then despite the fact that I have already abundantly declared His praises, I will nevertheless join them; I will praise Hashem while I live.*

According to Halachah, if someone is late for *Shacharis* and wants to "catch up" he may skip most of *Pesukei D'Zimrah,* reciting only *Baruch She'Amar, Ashrei,* and *Yishtabach.*[2] He has fulfilled the obligation to recite *Shacharis* — but what sort of a davening is this? He has not emulated Dovid, the נְעִים זְמִירוֹת יִשְׂרָאֵל, *sweet singer of Israel,*[3] who constantly sought to sing Hashem's praises.

Alive With Praise

אֲהַלְלָה ה׳ בְּחַיָּי אֲזַמְּרָה לֵאלֹהַי בְּעוֹדִי.
I will praise Hashem while I live,
I will make music to my God while I exist.

The word בְּעוֹדִי, *while I exist,* is related to עוֹד, *more* or *additional.* Dovid was never satisfied with praising Hashem today as he did yesterday. He constantly strove to gather his inner strength, thoughts, and emotions, and praise Hashem on yet a higher level.

Sometimes we see someone reciting *Tehillim* halfheartedly, his feet perched up on a stool or chair as he mumbles the words quickly. In this verse, Dovid is telling us his manner of singing Hashem's praises, one we should strive to emulate.

This verse contains another important message. Dovid praised Hashem בְּחַיָּי, by way of his very life. If one lives his life in accordance with Torah, living a life of *kiddush Hashem*, then everything he does brings honor and praise to the One Above. This is certainly true of one's Torah, tefillah, and good deeds, but it applies

---

2. On Shabbos and Yom Tov, one must also recite *Nishmas.*
3. See *Shmuel II* 23:1.

to his mundane activities as well. When a Jew eats in a refined, dignified way, not to fulfill his earthly desires but to strengthen his body so that he can better serve Hashem, then he has offered praise to Hashem through this mundane activity. When he walks in the street in a humble, pleasant manner, with his *yiras Shamayim* apparent, he has brought glory to His Name. Even one's sleep can be a form of praise of Hashem.

The Chiddushei HaRim of Ger and R' Yitzchak of Vorka once came to Warsaw and called on R' Yechezkel of Kuzhmir. When the rebbetzin informed them that the tzaddik was taking a nap, they requested and were granted permission to observe him as he slept.

They found him in a deep sleep. At one point, an insect landed on his head and bit him. R' Yechezkel, still asleep, pulled his sleeve over his hand and used it to massage the bite. One who scratches the hair of his head with his fingers is required to wash his hands.[4] *In his sleep, the tzaddik instinctively avoided this.*

Following our explanation of בְּעוֹדִי as *additional*, we can understand the end of this verse as referring to the secondary forms of *avodas Hashem*, the mundane activities we have mentioned above. Dovid is saying, "Not only do I praise Hashem through my performance of mitzvos, I also make music to Him through my eating, drinking, sleeping, and other physical activities."

The God of Yaakov

אַשְׁרֵי שֶׁאֵל יַעֲקֹב בְּעֶזְרוֹ שִׂבְרוֹ עַל ה' אֱלֹהָיו.

Praiseworthy is the one whose help is Yaakov's God, whose hope is in Hashem, his God.

Dovid speaks of Hashem as the "God of Yaakov" because Yaakov was the embodiment of *bitachon*, trust in Hashem. The

4. See *Shulchan Aruch, Orach Chaim* 4:18.

Midrash relates that Psalm 121 was said by Yaakov on his way to the house of Lavan:

> *[Yaakov said the following:] "When Eliezer [servant of Avraham] went to seek a wife for Yitzchak, he took with him ten camels laden with gifts, while I have come with not one earring or bracelet. . . . Shall I therefore lose my hope in my Creator? Heaven forfend! Rather, 'My help comes from Hashem, Maker of heaven and earth. He will not allow your foot to falter, your Guardian will not slumber. Behold, the Guardian of Israel neither slumbers nor sleeps.'*[5]
>
> *"Moreover, 'Hashem will protect you from all evil'*[6] *— from Esav and Lavan.*
>
> *" 'He will guard your soul' — from the Angel of Death.*
>
> *" 'Hashem will guard your departure and arrival' " — and with this confidence, Yaakov departed from Be'er Sheva and headed towards Charan.*[7]

Other Scriptural verses also point to a connection between Yaakov and *bitachon,* such as: *"Hashem, Master of Legions, is with us, a stronghold for us is the God of Yaakov, Selah."*[8]

Wholesome Brokenness

Regarding the words שִׂבְרוֹ עַל ה' אֱלֹהָיו, *whose hope is in Hashem, his God,* Zohar states: *Do not read the word* שִׂבְרוֹ, *his hope; rather [read it as if it were pronounced]* שִׁבְרוֹ, *his brokenness.* My master and teacher, R' Shraga Feivel Mendlowitz, explained:

Every person is destined to endure suffering and difficulties in this world, occurrences that can break him in body and sometimes in spirit. There are those who are "broken" by their pursuit of income in their desire to accumulate more money than they need.

5. *Tehillim* 121:2-4.
6. Ibid. v. 7.
7. *Bereishis Rabbah* 68:2.
8. *Tehillim* 46:12.

They work long hours, and even when they return home after a hard day's work their minds are filled with worry over their business. They fail to realize that whatever pleasure they are destined to derive from this world is carefully measured from Above, and that no amount of toil and expense will grant them any more material pleasure than has been decreed in Heaven.

A chassid came to R' Shloim'ke of Zhvil terribly distressed. "Rebbe," he said, "I lost my beautiful gold watch. Please bless me that I should find it!"

"Tell me," the Rebbe asked, "have you had some new, exceptional material pleasure as of late?"

The chassid replied, "Yes, we hung beautiful curtains in our dining room and I derive great pleasure from them."

"That," said R' Shloim'ke, "is the source of your loss. Material pleasure is decreed in Heaven in a very exact way. Because you allowed yourself the pleasure of those curtains, you lost your watch."

Suffering and loss are also decreed in exact measure. Years ago, Jews had a custom that when a glass or dish broke, they would say: הַפַּח נִשְׁבָּר וַאֲנַחְנוּ נִמְלָטְנוּ *(The snare broke and we have escaped).*[9] They viewed their loss as a great kindness. Perhaps it had been decreed that they should suffer physical harm, but Hashem, in His infinite mercy, allowed this decree to be fulfilled through material loss.

Life on this world is filled with difficulties, tests, and travails. This is how it is meant to be until the time of תֵּצֵא רוּחוֹ יָשֻׁב לְאַדְמָתוֹ, *when his spirit departs he returns to his earth.* Being broken and weary is a fact of life — but it is our choice to decide what sort of brokenness we want to experience.

There are many who do not make material pursuits the focus of their endeavors. These people place their trust in Hashem when their livelihood is concerned. They work, but they do not allow their livelihood to take over their lives. Rather, they devote significant portions of their day to Torah study, tefillah, and *chesed,*

9. Ibid. 124:7.

and it is regarding these pursuits that they allow themselves to be "broken." They invest much time and effort in their service of Hashem. They are broken, weary — and exhilarated at their spiritual achievement.

Fortunate is he who is "broken" because of ה' אֱלֹהָיו, as he dedicates himself to serving his Creator.

This concept is a formula for a wonderful, fulfilling life on this world. The more we exert ourselves in our performance of Torah, tefillah, and good deeds, the more we give *tzedakah* "until it hurts," leaving our bodies weary and our resources drained, the more we save ourselves from difficulties and losses in other areas.

Why, then, does not everyone adopt this formula as a way of life? Why do they place undue emphasis on earning a livelihood? The answer lies in the plain meaning of our verse. *Praised is he whose help is the God of Yaakov, whose hope is in Hashem, his God.* Only one with genuine *bitachon*, one who goes in the way of Yaakov Avinu, will understand where his primary efforts should be, and will act accordingly.

Do Not Rely on Nobles

This theme of *bitachon* relates to a verse earlier in this psalm. *Do not rely on nobles, nor on a human being, for he holds no salvation.* When a person does come to our aid, rescuing us from financial or material straits, we should not place our trust in him. Yes, we should feel gratitude to the person for having helped us, but at the same time, we must recognize the true Source of our rescue. We must never forget that this person was nothing more than Hashem's instrument in bringing about our salvation,

In *Hallel*, Dovid says, ה' לִי בְּעֹזְרָי וַאֲנִי אֶרְאֶה בְשֹׂנְאָי[10]. The plain meaning is: *Hashem is with me through my helpers, therefore I can face my foes.* There is also another way to translate the second half of the verse: *and I recognize the hand of Hashem through my foes.*

10. *Tehillim* 118:7.

Dovid perceived that whatever transpired throughout his difficult life was a manifestation of Hashem's will. When someone came to his aid, it was Hashem using this individual as His agent of rescue. And when his enemies tormented him, this was also an expression of Hashem's will.

When Dovid fled Jerusalem during the rebellion against him led by his son, Avshalom, he was met by Shimi ben Geira, who cursed him in public. One of Dovid's men wanted to kill Shimi for his blasphemy, but Dovid stopped him, saying, *"So shall he curse, for Hashem has said to him, 'Curse Dovid.'"*[11] Dovid did not mean that Shimi was absolved of his sin. What he meant was that if he, Dovid, had suffered this humiliation, then Heaven must have decreed it.

If people would have Dovid's outlook, they would not get upset every time someone slighted their honor or caused them distress. Instead, their lives would be filled with *ahavas Yisrael* and happiness.

Maker of Heaven and Earth

Continuing with the theme of *bitachon*, Dovid says: "Why worry about your livelihood, why be concerned if a competitor appears to be depriving you of customers? Hashem is עֹשֶׂה שָׁמַיִם וָאָרֶץ, אֶת הַיָּם וְאֶת כָּל אֲשֶׁר בָּם, *the Maker of heaven and earth, the sea and all that is in them.* Do you doubt, then, that He is capable of providing you with all that you need regardless of the apparent obstacles that you face?"

And if one falls on hard times and after engaging in *cheshbon hanefesh* (soul-searching) cannot find a sin or fault that would bring about such retribution, he should be aware that Hashem *safeguards truth forever.* Rashi comments: *"At the end of many generations, He upholds and safeguards the truth of His assurances."*

As the Torah states regarding Hashem's guidance of this world: *"The Rock — perfect is His work."*[12] We cannot fathom the work-

11. *Shmuel II* 16:10.

12. *Devarim* 32:4.

ings of Divine Providence; we cannot know how what happens today connects to happenings years ago or in a previous *gilgul.*[13] But we know that Hashem's ways are perfect, and if He has decreed that there be difficulties in one's life, He has done so with exacting precision.

Hope to Hashem

There are those who seem to have natural gifts for success. They are shrewd in business, politically savvy, charismatic. And then there are those who seem marked for failure, people who are easily exploited, poor, imprisoned in a web of problems, blind in the sense that they cannot seem to ever do things right, bent under the burden of familial, physical, or financial problems.

Do not lose hope, says Dovid. To the contrary, as he says elsewhere: קַוֵּה אֶל ה' חֲזַק וְיַאֲמֵץ לִבֶּךָ וְקַוֵּה אֶל ה', *Hope to Hashem, strengthen yourself and He will give you courage, and hope to Hashem.*[14] In this psalm, Dovid declares:

> עֹשֶׂה מִשְׁפָּט לַעֲשׁוּקִים, נֹתֵן לֶחֶם לָרְעֵבִים, ה' מַתִּיר אֲסוּרִים. ה' פֹּקֵחַ עִוְרִים, ה' זֹקֵף כְּפוּפִים, ה' אֹהֵב צַדִּיקִים.
>
> *Hashem does justice for the exploited, He gives bread for the hungry. Hashem releases the bound; Hashem gives sight to the blind; Hashem straightens the bent, Hashem loves tzaddikim.*

Just as Heaven decreed the difficulty, so can He decree that it shall end. Hashem can enlighten one who is feebleminded so that he will succeed in his venture;[15] He can remove the burden of one who is bent.

---

13. The term *gilgul* refers to a *neshamah* sent down to this world for an additional time or times, often to effect *tikkunim* (rectifications) for sins it committed in its earlier lifetime(s).

14. *Tehillim* 27:14.

15. Rav Wolfson explained that while פֹּקֵחַ עִוְרִים is commonly translated *Who gives sight to the blind,* the word פֹּקֵחַ is related to פִּקֵּחַ, *intelligent person,* and thus can mean that Hashem will enlighten someone who has been intellectually blind regarding a certain matter.

There are personal redemptions and there are national redemptions. In Egypt, the Jews merited that the exile, which had been decreed to last 400 years, should be calculated as beginning with the birth of Yitzchak. Regarding the Final Redemption, there is a date by which Mashiach must come, but if we are worthy, he can arrive earlier, on any given day. In a similar vein, because *Hashem loves tzaddikim*, their redemption from personal travail may be accelerated.

ה׳ שֹׁמֵר אֶת גֵּרִים.

Hashem protects converts.

Hashem carefully arranges the convert's personal redemption, so that his *neshamah* can gain shelter under the wings of the *Shechinah* at the precise moment decreed by Heaven.

יָתוֹם וְאַלְמָנָה יְעוֹדֵד.

He encourages orphans and widows.

Orphans and widows represent those who appear forlorn, bereft of the one who was their provider and protector. In fact, they are not forlorn at all; to the contrary, Hashem is "the Father of orphans and the Judge of widows."[16] The encouragement that Hashem lends to such individuals not only prevents them from failing, it often propels them to a level of success they never dreamed possible. What is important is that they place their trust in Him; the more one does so, the more he recognizes Hashem's guiding hand in his life.

In a letter to his sister whose husband passed away, leaving her a young widow with children, R' Yonason Eibeschutz wrote: If one would conduct a study he would find that orphans tend to be more successful than the average person. Hashem, their Father, ensures their success.

---

16. *Tehillim* 68:6.

וְדֶרֶךְ רְשָׁעִים יְעַוֵּת.

The way of the wicked He contorts.

The way Hashem deals with the wicked is also a lesson in faith. The wicked map out a path toward achieving their diabolical goals. Smugly, they launch their plans and are certain that they will succeed. And then suddenly they are stunned as unexpected turns of events destroy all their carefully constructed schemes.

Markings

יִמְלֹךְ ה' לְעוֹלָם אֱלֹהַיִךְ צִיּוֹן לְדֹר וָדֹר הַלְלוּיָהּ.

Hashem shall reign forever; your God, O Zion, from generation to generation, Halleluyah!

The entire world will recognize Hashem's reign at the End of Days when He returns the Jewish people to its homeland and the *Shechinah* dwells in Jerusalem once again.

The theme of this chapter, as we have seen, is *bitachon*. *Bitachon* is not easily acquired. In the Temple era, a primary method of acquiring *bitachon* was by visiting Jerusalem and the Beis HaMikdash. There, in the presence of the *Shechinah*, the Temple service, and the *Sanhedrin*, one gained *yiras Shamayim* and a heightened awareness of Hashem's involvement in his life. Therefore, Dovid concludes this chapter by declaring: *Hashem shall reign forever; your God, O Zion, from generation to generation, Halleluyah!*

While *Zion* refers to Jerusalem and the Beis HaMikdash, it is related to the word צִיּוּן, *marking* (as, for example, a marking that identifies a grave).[17] The Beis HaMikdash was a *tziyun* in that it identified a place on earth where the *Shechinah* dwelled, where one could gain an abundance of spiritual inspiration.

We have often said that there are parallels in *makom,* place; *zman*, time; and *nefesh,* soul. Though the *Zion* of *makom* has tem-

17. Yirmiyahu HaNavi says: הַצִּיבִי לָךְ צִיֻּנִים, *Make markers for yourself* (*Yirmiyahu* 31:20).

porarily been taken from us, those of *zman* and *nefesh* are still here. It is for us to utilize them to their fullest potential.

The day of Shabbos, if experienced properly, is such a signpost, as is the year of *Shemittah*. One can draw *bitachon* from the great Yom Tov of Purim, as well as other special days on the Jewish calendar.

And of course, the Torah itself is a great reservoir of faith and trust. One can strengthen his *emunah* and *bitachon* by immersing himself in the sweet waters of Torah.

We can gain *bitachon* by learning from and observing *tzaddikim*, who are living *sifrei Torah.* We gain *bitachon* by being close to God-fearing Jews, especially of the older generation, who were close to *tzaddikim* of yesteryear and can share stories of the *yiras Shamayim* and trust in Hashem that they exhibited.

Therefore, Dovid says, *[Hashem shall reign forever; your God,] O Zion, from generation to generation. Zion* is eternal; in every generation, it is available to us, in one form or another, for us to draw spiritual strength from it. When we realize this, we are overcome with joy and gratitude to Hashem. Therefore, Dovid concludes: הַלְלוּיָהּ, *Praise God!* Give thanks and praise to Hashem Who has given us the means to strengthen our trust in Him in every generation.

CHAPTER THIRTEEN

Psalm 147: A Song of Redemption and Faith

הַלְלוּיָהּ כִּי טוֹב זַמְּרָה אֱלֹהֵינוּ כִּי נָעִים נָאוָה תְהִלָּה.

Halleluyah! For it is good to make music to our God, for praise is pleasant and befitting.

This psalm continues the theme with which the previous one concluded: *Hashem shall reign forever* — a reference to the days of Mashiach when all of mankind will acknowledge Hashem's sovereignty. At that time, the entire world will perceive how good it is to sing Hashem's praises, how pleasant and befitting it is to acknowledge His greatness.

The name אֱלֹהִים denotes strict justice. The song that will be sung after Mashiach's arrival will be enhanced by the understanding of how all the difficulties of this long exile were truly for the benefit of the Jewish People.

Teshuvah and Song

There is a Yiddish expression, *A chazzan is a naar* (A cantor is a fool). R' Levi Yitzchak of Berditchev explains: In Heaven, the *Shaar HaNeginah* (Gate of Song) is near the *Shaar HaTeshuvah* (Gate of Repentance). The *chazzan* through his cantorial renditions merits to enter the *Shaar HaNeginah*; how foolish of him not to grab the opportunity and enter the *Shaar HaTeshuvah* as well.

There is a profound message in this thought. *Shirah* and *zimrah*, variations of song, can bring a person to *teshuvah.* In the Temple era, Levi'im would spend five years learning the art of song. So important was their singing and accompanying music that the service of the *korbanos* (sacrifices) was invalid without it. The atonement that the *korbanos* achieved would have been incomplete without *shirah*.

Seven Notes

In the writings of Kabbalah we find mention of the *Sefiros HaElyonos*, the Heavenly Emanations, attributes of Hashem through which He conducts the affairs of this world.[1]

There are seven *Sefiros,* corresponding to the seven days of the week. They represent *middos* of Hashem, as it were, attributes that we must strive to emulate and incorporate in our lives to be used in the appropriate way.

---

1. The *Seven Sefiros* are also discussed in "*Ahavas Yisrael* and Tefillah" (ch. 5).

The order of the seven *Sefiros* are: חֶסֶד, *kindness*; גְּבוּרָה, *power*; תִּפְאֶרֶת, *splendor*; נֶצַח, *eternity*; הוֹד, *glory*; יְסוֹד, *foundation*, and מַלְכוּת, *kingship*.

The number eight is beyond the *Sefiros*; it represents that which is לְמַעְלָה מִן הַטֶּבַע, *beyond the plane of nature*. Maharal[2] explains that the Chanukah miracles, which clearly were beyond the plane of nature, are represented by the eight days of that yom tov.

Teshuvah, too, is beyond the plane of nature. In the physical world it is often impossible to restore a damaged item to its original state, making it "as good as new," but *teshuvah* has the power to completely eradicate a sin's effect on the *neshamah*, restoring it to its original luster, and can even bring it to a higher level than it was before the sin.

Dovid HaMelech says: *"Before the mountains were born and You had not yet established the earth and the inhabited land . . . You say, 'Repent, O sons of man.'"*[3] From here, our Sages derive that *teshuvah* preceded this world,[4] for as we have said, it is beyond the plane of nature.

A musical octave consists of eight notes, the eighth being the same as the first. This represents the concept of *teshuvah*, whose literal meaning is *return*. Through sincere repentance, the *neshamah* returns to its original, pure, unsullied state.

In this psalm, Dovid says: *Halleluyah! For it is good to make music to our God, for praise is pleasant and befitting.* In the days of Mashiach, it will be very good, very beautiful, to sing to Hashem. Today many sweet, inspirational *niggunim* are composed with the seven musical notes. But when Mashiach comes there will be an eighth note. The Gemara states that the כִּנּוֹר, *harp*, used by the Levi'im in the Beis HaMikdash had seven strings, but in the days of Mashiach it will have eight,[5] as Dovid says: לַמְנַצֵּחַ בִּנְגִינוֹת עַל

2. In *Sefer Ner Mitzvah*.
3. *Tehillim* 90:2-3.
4. *Pesachim* 54a.
5. *Arachin* 13b.

הַשְּׁמִינִית, *For the Conductor, with instrumental music; on the eighth string.*[6] The *shirah* of the days of Mashiach will be of a more elevated level, beyond the plane of nature. The songs of that time will reflect a deeper understanding of Hashem's ways, of how all the happenings of history, even those that were tragic and exceedingly difficult, were all necessary to bring the world to its ultimate state of perfection.

Constant Building

בּוֹנֵה יְרוּשָׁלַיִם ה׳ נִדְחֵי יִשְׂרָאֵל יְכַנֵּס.
The Builder of Jerusalem is Hashem, the outcast of Israel He will gather.

Rambam writes:

> *If a king will arise from the House of Dovid who meditates in Torah and toils in mitzvos like his ancestor Dovid, in accordance with both the Written and Oral Torah; and he will prevail upon the entire Jewish people to go in its ways and to strengthen that which needs correction; and he will wage the wars of Hashem, then one can assume that he is Mashiach.*
>
> *If he did [all of the above] and was successful, and he built the Beis HaMikdash in its designated place and gathered in the outcast of Israel [to their Land], then surely he is Mashiach.*[7]

Thus, this verse, in its plain meaning, continues to speak of the time of the Final Redemption. Alternatively, the present tense, בּוֹנֵה, *He builds [Jerusalem],* alludes to the fact that Hashem is building the Jerusalem of the future *right now*, through the Torah and mitzvos of every single Jew. *Tzaddikim* of earlier generations

6. *Tehillim* 6:1. Rav Wolfson noted that R' Samson Raphael Hirsch translates לַמְנַצֵּחַ as related to נִצָּחוֹן (*victory*): *To the One Who grants victory through the power of music.*

7. *Hilchos Melachim* 11:4.

said that in Heaven, the Third Beis HaMikdash is almost complete; only a few more bricks are needed. Though we are a lowly generation in comparison to our ancestors, our Divine service is very beloved to Hashem and can put the finishing touches on that holy edifice.

We cannot fathom the great significance in Heaven of seemingly small acts. For example, when someone has an urge to say something negative about someone else and restrains himself, that act of self-control carries great weight in Heaven. The same applies to someone who has an urge to engage in mundane conversation in the midst of Torah study but restrains himself.

R' Yisrael of Apta[8] said that the reason this difficult *galus* has lasted so long is that the *Ribbono shel Olam* desires that our *neshamos* should achieve their *tikkun* (spiritual rectification) now so that we will be spiritually ready to greet Mashiach. Thus, our verse can mean: *The Builder of Jerusalem is Hashem* — Hashem is building Jerusalem now through our good deeds. And lest you wonder why our mitzvos have not yet "completed the edifice" and Mashiach has not yet come, the answer is because *the outcast of Israel He will gather*. Hashem is giving us time to ready ourselves spiritually.[9]

---

8. Author of *Sefer Ohev Yisrael.*

9. The Chofetz Chaim writes in a letter: "I am certain that Hashem is delaying our Redemption a bit more so that we can prepare ourselves for Mashiach's arrival, so that we will not go forward to greet him while sorely deficient in Torah and mitzvos.

"This can be likened to a wealthy man who invited his poor friends and neighbors to the wedding of his son. The man had invited some wealthy business acquaintances to the wedding and did not want to be embarrassed by the tattered rags which his relatives and neighbors were liable to wear. So he requested of them: 'Please make sure to come dressed presentably.'

"Hashem is likened to a groom and we are the bride, as it is written, *'As a bridegroom rejoicing over a bride, so will your God rejoice over you'* (*Yeshayahu* 62:5). As the time of redemption approaches, we must prepare ourselves with our spiritual garments — Torah and good deeds — so that we will be properly 'attired' to greet our Groom on that glorious day. Surely each one of us will want to greet Him and bask in the radiance of His Presence. However, if we will not be spiritually ready, and will be lacking in Torah and mitzvos, we will be forced to hide our faces in shame" (translation from *Chofetz Chaim: Lessons in Truth,* published by ArtScroll/Mesorah).

The Heart of the Earth

הָרוֹפֵא לִשְׁבוּרֵי לֵב וּמְחַבֵּשׁ לְעַצְּבוֹתָם.

He is the Healer of the broken-hearted, and the One Who binds up their sorrows.

Midrash and Zohar teach that this world can be viewed as a "body" comprised of the 248 "organs" that form the human body. Jerusalem is the earth's "heart," as Yeshayahu HaNavi says, *"Speak to the heart of Jerusalem ..."*[10] Just as the heart pumps life-giving blood through the body, so too is Jerusalem the place from which blessing and bounty go forth to the entire world.

It is not by chance that the entire world wants to call Jerusalem its own. Why should every religion, every nation, seek this small city for itself? Why should it bother mighty nations, rich in land and natural resources, that the Jewish people claim the Holy City as its own? The answer is that somehow they sense that Jerusalem is not just any city. It is the heart of the world, and therefore they want it for themselves.

And we, the Jewish people, are the "heart" of mankind. Our existence, our service of Hashem and allegiance to His Torah, give the world purpose. Therefore, whatever transpires in the world happens because of us.[11] A cursory study of world history will show that a disproportionate number of major historical events directly relate to the fortunes of the Jewish people.

Lofty Souls, Lowly Souls

As we have mentioned elsewhere, every Jew corresponds to a letter in the Torah. The name יִשְׂרָאֵל is an acronym for **יֵשׁ שִׁשִּׁים רִבּוֹא אוֹתִיּוֹת לַתּוֹרָה**, *There are 600,000 letters in the Torah.* The

10. *Yeshayahu* 40:2.

11. The Gemara states: "Retribution comes to the world only because of Israel" (*Yevamos* 63a).

greatest *neshamos* are rooted in the Torah's opening verses. Moshe Rabbeinu, says Zohar, is rooted in the large ב of בְּרֵאשִׁית, the letter with which the Torah opens.[12] The smallest *neshamos* are rooted in the last eight verses of the Torah, which begin, *"And there Moshe died."*[13] The smallest *neshamos* of all are rooted in the very last letter of the Torah, the ל of לְעֵינֵי כָּל יִשְׂרָאֵל, which, says *Rashi,* refers to Moshe's breaking of the First *Luchos* (Tablets).[14] These are broken, lowly souls, souls of *Ikvesa D'Meshicha*, the period preceding Mashiach's arrival. These souls are also alluded to in the enlarged ל of וַיַּשְׁלִכֵם אֶל אֶרֶץ אַחֶרֶת (*And He cast them to another land*).[15]

There is a huge distance between the beginning and end of the Torah. The great *neshamos* of the beginning seemingly have no connection to those at the end. However, there is one day of the year when the Torah's beginning and end are joined. Shemini Atzeres and its companion day, Simchas Torah, are days whose essence is borrowed from a future time, from the post-Messianic era, when the world will be filled with knowledge of Hashem and every *neshamah* will have achieved its *tikkun*. On Simchas Torah we dance in a circle, in which there is no beginning and no end. On Simchas Torah we read the final words of the Torah, לְעֵינֵי כָּל יִשְׂרָאֵל, and immediately afterwards we read the Torah's beginning, בְּרֵאשִׁית בָּרָא אֱלֹהִים. For when Mashiach comes, the lowly *neshamos* of *Ikvesa D'Meshicha* will reach unfathomable heights as they will be joined and uplifted by the lofty *neshamos* of earlier generations.

The final letter of the Torah, ל, and the opening letter, ב, together spell לֵב, *heart.* At present, there is a vast distance between these two letters, and the heart that is the souls of the Jewish people remains broken. However, *the Builder of Jerusalem is Hashem,*

12. The world was created for the sake of Moshe who is called רֵאשִׁית, as it is written (*Devarim* 33:21), וַיַּרְא רֵאשִׁית לוֹ, *He chose the beginning portion for himself* (cited by *Ramban* to *Bereishis* 1:1).

13. *Devarim* 34:5.

14. See *Rashi* to *Devarim* 34:12.

15. *Devarim* 29:27.

the outcast of Israel He will gather. And when that glorious time will finally come and the heart that is Jerusalem will be rebuilt, then Hashem Who is *the Healer of the broken-hearted, and the One Who binds up their sorrows* will heal our broken hearts. When Jerusalem will once again become the resting place of the *Shechinah* and the site of the Beis HaMikdash, then the souls of the lowly and the souls of the exalted will be united, and the לֵב will finally be whole.

Every Soul a Star

מוֹנֶה מִסְפָּר לַכּוֹכָבִים לְכֻלָּם שֵׁמוֹת יִקְרָא.
גָּדוֹל אֲדוֹנֵינוּ וְרַב כֹּחַ לִתְבוּנָתוֹ אֵין מִסְפָּר.

He counts the numbers of the stars, to all of them He assigns names. Great is our Lord and abundant in strength, His understanding is beyond calculation.

The stars that dot the heavens at night seem, to the uneducated, to be nothing more than that — a meaningless dot in the sky. One may not be aware that many stars are hundreds of times larger than planet Earth.

A believing Jew knows that not only are stars great in size, they also serve an important function. This must be so, despite the fact that modern science cannot discover the purpose of each star. For the *Ribbono shel Olam* would not have created something for no reason. Without a doubt, every star in every galaxy serves an important purpose.

The Jewish people are likened to the stars. A certain Jew may seem small of stature spiritually; it may appear as if he serves no important purpose in this world. Dovid HaMelech tells us that this is not so. *He counts the numbers of the stars, to all of them He assigns names.* Every star is assigned a number, indicating that its absence would be noted. And not only is it given a number, it is also given a name.

When the Jews were counted in the *Midbar,* Hashem told Moshe, *"Take a census of the entire assembly of Bnei Yisrael . . .* ***by number of the names,*** *each male according to their head count."*[16] A name indicates individuality, uniqueness. During the Second World War, the Germans, יִמַּח שְׁמָם, branded numbers on the Jews' arms, as if to say,"You're not a person, you're just a number." In the *Midbar,* the Jews had to be counted by name to demonstrate their individual importance.

This verse, then, returns to the theme with which this psalm began. *The Builder of Jerusalem is Hashem, the outcast of Israel He will gather in.* As explained above, the length of this *galus* has much to do with Hashem's desire that every Jew should achieve his *tikkun* so that he will be prepared to greet Mashiach. Hashem is concerned with every *neshamah,* no matter what his or her station in life or spiritual level. Hashem has a deep, unconditional, unfathomable love for every Jewish soul. Hashem views every *neshamah* as a giant star in the heavens, with its own unique name, individuality, and purpose. And He will bring every lost soul back to Jerusalem when the Final Redemption arrives.

Lest one wonder how it can be that every Heavenly body has its own unique purpose, how every *neshamah* has its own unique mission, and how every *neshamah* will achieve its *tikkun,* Dovid therefore says: *Great is our Lord and abundant in strength, His understanding is beyond calculation.* The term מִסְפָּר, *calculation,* indicates something that is finite, limited to this physical world. Hashem's wisdom is infinite, beyond human understanding. The human mind cannot fathom the deep, intricate planning through which He directs the happenings of the universe and the Jewish people in particular.

מְעוֹדֵד עֲנָוִים ה'. — *Hashem encourages the humble.*

He encourages and assists every individual to achieve his life's

16. *Bamidbar* 1:2.

misson. Sometimes, a person appears to be so plain and simple-minded, it is difficult for others to comprehend what his *tafkid*, spiritual mission, is on this world. But Hashem knows better and lends that person the help and encouragement that he needs. At the same time, מַשְׁפִּיל רְשָׁעִים עֲדֵי אָרֶץ, *He lowers the wicked down to the ground.* This refers to the wicked who will let nothing stand in their path to achieve their goals. If they see a need to step on others and in the process ruin their reputations or livelihoods, they will do so without remorse. Ultimately, the wicked man's fortunes will plummet as the *Ribbono shel Olam* takes him to task for the hurt he inflicted.

When the Clouds Will Part

Having spoken of the uniqueness and purpose of each Jewish soul and how this concept is deeply intertwined with the world reaching its ultimate state through the coming of Mashiach, Dovid HaMelech now returns to the theme with which he began:

עֱנוּ לַה׳ בְּתוֹדָה זַמְּרוּ לֵאלֹהֵינוּ בְכִנּוֹר.
Call out to Hashem with thanks,
with the harp sing to our God.

When Mashiach will arrive and the curtain on the stage of history will be lifted, everything that happened in this *galus*, its purpose and underlying goodness, will become clear. Then, we will erupt in a new expression of thanks to Hashem, and will play new, more sublime songs upon the eight-string harp, as mentioned above.

But we should not wait for Mashiach's arrival to burst forth with songs of thanksgiving. A Jew whose *emunah* is strong, who knows with certainty that redemption will come, can already *call out to Hashem with thanks, with the harp sing to our God.*

הַמְכַסֶּה שָׁמַיִם בְּעָבִים הַמֵּכִין לָאָרֶץ מָטָר הַמַּצְמִיחַ
הָרִים חָצִיר. נוֹתֵן לִבְהֵמָה לַחְמָהּ לִבְנֵי עֹרֵב אֲשֶׁר יִקְרָאוּ.
Who covers the heavens with clouds,
Who prepares rain for the earth,
Who makes mountains sprout with grass.
He gives to an animal its food,
to young ravens that cry out.

When thick, grey clouds cover the sky, the world appears dark and dreary. But everyone knows that those clouds are a blessing, for they herald the rains that will bring forth beautiful fields, orchards, and lush pastureland. The rains will provide sustenance for animals, birds, and of course for man.

Throughout our people's history, especially in our recent past, there have been times when the world was dark with clouds of war and persecution, and our nation bled. When Mashiach comes, we will perceive how all that transpired was the "rain" that produced the fruits of salvation, the rebuilding of the Beis HaMikdash, and the return of the Jewish people to its precious Land.

Anticipating the Redemption

לֹא בִגְבוּרַת הַסּוּס יֶחְפָּץ לֹא בְשׁוֹקֵי הָאִישׁ יִרְצֶה.
רוֹצֶה ה׳ אֶת יְרֵאָיו אֶת הַמְיַחֲלִים לְחַסְדּוֹ.
Not in the strength of the horse does He desire, and not in the thighs of man does He favor. Hashem favors those who fear Him, those who hope for His kindness.

In the world of falsehood that surrounds us, military might is what glorifies nations, and physical prowess, represented by the thigh, is what glorifies individuals. Neither has value in the eyes of the *Ribbono shel Olam*, Who favors those who have awe of Him and who faithfully hope for and anticipate the Final Redemption.

שַׁבְּחִי יְרוּשָׁלַיִם אֶת ה׳ הַלְלִי אֱלֹהַיִךְ צִיּוֹן. כִּי חִזַּק בְּרִיחֵי שְׁעָרָיִךְ בֵּרַךְ בָּנַיִךְ בְּקִרְבֵּךְ. הַשָּׂם גְּבוּלֵךְ שָׁלוֹם חֵלֶב חִטִּים יַשְׂבִּיעֵךְ.

Praise Hashem, O Jerusalem, laud your God, O Zion.
For He has strengthened the bars of your gates,
and blessed your children in your midst;
He Who makes your borders peaceful,
and with the cream of the wheat He sates you.

In our time, the Jews in our Holy Land seek to secure their borders, but peace eludes them. At the time of the Final Redemption, our Land's borders will be secure and true peace will reign.

הַשֹּׁלֵחַ אִמְרָתוֹ אָרֶץ עַד מְהֵרָה יָרוּץ דְּבָרוֹ.

He Who dispatches His utterance earthward;
how swiftly His commandment runs!

Hashem has decreed that ultimately, the Jewish people must be redeemed from *galus*, and He "dispatches" this utterance by way of the workings of Providence which will one day, hopefully soon, result in Mashiach's arrival. When the moment of Redemption comes, it will happen מְהֵרָה, *swiftly.*

The Purim redemption was a semblance of the great redemption that we anticipate. In discussing the Purim miracle, *Maharal* writes that when the moment of salvation arrived, everything happened very quickly: *"Then the king commanded: 'Tell Haman to* ***hurry*** *and fulfill Esther's wish.'"*[17] *"Then the king said to Haman: '****Hurry****, then, get the robe and the horse as you have said, and do all this for Mordechai the Jew.'"*[18] *"... and they* ***hurried*** *to bring Haman to the banquet which Esther had arranged."*[19] *"The couriers, riders of swift mules, went forth* ***in urgent haste*** *by order of the king."*[20] The salvation came from a Heavenly sphere that is beyond

17. *Esther* 5:5.
18. Ibid. 6:10.
19. Ibid. 6:14.
20. Ibid. 8:14.

time and space, and so events happened with incredible swiftness. It was a situation of וְנַהֲפוֹךְ הוּא *(and it was turned about)*;[21] with lightning speed, the situation turned around from impending doom to miraculous salvation, and the very events that seemed to bring about the Jews' downfall resulted in their rescue.

Similarly, when the moment of Yosef HaTzaddik's personal redemption arrived, *they* ***rushed him*** *from the dungeon.*[22]

This is how it will be when the time for the Final Redemption arrives. *He Who dispatches His utterance earthward;* ***how swiftly*** *His commandment runs!*

Tempering the Judgment

הַנֹּתֵן שֶׁלֶג כַּצָּמֶר כְּפוֹר כָּאֵפֶר יְפַזֵּר. מַשְׁלִיךְ קַרְחוֹ כְפִתִּים לִפְנֵי קָרָתוֹ מִי יַעֲמֹד. יִשְׁלַח דְּבָרוֹ וְיַמְסֵם יַשֵּׁב רוּחוֹ יִזְּלוּ מָיִם.

He Who gives snow like wool, He scatters frost like ashes. He hurls His ice like crumbs — before His cold, who can stand? He issues His command and it melts them, He blows His wind — the waters flow.

Cold, and the snow and ice that it brings, represents *din,* judgment. The whiteness of snow represents *hamtakas hadin,* the "sweetening" of Divine judgment when it is tempered with *rachamim*, Divine compassion.[23] However difficult the travails of

21. Ibid. 9:1.

22. *Bereishis* 41:14.

23. Rav Wolfson noted that the Beis HaMikdash was called לְבָנוֹן because it was מְלַבֵּן *(whitened)* the sins of the Jewish people.

On another occasion, Rav Wolfson quoted R' Mordechai of Lechovitz, who said that the whiteness of snow is a great kindness of Hashem. Imagine the gloom that would descend upon man if every time it snowed, the earth would be blanketed in black!

Man toils for his sustenance because of the curse that Adam received after he partook of the Tree of Knowledge. Nursing babies, however, are exempt from this curse. Their sustenance is readily available in the form of their mother's milk. The whiteness of milk represents this exemption from judgment.

The letters of the word חָלָב, *milk,* when rearranged are an acronym for לְהַגִּיד בַּבֹּקֶר חַסְדֶּךָ, *to relate Your kindness in the morning* (*Tehillim* 92:3 — *Bnei Yissoschor*).

The *Dor HaMidbar* was also exempt from this curse, as they were sustained for 40

galus are, the *Ribbono shel Olam* ensures our continued existence. *He Who gives snow like wool* means that when judgment represented by "snow" is meted out, we are provided with the protective "wool" that makes it possible to survive and tolerate it.

Tzaddikim offer a parable of a prince who has committed a terrible crime for which the punishment is that a heavy stone must be thrown upon him. Out of mercy for his beloved son, the king orders that the stone be crushed into powder and then the powder be thrown upon the prince. In a similar sense, *He scatters frost like ashes, He hurls His ice like crumbs.* Hashem takes the "frost" that has been decreed as punishment and scatters it like ashes, He takes the "ice" and breaks it into crumbs; that is, He delivers it in "small doses" so that the Jewish people will find it easier to bear. *Before His cold who can stand?* If not for His mercy in judgment, we would not be able to survive.

He issues His command and it melts them, He blows His wind — the waters flow. Eventually, the judgment comes to an end, like the frigid winter that eventually gives way to the warmth of spring. The snow and ice become water, which represents kindness and blessing from Above. Often in our history, we have seen how the most difficult judgments were followed by blessing of monumental proportions.

An illustration of this is the incredible growth of Torah learning since the end of the Second World War. There were those lacking in faith who thought that the war spelled the end of the yeshivos, ר"ל. Since the war the growth of Torah in Eretz Yisrael, America, and elsewhere has been truly miraculous. The snow melted and the waters that then flowed nurtured the soil of Jewish life, bringing forth unprecedented growth.

---

years by the *mann* that fell from Heaven. When Moshe rebuked *Bnei Yisrael* at the end of his life, he mentioned that they sinned at *"Lavan"* (*Devarim* 1:1). *Rashi* quotes R' Shimon bar Yochai who says that Moshe was rebuking them for disparaging the *mann*, which was *lavan*, white. The Torah identifies the *mann* by its color because its whiteness represented the special *chesed*, kindness, of this Divine blessing that allowed the entire nation to be sustained without any effort on its part.

Chok vs. *Mishpat*

מַגִּיד דְּבָרָיו לְיַעֲקֹב חֻקָּיו וּמִשְׁפָּטָיו לְיִשְׂרָאֵל.
לֹא עָשָׂה כֵן לְכָל גּוֹי וּמִשְׁפָּטִים בַּל יְדָעוּם הַלְלוּיָהּ.
He relates His word to Yaakov, His statutes and judgment to Yisrael. He did not do so for any other nation, such judgments — they know them not. Halleluyah!

A *chok* is a mitzvah whose reason has not been revealed to us, such as the prohibition against wearing *shaatnez*. A *mishpat* is a mitzvah whose reason is known. The term *chok* also represents happenings in our history or in our personal lives that, at the time of their occurrence, seemed incomprehensible. A classic illustration of this is *Akeidas Yitzchak*. Avraham Avinu was entrusted with a command that seemed to contradict Hashem's promise to him of "*... through Yitzchak will offspring be considered yours.*"[24] Avraham went to the *Akeidah* armed with his faith, passed the test, and then everything became clear. The *chok*, the incomprehensible command, had become *mishpat*, justice, something that was very clearly understood.

In a certain sense, mitzvos in general have an element of *chok* before one actually performs them. Dovid HaMelech says concerning the mitzvos: שֵׂכֶל טוֹב לְכָל עֹשֵׂיהֶם, *good understanding to those who practice them*.[25] R' Samson Raphael Hirsch explains that true appreciation for a mitzvah and how it impacts on our lives can come only through performing it.

Can someone who has never observed Shabbos understand the beauty and sanctity of this most precious day? Can someone who has never toiled over a *blatt Gemara* understand the indescribable joy that overwhelms the student when finally, the *sugya* (Talmudic topic) becomes crystal clear? Only one who has experienced Shabbos or Torah learning can perceive its beauty. Thus, a mitzvah

24. *Bereishis* 21:12.
25. *Tehillim* 111:10.

can be a *chok* of sorts before it is fulfilled, and becomes a *mishpat* afterwards.

He did not do so for any other nation, such judgments — they know them not. The nations of the world surely have no appreciation for our *chukim* and they cannot truly comprehend our *mishpatim*. They have no inkling of our deeply rooted *emunah*, an *emunah* that is our inheritance from our holy *Avos* and *Imahos*, and which gives us the strength to face the most difficult challenges. Our *chukim, mishpatim,* and *emunah* are priceless blessings that should inspire us to exclaim, *"Halleluyah!"*

CHAPTER FOURTEEN

Psalm 148: The Symphony of Creation

הַלְלוּיָהּ, הַלְלוּ אֶת ה׳ מִן הַשָּׁמַיִם, הַלְלוּהוּ בַּמְּרוֹמִים ...
Halleluyah! Praise Hashem from the heavens; praise Him in the heights ...

This psalm continues the theme of the days of Mashiach, when the entire spiritual and physical universe will join together in joyous praise of Hashem.

About the creation of Adam the Torah says: וַיְהִי הָאָדָם לְנֶפֶשׁ חַיָּה, *And the man became a living soul.*[1] Both the Maggid of

1. *Bereishis* 2:7.

Mezeritch and R' Chaim Volozhiner[2] offer a novel interpretation of these words: *And man became the living soul of the universe.* The purpose of Creation is for man to serve his Creator. When Adam was formed, he became the "soul of the universe," so that his actions would affect everything in the heavens above and the earth below.

This is the power with which Adam was invested. But in succeeding generations, instead of using this power for the good, mankind became corrupt, to the point that even animal life and plant life were adversely affected.[3] The world was destroyed by the *Mabul* (Flood) and Noach led a new beginning. Ten generations later, the world was steeped in idol worship, but one man, Avraham Avinu, recognized the One and Only God. And so Avraham and his descendants gave the world purpose and they alone remained the "soul of the universe." Thus, the words, deeds, and even thoughts of a Jew affect the workings of heaven and earth.[4]

All Hashem's creations sing *shirah* to Him, each in its own way. But this symphony of song must be initiated by man. And in this psalm Dovid, who possessed the *neshamah* of Adam and Mashiach,[5] invites all of Creation to join him in praising Hashem:

Halleluyah! Praise Hashem from the heavens, praise Him in the heights. Praise Him, all His angels; praise Him, all His legions. Praise Him, sun and moon; praise Him, all bright stars. Praise Him, the most exalted of the heavens and the waters that are above the heavens. Let them praise the Name of Hashem, for He commanded and they were created.

---

2. *Nefesh HaChaim* 1:4.

3. See *Rashi* to *Bereishis* 6:12.

4. R' Chaim Volozhiner writes that when a Jew commits a sin, he brings more harm to the world than Nevuchadnezzar and Titus did when they destroyed the Beis HaMikdash, for our actions affect the workings of Heaven, while theirs did not. That they were able to destroy the Beis HaMikdash was only because the sins of the Jewish people had already defiled it; it was we who had destroyed it, not they.

5. Dovid's soul will reappear in the person of Mashiach. Zohar states that אָדָם is an acronym for אָדָם, דָוִד, מָשִׁיחַ.

The Heavenly Song

What is the nature of the "song" of the celestial bodies? It is their natural functioning. When the sun rises in the morning to warm the earth and its inhabitants, when the moon appears in the evening to illuminate the darkness, each contributes its own "musical score" to the symphony of creation.

When Yehoshua caused the sun to stop its movement across the sky, he said: *"Sun, be silent in Givon ...."*[6] Its normal functioning is its *shirah*, and when this was temporarily suspended, it "fell silent."

Therefore, in our chapter, Dovid declares:

> וַיַּעֲמִידֵם לָעַד לְעוֹלָם, חָק נָתַן וְלֹא יַעֲבוֹר.
> *And He established them forever and ever, He issued a decree that will not change.*

Their unchanging functions, which bring endless blessing to this world, are their expression of song.

Heavenly Ornaments

Homiletically, the word [וַיַּעֲמִידֵם] לָעַד [לְעוֹלָם] can be translated *as an ornament,* as in הוֹרֵד עֶדְיְךָ מֵעָלֶיךָ, *remove your ornament from yourself.*[7] The *shirah* of the heavenly bodies is only an enhancement to that of mankind on this world. The sun, moon, and stars do not have *bechirah*, free will, as the plain meaning of this verse proclaims: *And He established them forever and ever, He issued a decree that will not change.* Man, on the other hand, does have *bechirah*. Therefore, if man lives his life in accordance with Hashem's will, then his life is the greatest form of *shirah* and his song is enhanced by that of the heavens, much as a piece of jewelry enhances the appearance of the one it adorns.

6. *Yehoshua* 10:12.
7. *Shemos* 33:5.

However, if man flouts God's will and chooses to live a life of sin, then the heavenly song is like a נֶזֶם זָהָב בְּאַף חֲזִיר, *golden ring in a swine's snout*;[8] its inherent beauty is unappreciated because the song of man has been corrupted.

The Earth and Its Components

Dovid now turns his attention to the earth and its various components:

הַלְלוּ אֶת ה׳ מִן הָאָרֶץ, תַּנִּינִים וְכָל תְּהֹמוֹת.
אֵשׁ וּבָרָד, שֶׁלֶג וְקִיטוֹר, רוּחַ סְעָרָה עֹשָׂה דְבָרוֹ.
Praise Hashem from the earth,
sea giants and all watery depths. Fire and hail,
snow and vapor, stormy wind fulfilling His word.

This last verse lists items that have destructive power. The term רוּחַ סְעָרָה, *stormy wind,* is found at the opening of Yechezkel HaNavi's great esoteric vision knows as *Maaseh Merkavah* ("The Workings of the Chariot"): *"Then I looked and behold! A stormy wind was coming from the north, a great cloud with flashing fire, and a brilliance surrounding it."*[9] This is a description of the אַרְבַּע קְלִיפּוֹת, *the four shells (of spiritual impurity)* that need to be penetrated in order to approach the Divine Presence. The outermost and most difficult to penetrate is רוּחַ סְעָרָה.

Destructive forces also sing a *shirah* of sorts, for their power too is an expression of Hashem's will. As a *tzaddik* put it, in a time of war, "Every bullet has its address." When storms, earthquakes, or tsunamis bring devastation and loss of life, it is only because Hashem willed that it should be. And it is He Who decrees who will merit to survive those disasters.[10]

---

8. *Mishlei* 11:22.

9. *Yechezkel* 1:4.

10. During the Second World War the great rosh yeshivah R' Yisrael Zev Gustman

Dovid then calls to three groups of earthly creations to express their praise of Hashem. He addresses the דוֹמֵם, *inanimate object*; צוֹמֵחַ, *plant life*; and חַי, *living creature*:

הֶהָרִים וְכָל גְּבָעוֹת, עֵץ פְּרִי וְכָל אֲרָזִים.
הַחַיָּה וְכָל בְּהֵמָה, רֶמֶשׂ וְצִפּוֹר כָּנָף.
[Praise Hashem] . . . Mountains and all hills, fruitful trees and all cedars. Beasts and all cattle, crawling things and winged fowl.

At the time of the Final Redemption, the inanimate mountains will join in a special joyous song, as Yeshayahu HaNavi prophesies: *"For in gladness shall you go out and in peace shall you arrive; the mountains and hills will break out in glad song before you, and all the trees of the field will clap hands."*[11]

Aside from its plain meaning, *fruitful trees* alludes to the Jew who is productive spiritually, through his Torah study, tefillah, and good deeds. The essence of his actions and words gives praise to Hashem. *All cedars* alludes to the haughty wicked who suffer retribution for their evil deeds, thereby bringing glory to Hashem's Name. Regarding the Ten Plagues with which Pharaoh and his people were smitten, *Ramban*[12] applies the verse *"I will be exalted and I will be sanctified, and I will make Myself known before the eyes of many nations . . . ."*[13]

Dovid then addresses the מְדַבֵּר, *speaking being*:[14]

---

spent five years hiding and fleeing from the Germans. More than 100 times it appeared his end might be near, and he recited *Viduy* each time. After the war he explained the secret of his survival: "The same *Ribbono shel Olam* Who decrees who shall die decrees who shall live. He decreed that I should live, so no matter what the Germans tried to do, they could not kill me."

11. *Yeshayahu* 55:12.

12. *Shemos* 7:3; see *Rashi* ad loc.

13. *Yechezkel* 38:23.

14. *Sefer Kuzari* states that the Jewish people are a fifth level of creation, for their souls are of a more exalted nature.

מַלְכֵי אֶרֶץ וְכָל לְאוּמִּים, שָׂרִים וְכָל שֹׁפְטֵי אָרֶץ ...

[Praise Hashem] kings of the earth and all governments, princes and all judges on earth. Young men and also maidens, old men together with youths.[15] Let them praise the Name of Hashem, for His Name alone will have been exalted; His glory is above earth and heaven.

Unwittingly, the leaders of nations also execute Hashem's will, for it is He Who turns their hearts in the direction that He chooses. As Shlomo HaMelech says: *"Like streams of water is the heart of a king in the hand of Hashem; wherever He wishes, so does He direct it."*[16] Nevertheless, like every human being, they have *bechirah*, free will, and will be held accountable for their wicked actions.[17] Dovid calls upon these leaders to exercise their free will to carry out Hashem's desire in a positive way. By doing so, they will have declared that *His name alone will have been exalted; His glory is above earth and heaven.* Because of his free will, the praise of Hashem expressed by man is a more exalted quality than that of the celestial bodies that have no choice but to function as He decreed. Therefore, in this verse Dovid places *earth* before *heaven.* The praise expressed by mortal man on earth exceeds that of the heavenly beings.

---

15. Rav Wolfson cited R' Yehudah HeChasid (1150-1217) in *Sefer HaChassidim* who notes the difference in the wording of the two halves of this verse. The first half says *young men* and also *maidens* [וְגַם] while the second half reads *old men* together *with youths* [עִם]. Dovid does not say that young men will be together with maidens because such mingling would be improper.

16. *Mishlei* 21:1.

17. See *Ramban* to *Shemos* 7:3 who explains why Pharaoh was punished for persecuting *Bnei Yisrael* despite the fact that Hashem "hardened his heart" so that he would not allow the Jews to leave Egypt. *Ramban's* words also explain why Pharaoh was held accountable despite the fact that the Egyptian exile had been decreed many years earlier. (See also *Rambam, Hilchos Teshuvah* 6:3.)

His Intimate Ones

In the world as we know it, the nations do not heed Dovid's call to join him in praising Hashem. They worship many things: false gods, false ideals, materialism, but not the One and Only Creator. At the time of the Final Redemption, they *will* heed his call.

In the world's present state, only the Jewish people praise Hashem — every day, morning, afternoon, and evening. Yet, despite our exalted status as Hashem's beloved, chosen nation and despite our faithfully clinging to His Torah and mitzvos, we remain downtrodden and despised, scorned and rejected. But when Mashiach will appear, all the world will recognize our close, unique relationship with Hashem. At that time . . .

וַיָּרֶם קֶרֶן לְעַמּוֹ תְּהִלָּה לְכָל חֲסִידָיו לִבְנֵי יִשְׂרָאֵל עַם קְרֹבוֹ הַלְלוּיָהּ.

He will have exalted the pride of His nation, causing praise for all His devout ones, for the Children of Israel, His intimate people. Halleluyah!

In the *Shemoneh Esrei* of the *Yomin Nora'im* we pray: *"And so, too, O Hashem, grant honor to Your people, praise to those who revere You . . . ."* We pray for the day when all will perceive that we, the Jewish people, are the "conductors" of the magnificent symphony of Creation as it sings the praises of Hashem.

In the final verse of this chapter, Dovid anticipates the time when this tefillah will be answered. Then, all the world will recognize that even as we suffered in *galus*, we were עַם קְרוֹבוֹ, *His intimate people.* May that day come speedily and in our lifetime.

CHAPTER FIFTEEN

Psalm 149: A New Song for a New World

הַלְלוּיָהּ שִׁירוּ לַה׳ שִׁיר חָדָשׁ ...

Halleluyah! Sing to Hashem a new song . . .

The arrival of Mashiach will usher in a new, more sublime level of existence. In *Rambam's* words:[1]

And at that time, there will be no hunger and no war; no jealousy and no strife. For there will be an abundant flow

1. *Hilchos Melachim* 12:5.

of goodness and all delicacies will be as common as sand. The world will be occupied with nothing but knowing Hashem. Therefore, the Jewish people will be men of great wisdom; they will know hidden matters and will attain an understanding of their Creator as much as a human being can, as it is written: "For the earth will be filled with knowledge of Hashem, like the water that covers the seabed."[2]

A new world requires a שִׁיר חָדָשׁ, *new song,* one that is more beautiful and spiritually uplifting than anything that was sung previously. As we noted in our discussion of Psalm 147, the כִּנּוֹר, *harp*, used by the Levi'im in the Beis HaMikdash had seven strings, but in the days of Mashiach it will have eight.[3] The *shirah* of the days of Mashiach will be of a more elevated level, beyond the plane of nature.

And who will lead the singing at that glorious time? תְּהִלָּתוֹ בִּקְהַל חֲסִידִים, *His praise is in the congregation of the devout.* A great celebration, known as the *Simchas Beis HaSho'eivah*, was held at the Beis HaMikdash on each night of Chol HaMoed Succos. The Mishnah states that חֲסִידִים וְאַנְשֵׁי מַעֲשֶׂה, *Devout men and men of good deeds,* would dance and juggle flaming torches while everyone else looked on.[4] So, too, at that joyous time of Mashiach's arrival, the singing will be led by the devout, those who faithfully clung to Hashem and His Torah throughout this difficult *galus.* And all of *Klal Yisrael* will join in and sing — יִשְׂמַח יִשְׂרָאֵל בְּעֹשָׂיו בְּנֵי צִיּוֹן יָגִילוּ בְמַלְכָּם, *Let Israel exult in its Maker, let the children of Zion rejoice in their King.* And the nations of the world will look on in awe.[5]

---

2. *Yeshayahu* 11:9.

3. *Arachin* 13b.

4. *Mishnah Succah* 5:4.

5. Zohar interprets יִשְׂמַח יִשְׂרָאֵל בְּעֹשָׂיו as *A Jew will rejoice with those who made him.* This means that when a Jew celebrates a wedding, *bris milah,* or other joyous mitzvah, his parents, grandparents, and earlier generations descend from their place in *Gan Eden* to be present at the *simchah.*

When the *Simchah* Will be Complete

The Midrash cites the words יִשְׂמַח יִשְׂרָאֵל בְּעֹשָׂיו, *Let Yisrael exult in its Maker,* alongside יִשְׂמַח ה' בְּמַעֲשָׂיו, *Let Hashem rejoice in His works.*[6] It expounds:

> *Israel never rejoiced [fully] with My world. It does not say* שָׂמַח *[Israel* ***rejoiced****] but rather* יִשְׂמַח *[****he will rejoice****]; they are destined [in the days of Mashiach] to rejoice with the works of HaKadosh Baruch Hu.*
>
> *And, as it were, HaKadosh Baruch Hu never rejoiced [fully] with His world. It does not say* שָׂמַח *[Hashem* ***rejoiced****] but rather* יִשְׂמַח *[****He will rejoice****]; HaKadosh Baruch Hu is destined in the future to rejoice with the deeds of the righteous.*[7]

Since the sin of Adam, Hashem has never found complete satisfaction with His world, and thus His joy over it has never been complete. Because Hashem's joy is lacking, it is not possible for man's joy to be complete. No matter how powerful or successful one has become, or how exciting and joyous is the occasion, the *simchah* is not complete. Only when Mashiach has arrived, when the *Ribbono shel Olam* will finally be completely happy with this world and its inhabitants, will man's happiness be complete as well.

Only once in history was man's joy complete, at a moment that provided a tiny glimpse of the world to come. Shlomo HaMelech was the 15th generation from Avraham Avinu. He represented סִיהֲרָא בְּאַשְׁלָמוּתָא, *the moon in its fullness* (which occurs on the 15th day of the lunar month). For the Jewish people are likened to the moon, as we say in *Kiddush Levanah*: *"To the moon He said that it should renew itself as a crown of splendor for those . . . destined to renew themselves like it."* Shlomo's reign, when the Jewish people was at peace with its enemies and was the envy of the nations, provided a semblance of the world of the future.[8]

---

6. *Tehillim* 104:31.

7. *Vayikra Rabbah* 20:2.

8. Rav Wolfson noted that according to Zohar, Shlomo is the *Ushpizin* (Exalted Guest)

There was one point in Shlomo's reign that provided not only a semblance but a "window" into the future. This was at the dedication of the Beis HaMikdash, a moment in history when Hashem's joy was complete. Of that moment the Mishnah applies the verse: *"Go forth and gaze, O daughters of Zion, upon the King Shlomo,*[9] *adorned with the crown His nation made Him on the day of His wedding and on the day of the joy of His heart."*[10]

> *"On the day of His wedding"* — this is the giving of the Torah.
> *"and on the day of the joy of His heart"* — this is the building of the Beis HaMikdash, may it be rebuilt speedily in our days, *amen.*[11]

With Dancing and Music

יְהַלְלוּ שְׁמוֹ בְמָחוֹל.

Let them praise His Name with dancing.

Literally, the word מָחוֹל means *a circle.* The Gemara states that in the days of Mashiach the *tzaddikim* will form a circle around Hashem. Each *tzaddik* will point to Hashem and declare: *"Behold! This is our God, in Him we placed our confidence so that He might save us. This is Hashem in Whom we placed our confidence, we shall rejoice and be happy in His salvation."*[12]

---

of Shemini Atzeres. As we have noted elsewhere, the number eight represents לְמַעְלָה מִן הַטֶּבַע, *beyond the plane of nature.* The day of Shemini Atzeres is a semblance of the world after Mashiach's arrival. In fact, *Chasam Sofer* writes that all the *yamim tovim,* including the holy day of Yom Kippur, are a progression that prepares for the awesome day of Shemini Atzeres — the center point [i.e. climax] around which the festival cycle revolves.

The *haftarah* of Shemini Atzeres (*Melachim I* 8:54-9:1) is about Shlomo's dedication of the First Beis HaMikdash. Its concluding words are: וְאֵת כָּל חֵשֶׁק שְׁלֹמֹה אֲשֶׁר חָפֵץ לַעֲשׂוֹת, *and every yearning of Shlomo that he desired to do.* For Shlomo's era, as we have explained, was a semblance of the perfect world of the future.

9. I.e. Hashem, מֶלֶךְ שֶׁהַשָּׁלוֹם שֶׁלּוֹ, *the King, to Whom peace belongs (Rav).*

10. *Shir HaShirim* 3:11.

11. *Mishnah Taanis* 4:8.

12. *Yeshayahu* 25:9.

And who will these *tzaddikim* be? The entire Jewish nation. For at that time, every sinful soul will repent and will be cleansed of his misdeeds. In a circle, there is no front and no rear; everyone is equally distant from the center. At that time, every Jewish soul, whatever his station in life had been previously, will feel an intense closeness to Hashem and will join in that joyous circle of dancers who will point to the *Shechinah* in the center.

בְּתֹף וְכִנּוֹר יְזַמְּרוּ לוֹ.

With drum and harp let them make music to Him.

The beat of the drum can disturb one's inner peace, while the sweet sound of the harp is soothing to the soul. However, when the drum accompanies the harp in proper rhythm, it enhances the song in a way that inspires and uplifts. The תֹּף, *drum,* represents the harsh sufferings that the Jewish people endured during this long, difficult *galus*. The כִּנּוֹר, *harp,* represents the periods of calm and blessing that our nation experienced as it migrated from country to country. The combined music of the drum and harp in the future will represent a recognition that all that transpired, even the suffering and persecutions, were ultimately for our good and were necessary for our redemption.

A Time to Appease

כִּי רוֹצֶה ה' בְּעַמּוֹ, יְפָאֵר עֲנָוִים בִּישׁוּעָה.

For Hashem favors His people,
He adorns the humble with salvation.

When Yosef HaTzaddik was called upon to interpret Pharaoh's dreams, the Torah states: וַיְרִיצֻהוּ מִן הַבּוֹר[13], which translated literally means *and they rushed him from the pit.* Zohar,[14] however, relates

13. *Bereishis* 41:14.

14. Vol. I p. 388.

the word וַיְרִיצֻהוּ to the word רוֹצֶה, which can mean *appease*. From the day he was kidnapped and sold into slavery, Yosef suffered terribly. In the house of Potiphar, he was subjected to the most difficult *nisyonos* (spiritual tests). Then he was thrown into a dungeon where he languished for 12 years. And suddenly, when those 12 years came to a close, he was rushed out of imprisonment, given a haircut and a set of presentable clothing, and brought before the king.

By the time his audience with Pharaoh ended, Yosef had gone from lowly prisoner to the viceroy who governed the Egyptian empire. At that time Yosef recognized with astonishing clarity that all the years of suffering had been a means of bringing him to this position. As he later told his brothers, "*... do not reproach yourselves for having sold me here, for it was as a supporter of life that God sent me here ... God has sent me ahead of you to ensure your survival in the land and to sustain you for a great deliverance.*"[15]

And so it will be when the Final Redemption comes: כִּי רוֹצֶה ה' בְּעַמּוֹ, *For Hashem will appease His nation.* He will help them to understand the goodness in all the trials and tribulations they endured. יְפָאֵר עֲנָוִים בִּישׁוּעָה, *He adorns the humble with salvation.* At the time of their salvation, the Jewish people will be adorned with a crown whose jewels will be the tests of exile that they successfully overcame and which served as the catalyst for their redemption.

Joyously Upon Their Beds

יַעְלְזוּ חֲסִידִים בְּכָבוֹד יְרַנְּנוּ עַל מִשְׁכְּבוֹתָם.
Let the devout exult in glory,
let them sing joyously upon their beds.

When a person is beset with worries, he seeks ways to distract himself as he goes about his day. However, when he lies in bed at night with nothing to distract him, his worries weigh heavily upon him.

15. *Bereishis* 45:5,7.

In the days of Mashiach, our worries will end. The Jew will sing joyously even as he lies in bed, secure in the knowledge that the world has entered an era of unparalleled peace and tranquility, as the nations of the world acknowledge our unique status as Hashem's Chosen People.

A Double-Edged Sword

רוֹמְמוֹת אֵל בִּגְרוֹנָם וְחֶרֶב פִּיפִיּוֹת בְּיָדָם.

The lofty praises of God are in their throats, and a double-edged sword is in their hand.

The Midrash teaches that when the voice of Yaakov is raised in Torah and tefillah, then the hands of Esav have no power.[16] The *lofty praises of God are a double-edged sword* in the hands of the devout.

Those who are truly close to Hashem do not wait for salvation to come to lift their voices in praise. Dovid says elsewhere, נְקַדְּמָה פָנָיו בְּתוֹדָה.[17] The word נְקַדְּמָה can be translated as *let us precede* (in offering thanks). A true man of faith knows that Hashem's salvation can come in the blink of an eye. He is aware that even in the darkest of times, Hashem is watching over him, carefully guiding all that transpires. As such, his songs of praise *precede* the moment of salvation.

Also, true men of faith do not need to wait for the days of Mashiach to sleep peacefully. Yaakov Avinu lay down in the darkness of night at the site of the future Beis HaMikdash. What did he have for protection? *"He took from the stones of the place which he arranged around his head and lay down in that place."*[18] What kind of protection was this? How could a few stones around Yaakov's head protect his entire body from the dangers lurking all around him?

16. *Bereishis Rabbah* 65:20.

17. *Tehillim* 95:2.

18. *Bereishis* 28:11.

Pirkei D'Rav Eliezer writes that these stones were from the altar upon which Avraham had brought Yitzchak at the *Akeidah*. To Yaakov, they were a "*mezuzah*" of sorts. Yaakov was confident that their sanctity would bring him protection from Above, and with that knowledge he was able to sleep peacefully.

One who possesses true *bitachon*, trust in Hashem, can find tranquility in the most difficult situation.

A Vengeance of Clarity

לַעֲשׂוֹת נְקָמָה בַּגּוֹיִם תּוֹכֵחֹת בַּלְאֻמִּים.

To execute vengeance among the nations, rebukes among the governments.

Rashi comments on the words וְאֵת כֹּל וְנֹכָחַת[19] that הוֹכָחָה means *to clarify matters*. A primary vengeance against our enemies at the End of Days will be their realization that throughout the millennia of this *galus*, Hashem never abandoned us. Nothing happened without His guiding hand allowing it to happen, and all the exiles, migrations, persecutions, and travails were necessary steps along the road to redemption. The clarity of this truth will infuse the Jewish people with unparalleled joy and will leave the nations of the world stunned and speechless.

לֶאְסֹר מַלְכֵיהֶם בְּזִקִּים וְנִכְבְּדֵיהֶם בְּכַבְלֵי בַרְזֶל.
לַעֲשׂוֹת בָּהֶם מִשְׁפָּט כָּתוּב ...

To bind their kings with chains, and their nobles with fetters of iron. To execute upon them written judgment ...

The future judgments against the nations are recorded in the writings of the *Nevi'im*. Every word of those prophecies will be fulfilled when Mashiach comes.

19. *Bereishis* 20:16.

הָדָר הוּא לְכָל חֲסִידָיו הַלְלוּיָהּ.

He is the majesty of all His devout ones — Halleluyah!

In the glorious days of the future, Hashem's greatness will be revealed on a level that surpasses anything mankind has yet experienced. May we soon witness that time.

CHAPTER SIXTEEN

Psalm 150: A Fitting Conclusion

The final chapter of *Sefer Tehillim*, and the last in *Pesukei D'Zimrah*, is an all-encompassing call to praise Hashem on earth and in heaven, with every means and in every situation.

הַלְלוּיָהּ הַלְלוּ אֵל בְּקָדְשׁוֹ הַלְלוּהוּ בִּרְקִיעַ עֻזּוֹ.

Halleluyah! Praise God in His sanctuary, praise Him in the firmament of His power.

The Midrash states that the Heavenly retinue is not permitted to sing its praises of Hashem until the Jewish people have praised Him on earth. For, as we have already explained, the purpose of creation is that we, the Chosen People, should serve Hashem, and our actions affect what occurs in both the upper and lower worlds.

Therefore, Dovid calls out to the Jewish nation: *Praise God in His sanctuary*, in His Beis HaMikdash, or in His *mikdash me'at* (miniature sanctuary), the *beis haknesses.* Then, he invites the angels on high: *Praise God in the firmament of His power.*

With Might and Greatness

הַלְלוּהוּ בִגְבוּרֹתָיו הַלְלוּהוּ כְּרֹב גֻּדְלוֹ.

Praise Him for His mighty acts, praise Him as befits His abundant greatness.

In *Sefer Divrei HaYamim,* Dovid sings a song of praise in which he makes mention of the seven *Sefiros* (Emanations), *middos* of Hashem that man should strive to emulate.[1] That verse is recited as part of *Pesukei D'Zimrah* and when the *sefer Torah* is carried to the *bimah* for the Torah reading:

> לְךָ ה' הַגְּדֻלָּה וְהַגְּבוּרָה וְהַתִּפְאֶרֶת וְהַנֵּצַח וְהַהוֹד כִּי כֹל בַּשָּׁמַיִם וּבָאָרֶץ לְךָ ה' הַמַּמְלָכָה ...
>
> *Yours, Hashem, is the greatness, the strength, the splendor, the triumph, and the glory, even everything in heaven and earth; Yours, Hashem, is the kingdom ...*[2]

The term גְּדֻלָּה, *greatness,* refers to Hashem's attribute of *chesed,* kindness. *Chesed* is גְּדֻלָּה because when one reaches out to help another, he is expanding his sphere of accomplishment, doing not just for himself but for others as well. גְּבוּרָה, *strength,* refers to Hashem's attribute of *din,* strict judgment.

In our verse, Dovid calls to one and all: *Praise God when His judgment is manifest, praise God when His kindness is manifest.* As the mishnah states: "A person is obligated to bless God for the bad just

1. See "*Ahavas Yisrael* and Tefillah" (ch. 5).

2. *Divrei HaYamim I* 29:11.

as he blesses God for the good."[3] For in essence, all that Hashem does is for the good and therefore warrants an expression of praise.

In *Hallel*, Dovid expresses this same theme: *"Trouble and sorrow I would find — and in Hashem's Name I will call,"*[4] and in that very same chapter he says, *"I will raise the cup of salvations — and in Hashem's Name I will call."*[5]

This idea is also the theme of the next verse in our chapter:

הַלְלוּהוּ בְּתֵקַע שׁוֹפָר הַלְלוּהוּ בְּנֵבֶל וְכִנּוֹר.

Praise Him with the blast of the shofar, praise Him with lyre and harp.

The sound of the shofar inspires fear and trembling, as it is written, *"Can a shofar be blown in a city and the people not tremble?"*[6] By contrast, the sweet sounds of the lyre and harp are soothing to the soul. The shofar symbolizes judgment, the lyre and harp allude to Hashem's bountiful goodness. A Jew gives thanks to his Creator in all situations.

הַלְלוּהוּ בְתֹף וּמָחוֹל הַלְלוּהוּ בְּמִנִּים וְעוּגָב.
הַלְלוּהוּ בְצִלְצְלֵי שָׁמַע הַלְלוּהוּ בְּצִלְצְלֵי תְרוּעָה.

Praise Him with drum and dance, praise Him with minim and ugav. Praise Him with clanging cymbals, praise Him with resonant trumpets.

The various instruments mentioned here represent a symphony of song.[7] The drum and symbols produce a loud, pounding sound

3. *Mishnah Berachos* 9:1.

4. *Tehillim* 116:3-4.

5. Ibid. v. 13. While the first verse continues, "Please, Hashem, save my soul!" the fact that in both places Dovid uses the exact same words — וּבְשֵׁם ה' אֶקְרָא *(and in Hashem's Name I will call)* — indicates that in both situations, Dovid was filled with gratitude and praise of Hashem.

6. *Amos* 3:6.

7. The commentators disagree on the definition of *minim* and *ugav. Targum* translates *minim* as חַלִּילִין, *flutes.* Meiri suggests that it refers to a type of organ. There are other

whose vibrations can be somewhat disturbing, but they are vital nonetheless. Without the rhythm of the drum and cymbals, the dance might lack coordination and the instruments might not play in unison. Similarly, all that transpires in this world, including that which affects us adversely (as the pounding of the drum often does) is part of a carefully choreographed "dance" and accompanying "orchestra." And the grand Conductor, the *Ribbono shel Olam,* is directing everything, down to the most minute detail, every moment of the day.[8]

The Song of the Soul

כֹּל הַנְּשָׁמָה תְּהַלֵּל יָהּ הַלְלוּיָהּ.
Let all souls praise God, Halleluyah!

The last five chapters of *Sefer Tehillim* focus on the song that will be sung upon Mashiach's arrival. Dovid concludes by declaring that at that glorious time, every Jewish soul will achieve its *tikkun* (spiritual rectification) and will join in that grandest of symphonies in praising Hashem. For Hashem is חוֹשֵׁב מַחֲשָׁבוֹת לְבִלְתִּי יִדַּח מִמֶּנּוּ נִדָּח (*He ponders thoughts so that no one be banished from Him*).[9] When the Final Redemption comes, every lost soul will return to its spiritual roots and will rejoice as it renews its closeness with its Father in Heaven.

Often, an author signs his name at the conclusion of his manuscript. As we have mentioned, the soul of Adam encompassed within it every soul that would descend to this world. As Zohar states, the soul of Adam later descended to this world in the person of Dovid HaMelech, and will descend once again in the person

opinions as well. *Targum* to *Bereishis* 4:21 identifies *ugav* as אַבּוּבָא, a type of flute.

8. A similar point was made in the previous essay regarding the combination of drum and harp.

9. Based on *Shmuel II* 14:14. *Ramchal* and others see that verse as alluding to the End of Days when every soul will achieve its *tikkun*.

of Mashiach, a scion of Dovid.[10] And so Dovid concludes *Sefer Tehillim* by saying:

> *I am* כֹּל הַנְּשָׁמָה, *the neshamah that encompasses all neshamos. Therefore, when I praise Hashem it is in a sense as if all Jewish souls are praising Hashem. And the day will yet come when all Jewish souls will in fact join together in praising Him.*

As we have mentioned, at the conclusion of Psalm 145, Dovid invites mankind to join him in praising the One Above. In Psalm 146, he declares: *I will praise Hashem while I live, I will make music to my God while I exist.* Though (in Psalm 145) he has uttered an all-encompassing song of praise, he still yearns to praise Hashem more.

In Psalm 147, Dovid invites everyone to join him in praising Hashem: *For it is good to make music to our God, for praise is pleasant and befitting.* There is no physical pleasure that can compare to the joy of attaching oneself to Hashem through tefillah, and Dovid invites one and all to participate in this pleasure.

In Psalm 148, Dovid calls out to all of creation to join in a symphonic song of praise: *Praise Hashem from the heavens, praise Him in the heights. Praise Him all His angels ... Praise Him, sun and moon ...*

In Psalm 149, he invites everyone to join him in the שִׁיר חָדָשׁ, *new song,* that will be mandated by the new, sublime world order of the days of Mashiach.

In this concluding psalm, Psalm 150, Dovid enhances his song with an array of musical instruments. He then concludes: *There is one instrument that is neither a drum nor a harp. It is silent and unseen. And yet, its song is the greatest song of all.*

It is the song of the neshamah. It is a song that is sung with feeling, with an outpouring of emotion. It is a song that is sung without ulterior motive, simply out of love of Hashem and recognition of His infinite goodness.

---

10. As we have noted, the word אָדָם is an acronym for אָדָם, דָּוִד, מָשִׁיחַ.

The literal meaning of ... כֹּל הַנְּשָׁמָה is *[Let] all souls . . .*; another translation is *The entire soul.* When a Jew stands before Hashem in tefillah, uttering each word with all his heart and soul, there is no greater *shirah* (song) in all of creation.

This is the concluding message of *Sefer Tehillim.*

CHAPTER SEVENTEEN

Az Yashir — The Song at the Sea

A major component of *Pesukei D'Zimrah* is *Shiras HaYam*, the Song at the Sea, which was led by Moshe and sung by the Jewish people after the great miracle of the splitting of the *Yam Suf.* Zohar teaches that one should recite *Shiras HaYam* with joy, and imagine as if he himself had experienced that miracle this very day.[1]

As the Sages relate, even a lowly maidservant merited an exalted level of prophecy at that time. The song represents the highest level of *emunah baShem,* faith in God. Reciting *Shiras HaYam* with joy and emotion strengthens one's *emunah.*

1. *Mishnah Berurah* 51:17 citing Zohar.

Sometimes, when suffering from a physical ailment, a person is presented with two options. He can purchase an expensive medication, or he can obtain an inexpensive or even free herb that can achieve the same results.

This can serve as a parable for curing the maladies of the soul.

In discussing various paths of *teshuvah, Sefer Chareidim* writes:[2]

> *After we have written about spiritual cures that are quite "expensive" [i.e. they are difficult, such as fasting and other forms of physical affliction], we should now investigate and seek cures that are inexpensive [i.e. which are relatively easy and are a sort of "segulah" (auspicious omen)] .... One should recite Shiras HaYam each day with proper kavanah, saying it in a raised voice and with great joy .... The Midrash states that the Jews achieved atonement for their sins when they recited the Song after crossing the Yam Suf. According to R' Shimon bar Yochai, there is an allusion in the Torah that we should recite the Song every day with great joy, like the time when it was first recited.*[3] *Surely, then, its spiritual power for those who recite it properly is the same as when it was said that first time.*

Mishnah Berurah[4] states: "Whoever recites [*Shiras HaYam*] with joy will have all his sins forgiven."

When Did They Sing?

There is an apparent contradiction in *Rashi* regarding the date when the *Shirah* was sung. In *Parashas Beshalach*, where the episode at the *Yam Suf* is recounted, *Rashi* states: "On the night, they

2. Ch. 73. *Sefer Chareidim* was authored by R' Eliezer Azkari (1533-1600).

3. The verse states: אָז יָשִׁיר ... וַיֹּאמְרוּ לֵאמֹר, *Then [Moshe and the Bnei Yisrael] sang ... and they said, saying.* The double terminology of וַיֹּאמְרוּ לֵאמֹר teaches that the *Shirah* should be recited in all future generations on a daily basis. According to R' Shimon bar Yochai, this means that it should be recited every day the same way it was recited that first time, with joy.

4. 51:17.

went down into the sea, in the morning they said the *Shirah*. This was the seventh day of Pesach. Therefore, we read the *Shirah* [at the public Torah reading] on the seventh day."[5]

Yet, at the conclusion of *Parashas Shelach*, where the mitzvah of *tzitzis* is given, *Rashi* states that the eight strands of *tzitzis* (on each corner) correspond to the eight days from when the Jews left Egypt until they sang the *Shirah*.[6] They left on the first day of Pesach, the 15th of Nissan. It would seem, then, that they recited the *Shirah* not on the seventh day of Pesach but on the following day.

The *Shirah* begins with the words אָז יָשִׁיר, which literally means *Then [Moshe and Bnei Yisrael] will sing*.[7] Why did the Torah use the future, rather than past *(Then they sang)* tense? *Rashi* cites the Midrash: "From here there is an allusion to *Techias HaMeisim* (the Resurrection of the Dead) in the Torah."[8]

Our Sages often use an expression: עִיקָר חָסֵר מִן הַסֵּפֶר, *The primary [point] is missing from the book*. The *Shirah* will be sung in the future, but the plain intent of the verse is that the Jewish people sang the *Shirah* after crossing the *Yam Suf*, in recognition of the great miracles they had witnessed. Why does the literal translation refer to the future?

Everything a Miracle

In a famous piece regarding the Exodus, *Ramban* writes:

> *Through [recalling and acknowledging] the great, manifest miracles [of the Exodus] a person ultimately acknowledges the hidden miracles [of everyday life], which are the foundation of the entire Torah. For a person has no share in*

5. *Shemos* 14:5.

6. *Rashi* to *Bamidbar* 15:38; see *Rabbeinu Bachya* there.

7. *Shemos* 15:1.

8. The 13th Principle of Jewish Faith, as formulated by *Rambam*, is: "I believe with perfect faith that there will be a *Techias HaMeisim* whenever the wish emanates from the Creator, Blessed is His Name and exalted is His mention, forever and for all eternity."

> *the Torah of Moshe Rabbeinu unless he believes that all our affairs and experiences are miracles; there is no element of "nature" or "the ordinary course of the world" whether regarding the community or the individual.*[9]

The Ten *Makkos* (Plagues) and the Splitting of the Sea were incredible, open miracles, witnessed by the entire Jewish nation. These miracles, *Ramban* teaches, were intended as a lesson that *everything* that transpires in this world occurs only through the will of Hashem.

An apple growing from a tree is no less miraculous than *mann* falling from Heaven. *Mann* is considered an open miracle because it happened only during one 40-year period in history, while apples have been a part of the seemingly "natural," constant way of the world since Creation.

Dovid HaMelech declares: לְעֹשֵׂה נִפְלָאוֹת גְּדֹלוֹת לְבַדּוֹ כִּי לְעוֹלָם חַסְדּוֹ, *To Him Who alone performs great wonders, for His kindness endures forever.*[10] Zohar offers a novel interpretation: *To the One Who alone knows of the wonders He performs ...* Only Hashem knows of the schemes of our enemies from which He saves us, without our even being aware that danger lurks. This is a major aspect of Hashem's hidden miracles for which we must eternally thank Him.

On the seventh day of Pesach, when the Jewish people crossed the *Yam Suf*, they sang the *Shirah* for the very first time, in recognition of the open miracles they had witnessed. But this was not the ultimate purpose of *Shiras HaYam*. That purpose was realized the next day, eight days after they had left Egypt, when nothing out of the ordinary occurred. On that day, they sang the *Shirah* in recognition of the daily, hidden miracles that Hashem constantly performs. As we say in the *Modim* blessing, "We gratefully thank You ... for Your miracles that are with us every day."

Praising Hashem for obvious miracles is certainly a worthy form of *avodas Hashem*. However, an even higher form of service is to

---

9. *Ramban* to *Shemos* 13:16.

10. *Tehillim* 136:4.

praise Hashem for miracles that are not obvious, but which one recognizes as being caused by Hashem's guiding, hidden Hand.

The future tense of אָז יָשִׁיר alludes not only to the *Shirah* at *Techias HaMeisim*, but to the *Shirah* that Moshe and *Bnei Yisrael* sang on the eighth day for the miracles of daily life. It alludes also to the *Shirah* that Jews have sung daily for millenia. This is the primary form of *Shirah.*

The *Shirah* is prefaced by the words וַיּוֹשַׁע ה' בַּיּוֹם הַהוּא, *And Hashem saved (Bnei Yisrael) on that day (from the hand of Egypt).*[11] The words בַּיּוֹם הַהוּא, *on that day,* seem superfluous. These words allude to the *Shirah* that Jews sing every day, the song of praise for daily miracles.

In the *Shirah* we say: עָזִּי וְזִמְרָת יָהּ וַיְהִי לִי לִישׁוּעָה, *God is my might and my praise, and was a salvation for me.*[12] When saying this verse we should have in mind: Hashem was a salvation ***for me*** — every day of my life, through the hidden miracles that He constantly performs.[13]

Tzitzis and the *Shirah*

Parashas Eikev opens with the words וְהָיָה עֵקֶב תִּשְׁמְעוּן (lit., *And it will be because of your listening*).[14] *Midrash Tanchuma*[15] understands the word עֵקֶב to mean *heel,*[16] meaning *If you will observe mitzvos that people tend to trample upon with their heel. Daas Zekeinim* says that this refers to the *tzitzis* on one's *tallis* "that tend to drag behind (and are inadvertently stepped on)."

As *Rashi* noted, the eight strands of the *tzitzis* correspond to the *Shirah* that the Jews recited on the eighth day following the Exodus which, as we have explained, was for everyday miracles.

11. *Shemos* 14:30.
12. Ibid. 15:2.
13. In *Hallel*, Dovid HaMelech says these exact words: עָזִּי וְזִמְרָת יָהּ וַיְהִי לִי לִישׁוּעָה.
14. *Devarim* 7:12.
15. Cited by *Rashi.*
16. As in *Bereishis* 25:26.

The *tzitzis* themselves, which tend to drag, represent our lowly generation, that of *Ikvesa D'Meshicha*, the period before Mashiach. Dovid HaMelech said of our generation, *"For bent down to the dust is our soul, stuck to the earth is our belly."*[17] The knots of the *tzitzis* represent the fact that despite our lowly level in comparison to previous generations, we nevertheless remain bound faithfully to Hashem in every situation, at all times. The word קֶשֶׁר *(knot)* has the same *gematria* as וְאַבִּיטָה נִפְלָאוֹת (*that I may perceive wonders* — 600).[18]

In a world of immorality and heresy, we are charged with the challenge of maintaining a pure, firm *emunah* in Hashem, of recognizing Hashem's guiding Hand in every aspect of our lives.[19] In a time of *hester panim*, Divine concealment, when world events are confusing, when the wicked seem to prevail, we continue to cling steadfastly to Hashem and His Torah and draw strength from the *Shirah* that we recite joyfully each morning. Our *Shirah* is exceedingly precious to the *Ribbono shel Olam.*

In the Shabbos day *zemer* that begins ... בָּרוּךְ ה' יוֹם יוֹם, we praise Hashem for rescuing us from the various exiles. The stanza regarding the current exile concludes with a verse from *Tehillim*: אֶהֱבוּ אֶת ה' כָּל חֲסִידָיו אֱמוּנִים נֹצֵר, *Love Hashem, all His devout ones, His faithful ones He safeguards.*[20] The words אֱמוּנִים נֹצֵר *(His faithful ones He safeguards)* have the same *gematria* as וַיּוֹשַׁע ה' בַּיּוֹם הַהוּא (*And Hashem saved [them] on that day* — 493).[21] As noted above, the words בַּיּוֹם הַהוּא represent the *Shirah* sung daily in every generation. It is a great expression of faith and earns us Hashem's love and protection.

The Gemara relates that when Mashiach comes, *tzaddikim* will form a circle around the *Shechinah*:

---

17. *Tehillim* 44:26.

18. Ibid. 119:18.

19. This concept is discussed in "Tefillah: An Expression of Faith" (ch. 2), and in Appendix A.

20. *Tehillim* 31:24.

21. *Shemos* 14:30.

וְאָמַר בַּיּוֹם הַהוּא הִנֵּה אֱלֹהֵינוּ זֶה קִוִּינוּ לוֹ וְיוֹשִׁיעֵנוּ זֶה ה׳ קִוִּינוּ לוֹ נָגִילָה וְנִשְׂמְחָה בִּישׁוּעָתוֹ.

He will say on that day: Behold, this is our God; we have directed our hope to Him that He would save us; this is Hashem to Whom we directed our hope, let us rejoice and be happy in His salvation.[22]

Note that this verse uses the term בַּיּוֹם הַהוּא which alludes to our daily expression of faith through reciting *Az Yashir*. On that great day in the future, *tzaddikim* will point to the *Shechinah* and joyfully declare, *"Behold, this is our God; we have directed our hope to Him that He would save us . . ."* They will joyfully recall the *emunah* in Hashem that kept us bound to Him throughout this long and difficult *galus*, an *emunah* that found expression in our daily, joyous recital of *Shiras HaYam.*

22. *Yeshayahu* 25:9; see *Taanis* 31a.

CHAPTER EIGHTEEN

The Shema and Its Introductory Blessings

Twice a day, every day of our lives, we fulfill the Scriptural mitzvah to recite the *Shema*.[1] When reciting the opening verse, we fulfill the mitzvah to acknowledge the oneness of God and accept upon ourselves His absolute sovereignty *(kabbalas ol malchus Shamayim)*.[2] In the second verse we fulfill the mitzvah to love Hashem and declare our willingness to subjugate our desires, and to sacrifice our possessions and even

1. *Sefer HaChinuch* mitzvah #420. There is an additional Rabbinic requirement to recite the *Shema* prior to retiring for the night (see *Shulchan Aruch, Orach Chaim* ch. 239).

2. Ibid. mitzvah #417.

our very lives for His sake.[3]

When we have in mind when saying וּבְכָל נַפְשְׁךָ *([And you shall love Hashem] ... with all your soul)* that we are willing to die for the sake of His Holy Name, we achieve atonement for all our sins, even the grievous sin of *chillul Hashem.*[4] This is because when we express with our lips and ponder in our minds our willingness to die *al kiddush Hashem*, it is considered as if we have actually sacrificed our lives. Thus does Dovid HaMelech say, *"Because for Your sake we are slain all day long."*[5] *Rashba* explains that this verse refers to the daily recital of *Shema.* A Jew's sincere commitment to martyrdom is considered as if he actually gave his life.[6]

In the second portion of *Shema*, we accept upon ourselves *ol mitzvos*, to faithfully observe all the Torah's commandments.

The final portion of *Shema* contains the mitzvah of *tzitzis* which, as *Rashi* states, corresponds to all 613 mitzvos. With its final verse, we fulfill the daily (and nightly) mitzvah to recall the Exodus from Egypt. As we have mentioned elsewhere, the redemption from Egypt is a cornerstone of Jewish faith, because it demonstrated for all time that there is an all-powerful God Who guides the happenings of this world with incredible precision, rewards those who obey His will, and punishes those who do not.

The *Aseres HaDibros* begins, *"I am Hashem, your God, Who took you out of Egypt from the house of slavery."*[7] *Ramban* writes that the second half of the verse complements the first, because along with belief in the existence of the One and Only God must go the belief in that which the Exodus made clear to all.

---

3. Ibid. mitzvah #418.

4. *Rabbeinu Yonah* writes that only death, not suffering alone, is an atonement for *chillul Hashem.* However, *kiddush Hashem,* sanctifying the glory of Hashem's Name through positive deeds, does serve as an atonement for *chillul Hashem.*

5. *Tehillim* 44:23.

6. Zohar states that when reciting the words וּבְכָל נַפְשְׁךָ one should have in mind that he is willing to sacrifice his life in a *sha'as hashemad*, when our enemies attempt to force us to transgress the Torah. This, says Zohar, is considered as if one actually sacrificed his life and is a great source of atonement for one's sins.

7. *Shemos* 20:2.

Krias Shema begins with a Jew's declaration of faith that Hashem is the One and Only God. That declaration, however, is not complete until we recite the very last verse of *Shema* in which we recall *Yetzias Mitzrayim*.

An Awesome Sanctity

When a Jew recites the *Shema* with proper *kavanah*, he draws upon himself an awesome sanctity that affects both body and soul. *Midrash Hane'elam*[8] states:

> *R' Yehudah said: "It will be healing to your navel and marrow to your bones."*[9] *The Torah is a healing for the body and bones, in this world and the next. For R' Nehurai said in the name of R' Nechemia: In Krias Shema there are 248 words, corresponding to a person's limbs. When a person recites Shema in the correct manner, each limb takes one of the words and is healed by it.*

In Time and Place

The power of *Shema* goes further. As stated in *Sefer Yetzirah*, there are parallels in נֶפֶשׁ, *soul*; מָקוֹם, *place*; and זְמַן, *time*. For example, the *Kohen Gadol* is the holiest *soul*; the *Kodesh HaKodashim* is the holiest *place*; and Yom Kippur is the holiest *day*. On Yom Kippur all three come together, when the *Kohen Gadol* enters the *Kodesh HaKodashim*.

The days of the year, like the human body, correspond to the mitzvos of the Torah. Each day is a "limb" of the year and therefore each one corresponds to a specific mitzvah or mitzvos.[10] Rosh Hashanah, a day that encompasses within it all the

---

8. Cited in *Mishnah Berurah* 61:6; see *Tur, Orach Chaim* 61:3.

9. *Mishlei* 3:8.

10. This is more obvious with the Torah's 365 negative commandments which correspond to the 365 days in a solar year.

days of the coming year, corresponds to *Krias Shema.* On Rosh Hashanah, we declare our acceptance of Hashem's sovereignty and pray that the day will soon come when all of mankind will recognize that He alone is Master of all. In the *Mussaf Shemoneh Esrei* of Rosh Hashanah, we recite the first verse of *Shema* and we beseech Hashem that the time soon come when *"All the world's inhabitants will recognize and know that to You every knee should bend . . ."*

And just as the human body is comprised of 248 limbs, so it is with the *makom,* place, that is this planet. In *Tanach,* we find verses that refer to the "arms of the world,"[11] the "eye of the world,"[12] and "the heart of the earth," which is a reference to Jerusalem.[13] When a Jew recites *Shema* with *kavanah*, accepting upon himself Hashem's sovereignty in every aspect of his life, he infuses this entire world — all of its "248 limbs" — with *yiras Shamayim.* This can have a profound influence, particularly upon other Jews, wherever they may be.

Perhaps on the other side of the world there is a Jew who, unfortunately, finds himself overcome by his *yetzer hara.* He is poised to commit a terrible sin — at the very moment that you are reciting *Shema* with great intensity. The *yiras Shamayim* that you have brought to the world may influence that Jew to refrain from committing that sin. He will find himself unable to do what he had prepared and planned for, though he will never know that it is you whom he has to thank for this.

At times, we ourselves are the beneficiaries of someone else's *Krias Shema.* We may find ourselves facing a *nisayon* (spiritual test) that we feel unable to overcome. Suddenly, we are infused with *yiras Shamayim* and resist the temptation. It may very well be that at that moment a *tzaddik* somewhere in the world was reciting *Shema* with great fervor.

---

11. *Devarim* 33:27. In that verse, the plain meaning of זְרוֹעֹת (*arms*) is *mighty ones.*

12. *Bamidbar* 22:5. In that verse, the plain meaning of עֵין (*eye*) is *surface.*

13. *Yeshayahu* 40:2.

Our *Krias Shema* does not only affect humanity. All of creation and even the Heavenly angels are influenced by our acceptance of Hashem's sovereignty. In the opening *Bircas Shema,* we say of the angels, *"They all do the will of their Creator with awe and reverence."* When a Jew recites *Shema* properly he draws *yiras Shamayim* upon himself, and with this he affects all that exists in both the lower and upper worlds.

In *Ashrei* we say *"to inform human beings of His mighty deeds."*[14] In its plain meaning, the verse is referring to Hashem's mighty deeds. Homiletically, said R' Boruch of Mezhibuzh,[15] it refers to us. A Jew must be cognizant of the power of his own deeds. If we bear in mind the great power of our tefillah and in particular our *Shema,* we will strive to pray with true *kavanah* so that our tefillos will have their desired effect.

And when a Jew recites *Shema* properly and in doing so brings light to all of creation, Hashem rewards him in kind, illuminating his path in his service of Hashem, filling his heart with spiritual light and with all that a God-fearing Jew yearns for.

With Awe

The morning *Shema* is preceded by two lengthy blessings and followed by one.[16] The first of these blessings focuses on the greatness of Hashem: *"Who forms light and creates darkness ... How great are Your works ... Master of wars ... creates cures ... is too awesome to praise ..."* It is a preparation for our *kabbalas ol malchus Shamayim* when we recite the opening verse of *Shema.*

In this blessing we also make mention of the praises uttered by the heavenly angels: *"... all of Whose ministering angels stand at the*

14. *Tehillim* 145:12.

15. A grandson of the Baal Shem Tov.

16. The evening *Shema* is preceded by two blessings and followed by two. *Tur* (*Orach Chaim* 58:1) writes that Dovid HaMelech alluded to these seven blessings (three morning and four evening) when he said, *"Seven times a day I have praised You for Your righteous ordinances"* (*Tehillim* 119:164).

summit of the universe and proclaim ..." Note that the angels stand as they sing their praises, while it is our custom to sit when we recite the *Shema* and its accompanying blessings. This is because, as we have previously noted,[17] *Shema* and its accompanying blessings bring us into the עוֹלָם הַבְּרִיאָה, the world of the כִּסֵּא הַכָּבוֹד, God's Throne of Glory. At this point we become a מֶרְכָּבָה (lit. *chariot),* a bearer of God's Presence, through our recitation of this portion of tefillah. The Jewish people, not the heavenly angels, are the bearers of Hashem's Presence. This illustrates the utter closeness between Hashem and His beloved people, which is the focus of the second of the *Shema* blessings.[18]

With Love

As mentioned above, the second verse of *Shema* is the mitzvah to love Hashem. The question is asked: How is it possible to command someone to love? Can someone be told to experience an inner emotion that he simply does not feel?

Sfas Emes answers that deep within every Jewish *neshamah*, there is an *ahavah mesuseres*, a hidden, burning love for Hashem. The source of this love is the intense, unconditional love that Hashem has for us. In the words of Zohar, "If people would know the degree of love with which *HaKadosh Baruch Hu* loves the Jewish people, they would roar like a young lion and run after Him."[19] As Shlomo HaMelech says, *"As water reflects a face back to a face, so one's heart is reflected back to him by another."*[20] Our soul perceives

17. See *"Pesukei D'Zimrah:* Breaking Through the Barriers" (ch. 8) in this volume.

18. *Be'er Heitev* (*Shulchan Aruch* 59:1 citing *Ateres Zekeinim*) discusses the precise wording of this *berachah*, how some of its initial letters combine to form various Names of Hashem, and that one who concentrates on these Names when reciting those words "will not be harmed that entire day." This illustrates how, as R' Chaim Volozhiner writes (in *Nefesh HaChaim*) of *Shemoneh Esrei,* the words of davening, as composed by the *Anshei Knesses HaGedolah*, are laden with deep, esoteric meaning. Our task is to do our best to concentrate on their basic meaning, while realizing the enormous hidden power that they contain.

19. *Zohar*, *Parashas Shemos*.

20. *Mishlei* 27:19.

Hashem's love and responds in kind.[21]

Hashem's love for us is evident in many places in *Tanach.* Prominent among them is the sad *haftarah* of *Shabbos Chazon*, the Shabbos preceding Tishah B'Av. In it, Yeshayahu HaNavi chastises the generation of the Destruction of the first Beis HaMikdash for having strayed from Hashem's path. His first words are: *"I have raised children and elevated them, but they have rebelled against Me."*[22]

The very first word of this prophecy is בָּנִים, *children.* The people had sinned grievously, but Hashem still considered them His children. And He always will.

The last prophet was Malachi. His prophecy had to carry our people through 2,000 years of exile, until the next prophet, Eliyahu, will appear. His prophecy, therefore, opens: *"I loved you, says Hashem."*[23]

The blessing of *Ahavah Rabbah*[24] begins and ends with an

---

21. The Chofetz Chaim writes: "I would also like to alert everyone to that which the Gemara states: *'Ula said: Whoever recites [the morning] Shema without [wearing] tefillin is considered as if he testifies falsely about himself'* (*Berachos* 14b). For he says, *"And you shall bind them ([i.e. the tefillin] (as a sign upon your arm)"* — but he is not binding [them if, at that moment, he is not wearing them].'

"It seems obvious that the same applies to that which is said [in *Shema*], *'And you shall love Hashem, your God,'* that one must bring love of Hashem into his heart. As [*Sefer*] *Chovos HaLevavos* writes (*Shaar Ahavas Hashem,* ch. 3), one must ponder Hashem's greatness and loftiness [for He sustains all worlds], and contrast this with his own puniness and that of his fellow man. Then, he should recognize the abundant goodness that the Creator has constantly bestowed upon him from the time he was born — and not because he earned it. [He should also reflect upon how] He conceals his sins from others and is slow to anger [when he sins].

"If one finds it difficult to think about this while saying *Shema,* he should at least reflect upon it once a day. Is the fact that it [love of Hashem] is a constant mitzvah that is not dependent on a specific time, as is well known, reason that it should be so neglected as to not be fulfilled at least once a day?

"It is good to reflect upon this at the conclusion of tefillah, before one enters his home for his [morning] meal, as with other mitzvos in which one is obligated such as *tefillin* and *lulav* [on Succos] where [halachah states that] one should not eat before fulfilling them" (Sefer *Shemiras HaLashon,* part II, Conclusion, ch. 2).

22. *Yeshayahu* 1:3.

23. *Malachi* 1:2. The last two verses of Malachi's prophecy foretell Eliyahu's arrival: *"Behold, I send you Eliyahu HaNavi before the coming of the great and awesome day of Hashem ..."*

24. Or *Ahavas Olam,* depending on one's *nusach.*

expression of Hashem's deep love for the Jewish people. *"With an eternal love have You loved us, Hashem, our God ..."* Lest one think that he can comprehend the deep, unfathomable love that Hashem feels towards every Jew, the blessing continues: חֶמְלָה גְדוֹלָה וִיתֵרָה חָמַלְתָּ עָלֵינוּ ..., *with exceedingly great mercy You have been merciful to us ...* The word וִיתֵרָה, *exceedingly,* means that however great we perceive Hashem's mercy upon us, it is even greater than that.

In this blessing we beseech Hashem to grant us understanding of His holy Torah, which He imparted to us with love, and to speedily bring about our redemption from this long exile. The theme of the blessing's conclusion is the same as its beginning: *Blessed are You, Hashem, Who chooses His people, Israel, with love.*

The Third *Parashah*

The third and final portion of *Shema* is the *parashah* of *tzitzis.* These verses are found at the conclusion of *Parashas Shelach,* in which the tragic episode of the *Meraglim* (Spies) is related. The *Meraglim* erred in their description and understanding of the precious land of Eretz Yisrael. They erred because they went about their mission as emissaries of the people. Had they seen themselves as emissaries of Hashem they would have viewed the land in a totally different light.

Some commentators explain that the *tzitzis* are like a string that one winds around his finger as a reminder of something. Looking at the *tzitizis* threads reminds us Whose emissaries we are.

The *tzitzis* carry yet a deeper message. There is a spiritual power in *tzitzis* to awaken the *neshamah* to its true calling and, in so doing, prevent us from sinning.[25] This power is alluded to in the Torah. *"It shall constitute tzitzis for you, that you may see it and remember all the mitzvos of Hashem and perform them;* ***and not explore after your heart and after your eyes after which you stray.***"[26]

25. The Gemara relates that a certain scholar felt overcome by an urge to commit a terrible sin, until his *tzitzis* lifted themselves up and slapped his face (*Menachos* 44a).

26. *Bamidbar* 15:39; see *Keren Orah* to *Menachos* 44a.

Our National *"Tallis"*

In the prayer recited before donning a *tallis* we say, *"And just as I wrap myself in a tallis in this world, so may I merit the garb of the rabbis and a beautiful tallis in the World to Come."* A Jew's purpose in this world is to weave for himself a *"tallis"* that will be his in the Next World. The fabric of this *tallis* is created from the mitzvos that he performs during his lifetime. If he has succeeded in performing the 613 mitzvos to the best of his ability, then he will have woven a complete, beautiful *tallis.*

The collective Jewish people also weave a *"tallis"* through the course of their history since the giving of the Torah. This is the *tallis* that we will present to Mashiach upon his arrival.

In the *parashah* of *tzitzis* we say, *"And say to them, that they are to make for themselves tzitzis on the corners of their garments throughout the generations."*[27] These words allude to this *tallis,* woven through the spiritual effort of all Jews throughout the generations. Our generation of *Ikvesa D'Meshicha* is honored with the task of weaving the very last strands of this *tallis,* the threads that will make it complete and to which the *tzitzis* will be attached.

Of Mashiach, Yeshayahu HaNavi says, וְיָצָא חֹטֶר מִגֵּזַע יִשָׁי, *A staff will grow from the stump of Yishai.*[28] וְיָצָא חֹטֶר has the same *gematria* as עַל כַּנְפֵי בִגְדֵיהֶם *([... and they shall make for themselves tzitzis] on the corners of their garments* — 324).[29] Mashiach will arrive when the last generation will complete the corners of our national *tallis.*

The generations of Jews since Avraham comprise a collective "body" with each generation corresponding to a different part. Our lowly generation corresponds to the עֲקֵבִים, *heels,* the very bottom of the body. We also correspond to the very last of the 248 words that comprise the "body" that is *Shema.* The last word, as

27. *Bamidbar* 15:38.
28. *Yeshayahu* 11:1.
29. *Bamidbar* 15:38.

stated in Halachah, is not found in the three portions of *Shema*. It is the word אֱמֶת, *truth,* with which the next blessing begins.

The final mishnah in *Masechta Sotah* describes the state of the world before Mashiach's arrival.[30] Among the failings of that time is that "truth will be absent." The world in which we live is one of falsehood, as we know only too well.

In many communities it is customary to say the word אֱמֶת aloud when completing the *Shema*. This must be our declaration wherever we are, in every situation. In word, thought, and deed, a Jew must proclaim, "!אֱמֶת" We do this by holding steadfast to our *emunah*, our faith in Hashem, and resisting the spiritual chaos that surrounds us.

30. The mishnah truly describes the world in which we presently live: "In *Ikvesa D'Meshicha* chutzpah will increase and costs will soar . . . government will turn to heresy and there shall be no rebuke. The meeting places will be used for immorality . . . those who fear sin will be despised and truth will be absent. Youths will blanch the faces of elders . . . the face of the generation is like the face of a dog . . . Upon what, then, can we rely? Upon our Father in Heaven" (*Sotah* 49b).

CHAPTER NINETEEN

Emes V'Yatziv

The Gemara states: "Whoever does not recite [the blessing of] *Emes V'Yatziv* in the morning and *Emes Ve'Emunah* in the evening has not fulfilled his obligation."[1] The blessing that begins with אֱמֶת וְיַצִּיב (*True and certain*)[2] immediately preceding the *Shemoneh Esrei* of *Shacharis* is an enhanced fulfillment of *zechiras Yetzias Mitzrayim,* remembering the Exodus from Egypt, and a powerful declaration of faith. How unfortunate that this precious blessing is often recited hurriedly.

The letters of the word מִצְרַיִם, *Egypt,* can also be read מְצָרִים, *narrow straits* [i.e. difficulties].[3] The miracles of *Yetzias Mitzrayim* are

1. *Berachos* 12a.

2. Halachah requires that the blessing's opening word, אֱמֶת, be said with the concluding words of *Shema,* ה' אֱלֹהֵיכֶם [אֱמֶת].

3. As in כָּל רֹדְפֶיהָ הִשִּׂיגוּהָ בֵּין הַמְּצָרִים, *All her pursuers overtook her in narrow straits* (*Eichah* 1:3).

the source of salvation from all future exiles. In fact, Zohar states that the four times the word *emes* (true) appears in *Emes V'Yatziv* allude to the Four Exiles, for all future redemptions are rooted in *Yetzias Mitzrayim.*

An individual's redemption from personal travails and sufferings also has its roots in the redemption from Egypt. When a Jew fulfills the mitzvah to recall the Exodus and internalizes the belief that nothing is beyond Hashem's power, he has achieved a great source of salvation from any difficulties he may be experiencing in his personal life.

In Every Generation

The Torah states:

> *Perhaps you will say in your heart: "These nations are more numerous than I; how will I be able to drive them out (of Canaan)?"*
>
> *Do not fear them! You shall remember what Hashem, your God, did to Pharaoh and to all of Egypt.*[4]

Chasam Sofer interprets: In every generation, when Jews face bitter enemies who seek to harm them, they should recall the miracles of the Exodus. This will initiate a Divine flow of salvation that will protect them from all harm.

This is what we do when we recite *Emes V'Yatziv*, which immediately follows our mention of the Exodus in the final verse of *Shema.* We declare:

> *His sovereignty and faithfulness endure forever. His words are living and enduring, faithful and delightful forever and to all eternity; for our forefathers and for us, for our children and for our generations . . .*

Then we proceed to declare, in detail, the great wonders that Hashem performed for us as we left Egypt:

---

4. *Devarim* 7:17-18.

From Egypt You redeemed us, Hashem, our God, and from the house of slavery You liberated us. All their first-born You slew, but Your firstborn, Israel, You redeemed; the Sea of Reeds You split for them; the willful sinners You drowned ...

As in the second blessing of *Shema*, we make mention here of Hashem's love for us: *the dear ones You brought across ... for this, the beloved offered praise to God ...* The *Shirah* the Jews sang after crossing the *Yam Suf* was an outgrowth of their knowledge that they were beloved by Hashem.

The Beis Aharon of Karlin once declared: "All I need are ten Jews who together with me can shout, 'עֶזְרַת אֲבוֹתֵינוּ אַתָּה הוּא מֵעוֹלָם (*The help of our forefathers You have been, always*)'" — the concluding paragraph of this precious blessing.

The legendary Mashgiach of Mir and later Ponovezh, R' Chatzkel Levenstein, would lament the haste with which *Ezras Avoseinu* is often said. He would refer to it as a "miniature *Nishmas*," the precious prayer of praise and thanksgiving that we recite every Shabbos and Yom Tov morning.[5]

Emes V'Yatziv, of which *Ezras* is a part, is filled with priceless gems and contains the very foundations of our faith. Reciting it with *kavanah* is an ideal way to strengthen one's *emunah*.

---

5. In *Reb Chatzkel — Guardian of Torah and Mussar* (published by ArtScroll/Mesorah), an entire chapter is devoted to describing the Mashgiach's efforts in tefillah. There we find: "... Of particular importance to him was the blessing of *Ezras Avoseinu* after the morning *Shema* and *Ve'Emunah Kol Zos* in the evening. To hear Reb Chatzkel say these prayers in his loud and deliberate voice was to hear someone commenting on events in which he was actually participating" (p. 41). A footnote there continues: "This is an observation conveyed by many *talmidim* and found in many sources. The Mashgiach was renowned for his deep penetration into the meaning of these prayers. No *talmid* from Reb Chatzkel's years in Ponovezh can forget his emphasis on the importance of *Ezras Avoseinu* and *Ve'Emunah Kol Zos*."

Reb Chatzkel once likened rushing through *Ezras Avoseinu* to someone who places a piece of delicious meat into his mouth, only to have it snatched away before he can enjoy its taste (heard from a *talmid*).

When All the Waters Split

... וְיַם סוּף לָהֶם בָּקַעְתָּ ...
... the Sea of Reeds You split for them ...

The Midrash[6] draws a comparison between the Beis HaMikdash and the Splitting of the Sea, citing the verse לְגֹזֵר יַם סוּף לִגְזָרִים כִּי לְעוֹלָם חַסְדּוֹ, *To Him Who divided the Sea of Reeds into parts, for His kindness endures forever.*[7]

The Beis HaMikdash was the place that connected the Jewish people to their Father in Heaven. It was from that place that the tefillos of Jews everywhere ascended.

From Scriptural sources and the words of our Sages, we see that each *shevet* (tribe) had its own gate through which it entered the Beis HaMikdash area. This alludes to the teaching that each *shevet* has its own Heavenly gateway through which its tefillos ascend. In this vein, *Chasam Sofer* explains the requirement that each *shevet* have its own *Sanhedrin* (High Court). It is by way of its Heavenly conduit that each *shevet* receives its Divine flow of Torah insight. The receptacle of this flow is the *Sanhedrin* of each *shevet*. This is the meaning of *Judges and officers shall you appoint in all your gates [i.e. cities] ... for your shevatim (tribes).*[8] Because each *shevet* has its own Heavenly gate, therefore it requires its own judges and court officers.

Targum Yonasan and the Midrash state that at the Splitting of the Sea, the Sea of Reeds divided into 12 paths, one for each *shevet*. What was the purpose of this?

Regarding the words וַיִּבָּקְעוּ הַמָּיִם, *And the waters split,* our Sages teach that at the moment when the sea split, all the waters in the world split as well. Why was this necessary?

This miracle was much more than a phenomenon that overrode the laws of nature. The splitting of the waters so that the

6. *Yalkut Shimoni* to *Shir Hashirim* 4:4.
7. *Tehillim* 136:13.
8. *Devarim* 16:18.

Jews could pass through represented the destruction of spiritual impediments that sought to divert a Jew's mind from Hashem. When all the waters in the world split, it represented the fact that at that moment, every spiritual force that sought to deprive a Jew from experiencing a close relationship with Hashem had been vanquished.

The Last Generation

The Arizal taught that the 12 months of the year correspond to the 12 *shevatim,* according to the order of how they traveled in the Wilderness. Yehudah corresponds to the first month of the Jewish year, Nissan. The last three months of the year, Teves, Shevat, and Adar, correspond to Don, Asher, and Naftali. *Sefer HaTanya* writes that the generations since the giving of the Torah also correspond to the 12 *shevatim.* The last generations correspond to the camp of Don, with the very last generation before Mashiach corresponding to Naftali.

The name נַפְתָּלִי has the same letters as נָפַלְתִּי, *I have fallen*, an apt description of our generation. We are a lowly generation in a very lowly world. But we need not despair. The sea split separately for each of the 12 *shevatim,* for its effects reach every generation, including our own. Through *mesiras nefesh* (self-sacrifice), sincere service of Hashem, and effort in Torah and tefillah, we can destroy every sort of spiritual blockade that the Satan seeks to place in our path.

Therefore, we say in this blessing of *Emes V'Yatziv, "... [You are a] Shield and Savior for them and their children after them* ***in every generation****." "True — You are the Master for Your people and a mighty King to fight their battles* ***for fathers and sons****."*

And we declare: *"True — You are the First and You are the Last."* In every generation, including the final one, Hashem helps His beloved children to overcome every difficulty and challenge.

With Joy and Vitality

מֹשֶׁה וּבְנֵי יִשְׂרָאֵל לְךָ עָנוּ שִׁירָה בְּשִׂמְחָה רַבָּה וְאָמְרוּ כֻלָּם, מִי כָמֹכָה ...

Moshe and Bnei Yisrael exclaimed a song to You with great joy and they all said, "Who is like You ..."

Twice a day, in the *Birchos Shema* of both *Shacharis* and *Maariv,* we say these words. While it is reasonable to assume that the Jewish people sang *Shiras HaYam* with great joy, nowhere does the Torah state this explicitly. What is the source for this, and why is it so important to mention it twice daily?

When Adam sinned by partaking of the Tree of Knowledge, confusion between good and evil, light and darkness set in, and *nitzotzos*, sparks of holiness, became dispersed throughout the world, becoming trapped by the *klipos* (shells of impurity). The mission of the Chosen People, as stated in the writings of Kabbalah, is to reunite these sparks, thereby reestablishing the Divine radiance that illuminated the world at the time of Creation.[9]

When a Jew fulfills his *avodas Hashem* in the proper way, he frees these *nitzotzos* from their entrapment and in so doing brings added *chiyus*, spiritual vitality, to his soul.[10] And he brings the world closer to the *tikkun* (rectification) it needs to be fit for Mashiach's arrival.

The concentration of sparks of holiness in any given place is in proportion to the *tumah*, spiritual impurity, of that place. The greater the *tumah*, the greater the concentration of *kedushah* trapped in the *klipos* of that place.

9. See *Ohr HaChaim* to *Bereishis* 46:3 where this concept is elaborated upon.

10. Rav Wolfson, quoting holy writings, said that the degree to which one is successful on any given day in drawing out these *nitzotzos* will be reflected in the manner with which he davens *Shacharis* the following morning. An impassioned tefillah, in which he focuses on the meaning of the words, indicates that his previous day was successful.

Egypt was עֶרְוַת הָאָרֶץ (lit. *the land's nakedness*),[11] the seat of moral decadence. In its land, people, and possessions lay the greatest concentration of hidden sparks of any place in the world at that time. Thus, it offered the greatest possibility for the nation of Hashem to raise itself to the level worthy of receiving the Torah at Sinai. This is why Providence decreed that Egypt be the כּוּר הַבַּרְזֶל, *iron furnace,*[12] in which the family of Yaakov Avinu became the Chosen People.

Of Death and Life

In its account of the Exodus from Egypt, the Torah states: וַיְנַצְּלוּ אֶת מִצְרָיִם, *And they [Bnei Yisrael] emptied Egypt.*[13] The Gemara comments: "They transformed Egypt into the equivalent of the depths of the sea where there are no fish."[14] In its plain meaning, this refers to the Egyptians' valuables which the Jews took with them when they left. In a deeper sense, it refers to the sacred sparks that had been encrusted beneath the layers of spiritual filth of that sinful land. During their 210-year sojourn there, the Jews succeeded in drawing out every last spark of holiness; when they finally left Egypt, it was bereft of its last shred of spirituality — like the depths of the sea that is empty of fish, which generally live near the surface of the water.[15]

In the midst of the narrative of the Exodus, the Torah states a prohibition against returning to Egypt.[16] The Arizal explains this prohibition in light of the above. Whatever *galus* is supposed to accomplish, the Egyptian exile accomplished in totality. The land was left totally devoid of spirituality, and thus there is no longer

11. *Bereishis* 42:12.

12. See *Devarim* 4:20.

13. *Shemos* 12:36.

14. *Berachos* 9b.

15. See *Ben Yehoyada* (ad loc.) who interprets that Gemara in this vein.

16. *Shemos* 14:13. See essay on *Modim* (ch. 21) where this prohibition is further discussed.

any reason to return there. The Egyptians that remained alive after the Jews left were like a creature that has been killed but still thrashes about in the moments following death. Physically they were alive, but spiritually they were dead.

The Midrash states that after the Egyptians drowned at the Sea of Reeds, the Angel of Egypt complained that he was now an angel without a mission. In response, he was appointed angel over the dead. In fact, he was still Angel of Egypt. Only now, the Egyptians, being totally divested of any iota of spirituality, were like the dead.

Healing for the Jews

Zohar states that each of the Ten Plagues was a punishment for the Egyptians and healing for the Jews.[17] As the Egyptians were smitten with spiritual death, the Jews became ever more energized with spiritual vitality.

The Torah states:

> וַיַּרְא יִשְׂרָאֵל אֶת מִצְרַיִם מֵת עַל שְׂפַת הַיָּם ... אָז יָשִׁיר מֹשֶׁה וּבְנֵי יִשְׂרָאֵל אֶת הַשִּׁירָה הַזֹּאת ...
>
> *Yisrael saw the Egyptians dead on the seashore ... Then Moshe and Bnei Yisrael sang this song to Hashem ...*[18]

To the words אָז יָשִׁיר מֹשֶׁה, which literally mean *Then Moshe **will** sing,* our Sages comment: "From here is a hint to *Techias HaMeisim* (the Resurrection of the Dead) from the text of the Torah."[19] We can interpret this to mean that at the same time that the Egyptians were spiritually dead in the fullest sense, devoid of any trace of *kedushah*, the Jews experienced a *"techias hameisim"* of sorts, becoming infused with newfound spiritual life, a level of spirituality that inspired the prophetic *Shiras HaYam* (Song at the Sea).

---

17. *Zohar*, vol. II, p. 36a.
18. *Shemos* 14:30,15:1.
19. See Rashi ad loc.

The Mishnah states that a *lulav* that is dry is unfit for the mitzvah of *arbaah minim* on Succos. Talmud Yerushalmi[20] cites a verse as a reason for this halachah: לֹא הַמֵּתִים יְהַלְלוּ יָהּ, *The dead cannot praise God.*[21] Just as the entire universe sings *shirah* to Hashem, each creation in its own unique way, so too on Succos when a Jew recites *Hallel,* the four species that he holds in his hands join him in praising their Creator. But a *lulav* that is dry, devoid of life, cannot sing *shirah.* Similarly, when someone mouths the words of *Hallel* without any feeling or thought, that is not *Hallel.*

The same applies to the study of Torah. Dovid HaMelech says of the Torah: זְמִרוֹת הָיוּ לִי חֻקֶּיךָ בְּבֵית מְגוּרָי, *Your statutes were music to me in my dwelling place.*[22] When Dovid studied Torah, he did so with ecstasy and delight, with feelings of love and gratitude to Hashem. This is how Torah should be studied, as we say each night in *Maariv, "... and we will rejoice with the words of the study of Your Torah ..."* Torah study devoid of joy is lacking a basic component of this greatest of mitzvos.

Therefore, it was obvious to our Sages that when the Jews sang *shirah* after crossing the Sea of Reeds, they did so with great joy. As the Egyptian nation, both at home and at sea, died a spiritual death, the Jews were becoming infused with the sparks of holiness that they had taken from their land of bondage. This spiritual vitality brought them to such heights that they were inspired to sing a prophetic song — a song that can be defined as *"shirah"* only because it was sung with intense joy.

Therefore, morning and evening, every day of our lives, we proclaim:

מֹשֶׁה וּבְנֵי יִשְׂרָאֵל לְךָ עָנוּ שִׁירָה בְּשִׂמְחָה רַבָּה וְאָמְרוּ כוּלָּם ...

---

20. *Succah* 3:1.

21. *Tehillim* 115:17. According to *Talmud Bavli,* a dry *lulav* is disqualified because it is not הָדָר, *beautiful.*

22. Ibid. 119:54.

The 15th of Shevat

The reading of *Parashas Beshalach*, in which *Shiras HaYam* is found, always falls on or around the 15th of Shevat, *Rosh Hashanah La'Ilanos* (The New Year for Trees).[23] It is at that time that the trees begin to shed their "burial shrouds" of winter and their rejuvenation begins. Though we cannot see it, the process that will produce buds, and eventually that year's fruits, has already begun.

The trees are experiencing their own *"techias hameisim."*

At the time of year when we read the Torah's hint to human *Techias HaMeisim,* the trees call out to us, "Take a lesson from us. For months we were barren, covered in white, seemingly devoid of life. And now, we are being revived. Soon we will be in full bloom, accomplishing the purpose for which we were created.

"You can do the same. If until now your service of Hashem has been devoid of life, without feeling, effort, and emotion, it is not too late to begin anew. Let today mark a new beginning, a day when you go about your Torah study, tefillah, and mitzvah performance with joy, vitality, and excitement."

Beginnings

As we have discussed, the wanderings of the Jewish people in exile are a result of the sin of Adam and Chavah. Their punishment of death was an indication of the damage that their sin had caused.

Beginnings are full of unlimited potential. Beginnings are embarked upon with a burst of energy, freshness, and zeal. Adam was the רֵאשִׁית, *beginning* [i.e. *first* and *primary*] of mankind. His soul encompassed that of every Jew who would ever be born. Adam was blessed with unlimited spiritual potential. His sin severely compromised his very promising beginning and changed his mission in this world.

---

23. This has halachic ramifications. See *Mishnah Rosh Hashanah* 1:1.

As we have mentioned elsewhere, there are parallels in *nefesh*, soul; *makom*, place; and *zman*, time. Adam was created on Rosh Hashanah, the day that is רֵאשִׁית in *zman* and which encompasses within it all the days of the coming year.

The site of the Beis HaMikdash is the רֵאשִׁית of *makom.* It is the site of the אֶבֶן שְׁתִיָּה, *foundation stone,* with which creation of this earth began. It is the site of the *Mizbei'ach* (Altar), the place from whose earth Adam was fashioned. And of course, it is the site of the House of Hashem, where He chose to rest His Presence and where His beloved nation served and will serve Him.

Adam, the רֵאשִׁית of all souls, who was formed from the earth of the place of רֵאשִׁית, on the day of רֵאשִׁית, had misused the *chiyus*, incredible spiritual vitality, with which he had been blessed. Therefore, in place of *chiyus*, death was decreed upon him.

With Renewed Energy

The Gemara states that sleep is one-sixtieth of death. In the days of *Selichos* preceding Rosh Hashanah, Jews sacrifice some sleep as they arise early for tefillah. This merit serves them well on Rosh Hashanah, the day of רֵאשִׁית, so that the potential for freshness and vitality inherent in this awesome first day will remain with them throughout the year.

Halachah states that one should not sleep on the day of Rosh Hashanah.[24] The day of רֵאשִׁית should be one of renewed energy, of spiritual accomplishment, not one of lethargy and sleep.

As the place of רֵאשִׁית, the Beis HaMikdash represents *chiyus*, vitality. In the presence of the *Shechinah* one is on a spiritual "high"; his service of Hashem is full of life, energy, and joy.

The *Lechem HaPanim,* which sat on the golden Table in the Beis HaMikdash for an entire week, was still oven-fresh and warm on the day it was removed, because the concept of aging and spoilage did not exist there.

24. *Rema, Orach Chaim* 583:2.

When Yaakov Avinu awoke from his prophetic dream on the Temple Mount, he said, *"Surely Hashem is in this place and I did not know!"*[25] Yaakov was saying, "Had I known that Hashem was here, I would not have slept here."[26] Yaakov understood that the place of רֵאשִׁית on this earth is a place of *chiyus,* vitality, and sleep in such a place is inappropriate.

Similarly, as Dovid searched to determine the exact spot upon which to build the Beis HaMikdash, he swore: *"If I go upon the bed that is spread for me, if I allow sleep to my eyes, slumber to my eyelids. Until I find a place for Hashem, a resting place for the Strong One of Yaakov."*[27]

Dovid HaMelech says, שְׁתוּלִים בְּבֵית ה' בְּחַצְרוֹת אֱלֹהֵינוּ יַפְרִיחוּ. עוֹד יְנוּבוּן בְּשֵׂיבָה דְּשֵׁנִים וְרַעֲנַנִּים יִהְיוּ, *Planted in the house of Hashem, in the courtyards of our God they will flourish. They will still be fruitful in old age . . .*"[28] When someone is "planted in the house of Hashem," he remains young and vigorous even in his old age. The words דְּשֵׁנִים וְרַעֲנַנִּים יִהְיוּ have the same *gematria* as בֵּית הַמִּקְדָּשׁ and רֹאשׁ הַשָּׁנָה (861).

Dovid pleads, אַל תַּשְׁלִיכֵנִי לְעֵת זִקְנָה כִּכְלוֹת כֹּחִי אַל תַּעַזְבֵנִי, *Do not cast me off in time of old age, when my strength fails — forsake me not.*[29] *Sfas Emes* explains: A person can be old in years and serve Hashem with the freshness and vigor of youth, and he can be young in years and serve Him in an aged, listless manner. Dovid begged that his *avodas Hashem* not be old and stale, devoid of passion and joy.

The Gemara relates[30] that each day at the conclusion of *Shemoneh Esrei,* R' Elazar would pray: "... and may we rise [each morning] and find that the yearning of our heart is to fear Your Name." How we begin our day impacts upon our entire day. Let

25. *Bereishis* 28:16.
26. *Rashi* citing Midrash.
27. *Tehillim* 132:3-5.
28. Ibid. 92:14-15.
29. Ibid. 71:9.
30. *Berachos* 16b.

us make every effort to rise each morning with zeal and joy, grateful for the opportunity to serve Hashem for yet another day. In this way, our davening and Torah study will be with energy and passion, and our business dealings will be with integrity and trust in Hashem. We will be cognizant that whatever transpires in our lives is decreed by Hashem, and that every moment of the day and night is an opportunity to serve Him with *chiyus* and love.

And let us make sure to fill our hearts with joy and faith each morning as we recite *Emes V'Yatziv* with fervor and passion.

CHAPTER TWENTY

Shemoneh Esrei: In the Merit of Our Forefathers

As we begin *Shemoneh Esrei,* we enter the highest spiritual world where we come directly before Hashem. This is reflected in the halachah that mandates that when saying *Shemoneh Esrei,* one should focus his thoughts towards Eretz Yisrael, as it is written: "*. . . and they will pray to You by way of their land.*"[1] He should also focus his thoughts towards Jerusalem and the Beis HaMikdash and picture himself as if he were standing in the *Kodesh HaKodashim*, the holiest place on earth, in front

1. *Melachim I* 8:48.

of the *Aron* where Hashem's Presence rested.[2]

To enter the Courtyard of the Beis HaMikdash, one had to ascend 15 steps.[3] The first 15 words of the *Emes V'Yatziv* blessing that precedes *Shemoneh Esrei* each begin with the letter ו. When we recite these words, it is as if we are ascending the 15 steps as we make our way to the *Kodesh HaKodashim.*

Opening Our Lips and Hearts

אֲדֹנָי שְׂפָתַי תִּפְתָּח וּפִי יַגִּיד תְּהִלָּתֶךָ.

My Lord, open my lips so that my mouth may declare Your praise.[4]

As we have mentioned in the preceding essay, the blessing of *Emes V'yatziv* is a magnificent remembrance of the wonders that accompanied the Jewish people as they left Egypt and a declaration of the fundamental truths of our faith. It concludes with *"Blessed are You, Hashem, Who redeemed Israel."*

The Egyptian bondage was both physical and spiritual; according to the Arizal, the spiritual bondage was primary. The Jews felt distant from Hashem; they found it difficult to open their hearts and pray to Him with genuine feeling. Immediately preceding Hashem's first revelation to Moshe Rabbeinu, Hashem opened a pathway for them, and their spiritual chains loosened. "... *They cried out, and their cry because of the work went up to God. God heard their cries, and God remembered His covenant with Avraham, Yitzchak, and Yaakov.*"[5]

At the Splitting of the Sea their spiritual redemption was complete. We make mention of this in *Emes V'Yatziv*:

---

2. *Mishnah Berurah* 94:7.

3. Corresponding to these steps, Dovid composed the 15 chapters beginning with the words *Shir HaMaalos* (Song of the Ascents) in *Sefer Tehillim* (ch. 120-134).

4. *Tehillim* 15:17.

5. *Shemos* 2:23-24.

From Egypt You redeemed us, Hashem, our God, from the house of slavery You liberated us .... For this, the beloved offered praise and exaltation to God; the dear ones offered hymns, songs, praises, blessings, and thanksgiving to the King, the living and enduring God ....

Chassidic writings offer a novel interpretation of the word פֶּסַח, *Pesach*, by which the Yom Tov is known: פֶּה שָׂח, *the mouth was able to speak*,[6] for upon redemption, the Jews were finally able to express their innermost emotions to Hashem in tefillah and song.

As individuals, we sometimes find ourselves in a personal bondage of sorts. We want very badly to experience tefillah as a true service of the heart, but find ourselves unable to do so. This is why as a preface to *Shemoneh Esrei* we recite the above words of *Emes V'Yatziv*. It is our hope that we too will be granted our personal redemption and be permitted to express our deepest feelings of love and closeness to Hashem as we stand before Him in prayer. And it is for this reason that as we are about to begin *Shemoneh Esrei* we beseech Hashem, *"Open my lips so that my mouth may declare Your praise."*

Connecting to Our *Avos*

As stated in *Shulchan Aruch*, it is imperative that we recite at least the first blessing of *Shemoneh Esrei* with *kavanah*, having in mind the simple meaning of the words. Otherwise, according to *Beis Yosef*, we must repeat *Shemoneh Esrei*. However, as *Rema* writes, already in his time the custom was not to repeat *Shemoneh Esrei*. This is out of concern that the repetition would not be an improvement, for one might not have proper *kavanah* the second time either.

At the start of this first blessing, we mention the fathers of our nation, Avraham, Yitzchak, and Yaakov. As the Gemara tells us, it

6. In *Lashon HaKodesh*, the letters ס and שׂ have the same pronunciation and are often interchanged.

was they who established the three daily tefillos. *Kavanah* is crucial when saying this blessing because through it we strengthen our connection to our forefathers, our roots. We connect ourselves to their unshakable *emunah*, their superlative *middos*. They are called *Avos*, Fathers, because we do not relate to them as if they are ancestors from many generations ago. Avraham, Yitzchak, and Yaakov are *fathers* to every Jewish soul that will ever live.[7]

Our Inheritance

In *Parashas Lech Lecha* Avraham asks Hashem, *"What can You give me seeing that I go childless, and the steward of my house is Eliezer from Damesek?"*[8] Our Sages see the word דַּמֶּשֶׂק as a contraction of דּוֹלֶה וּמַשְׁקֶה, *he draws from and gives to drink [from the Torah of his master to others].*[9] As an able disciple of Avraham, Eliezer absorbed the Torah he learned from his master and then taught it to others.

Why did Avraham see fit to mention this when he was asking Hashem about the promise that he would have children?

Avraham had two important missions in this world. He spread belief in Hashem to the masses, and Eliezer was a most able disciple in helping him to carry out this mission. Avraham recognized that. But he had another very important mission as well. He had developed in himself exalted levels of *emunah* and *chesed*, faith and kindness. While he could teach others through word and example about these qualities, there was another crucial way to transmit them — through spiritual "genes." When Avraham and Sarah

7. Rav Wolfson noted that while reviewing the weekly *parashah* is a mitzvah every week of the year, it is especially important to study in depth the *parshiyos* from *Lech Lecha* through *Vayechi*, which begin with Avraham and conclude with the passing of Yaakov (and his son Yosef). Studying these *parshiyos* is another important way of strengthening our connection to the *Avos*. And when we learn of their *emunah*, their love of Hashem, their awe of Him, the joy with which they served Him, and their concern for others, we become better people.

8. *Bereishis* 15:2.

9. *Rashi* ad loc. from *Yoma* 28b.

would merit a child, that child would inherit in its soul the *emunah* and *chesed* that had become the very essence of this great couple.

In truth, these two missions of Avraham were in fact one. It was not sufficient that Avraham and his family spread the Name of God among mankind. For their words to truly have a lasting impact on those whom they sought to influence, it was necessary that they possess exemplary *middos*. If in their dealings with their fellow man the family of Avraham would behave in an exceptional manner, one that would bring glory to God's Name, then their mission to spread belief in the true God would succeed. It was for this reason that Avraham greatly yearned for a child.[10]

An allusion to this is found in the verse in which Hashem reassures Avraham that indeed he and Sarah would be blessed with offspring. The words אֲשֶׁר יֵצֵא מִמֵּיעֶךָ, *the one who shall come forth from within you (will inherit you),*[11] has the same *gematria* as אֱלֹהֵי אַבְרָהָם אֱלֹהֵי יִצְחָק וֵאלֹהֵי יַעֲקֹב (782).

A Jew's Primary Traits

Rambam writes that when seeking a partner in life one should look for someone who possesses the three traits that are most basic to a Jew: חֶסֶד, *kindness;* בּוּשָׁה, *shame* [i.e. modesty]; and רַחְמָנוּת, *compassion.*[12] *Chesed* was transmitted to us from Avraham; *modesty* from Yitzchak; and *compassion* from Yaakov. These precious qualities are gifts that our *Avos* bequeathed to us. It is our responsibility to preserve them, nurture them, and not, God forbid, corrupt them.

---

10. Two successive *mishnayos* in *Pirkei Avos* speak of Avraham. In the first (5:3) he is called "Avraham," but in the second he is called "Avraham Avinu (Our Father)." The first discusses the generations from Noach until Avraham, so mentioning his being "our father" is irrelevant. The second mishnah, however, speaks of the ten *nisyonos* (spiritual tests) that Avraham successfully passed. The levels of faith that he attained by passing these test were transmitted to his descendants in our spiritual "genes." Therefore, it is important to state here that he is Avraham "Avinu" (R' Chaim Volozhiner in *Ruach Chaim* to *Avos*).

11. *Bereishis* 15:4.

12. *Hilchos Issurei Biah* 19:17.

While Avraham, Yitzchak, and Yaakov are all mentioned in the opening blessing of *Shemoneh Esrei,* this blessing is primarily that of Avraham, as it concludes, *"Blessed are You, Hashem, the shield of Avraham."* Avraham's primary attribute was *chesed,* kindness, and in this blessing we say: וְזוֹכֵר חַסְדֵי אָבוֹת, *and Who recalls the kindnesses of the Patriarchs. Chesed* is related to *ahavah,* and with these words we also allude to the love that our forefathers had for Hashem.

The second blessing, which speaks of Hashem's might, is that of Yitzchak, whose overriding attribute was *gevurah,* inner strength. *Chesed* and *gevurah* correspond to *ahavah* and *yirah,* love and awe, two contrasting *middos* that complement each other in service of Hashem. *Yirah* is related to *shame* [i.e. modesty] as it is written, "*... so that His awe shall remain upon your face [i.e. shall be apparent upon your modest countenance] so that you will not sin.*"[13]

The third blessing is that of *kedushah,* sanctity, the attribute of Yaakov, as it is written, "*... and they sanctify the Holy One of Yaakov.*"[14]

The Gemara tells us that when the teachings of a deceased scholar are quoted in this world, his "lips move in the grave," meaning that, in a certain sense, that scholar learns his insight with the one who repeats it.[15] This is because when a Jew propounds a *chiddush* (new insight) in Torah, that thought becomes bound up with his *neshamah* and remains a part of his very essence. When the *chiddush* of a deceased scholar is repeated, his soul in the Next World is stirred.

In a similar vein, Talmud Yerushalmi states that when someone repeats the teaching of a deceased scholar, he should imagine "as if the master of that teaching is standing opposite him." The names of the *Tannaim* and *Amoraim* mentioned in Gemara are themselves a part of Torah. When we say their names and repeat their teachings, their *neshamos* come and learn with us.

---

13. *Shemos* 20:17.
14. *Yeshayahu* 29:23.
15. *Yevamos* 97a and *Bechoros* 31b.

If someone recites the first blessing of *Shemoneh Esrei* — and even better, the first *three* blessings — with proper *kavanah,* then the souls of Avraham, Yitzchak, and Yaakov pray along with him and they bring his requests before Hashem's Throne. And if he strives to go in their ways and seeks to develop in himself the traits of *ahavah, yirah,* and *kedushah,* then he has bound himself to his forefathers in a very meaningful way and they will certainly advocate that his tefillos be accepted on High.

CHAPTER TWENTY-ONE

Shemoneh Esrei: Modim

In *Modim,* the 18th *berachah* of *Shemoneh Esrei,* we thank Hashem for His daily miracles. We know that the functioning of the human body, with its intricate composition of organs, veins, and arteries, is a constant amazing miracle for which no degree of thanks is sufficient. But there is much more for which to thank the *Ribbono shel Olam.*

Dovid HaMelech says: לְעֹשֵׂה נִפְלָאוֹת גְּדֹלוֹת לְבַדּוֹ כִּי לְעוֹלָם חַסְדּוֹ. The literal translation is: *To Him Who alone performs great wonders, for His kindness endures forever.* However, another interpretation is: *To Him Who alone* ***knows*** *of the great wonders He performs …* Only Hashem knows of the illness He saves us from without our even being aware of it, of the accidents and other mishaps that He saves us from at times when we are not even aware of the danger.

Often, we are in ignorance of the complex workings that Heaven has arranged to ensure that our needs are provided for. And only He is aware of happenings in the far-off corners of the earth that are being effected for the sake of the Jewish people.

This is what we are expressing gratitude for when we thank Hashem עַל נִסֶּיךָ שֶׁבְּכָל יוֹם עִמָּנוּ, *for Your miracles that are with us every day.*

Hoda'ah, thanksgiving, is the underlying concept of *pirsumei nisa*, mitzvos that involve publicizing Hashem's miracles, such as the kindling of the Chanukah lights and the reading of the Megillah on Purim. This is why *pirsumei nisa* takes precedence over the performance of other mitzvos.[1] *Hoda'ah* obligates us to go about our service of Hashem with greater effort and focus. As Dovid expresses it: *"How can I repay Hashem for all His kindness to me?"*[2] A Jew who feels true *hakaras hatov* to Hashem will ask himself, "How can I not improve my *avodas Hashem;* how can I disappoint the One Who does so much for me, day in, day out?"

Returning to Give Thanks

The importance of *hoda'ah* is illustrated by a novel interpretation of the *Chasam Sofer.*

As the Jewish people headed toward the Yam Suf after leaving Egypt, they grew frightened when they saw the Egyptians in hot pursuit. Moshe told them:

> *Do not fear! Stand fast and see the salvation of Hashem that He will perform for you today; for that which you have seen Egypt today, you shall not see them ever again!*
>
> *Hashem will do battle on your behalf, and you shall remain silent.*[3]

---

1. See *Megillah* 3a-b. Rav Wolfson added that this is why women, though they are normally exempt from time-related mitzvos, are obligated in mitzvos that involve *pirsumei nisa*, even those that are rabbinic.

2. *Tehillim* 116:12.

3. *Shemos* 14:13-14.

Mechilta sees the words "*[that which you have seen Egypt today,] you shall not see them ever again!*" as a prohibition against a Jew returning to Egypt. But why is this prohibition stated in the middle of the narrative of the Exodus? Why is it necessary to mention this here?

Chasam Sofer answers this question with another question. Hashem's way of judgment in the world is *middah k'neged middah* (measure for measure); the punishment reflects the sin that was committed. The Egyptians had drowned Jewish babies in the Nile. It would have seemed appropriate, then, for the Egyptian armies to have drowned in the Nile as punishment. Why was it decreed that they drown in the Yam Suf?

The answer lies in the teaching that *"One who sees a place where miracles were performed on behalf of the Jewish people recites: 'Blessed are You, Hashem . . . Who performed miracles for our ancestors at this place.'"*[4] In the *Chasam Sofer's* words:

> *It was Hashem Yisborach's will that the miracle [of the Egyptians' drowning and the Jews' rescue] should happen at a place to which the Jews could return and recall the miracles at a future time. They would remember Hashem's kindness in performing these miracles and wonders, and they would praise and bless Hashem for this. However, Hashem had commanded them never to return to Egypt, so they would never have been able to return to the Nile had the miracles of the Egyptians' drowning and the water splitting happened there. Therefore, Hashem drowned them in the Yam Suf which is outside Egypt's borders, so that the Jews could return there and bless Hashem.*[5]

Chasam Sofer interprets the second verse as a question, not a statement: *Hashem will do battle on your behalf, and you shall remain silent?* Certainly, the Jewish people will want to express its gratitude to Hashem for these incredible miracles. Therefore, these miracles had to take place at the Yam Suf.

---

4. *Berachos* 54a.

5. *Toras Moshe* to *Shemos* 14:13.

Modim D'Rabbanan

Our Sages instituted that when the *chazzan* says this *berachah* during his repetition of *Shemoneh Esrei*, the congregation recites *Modim D'Rabbanan*, The Rabbis' *Modim*. For every other *berachah* of *Shemoneh Esrei*, the congregation merely responds *"Amen"* to the *chazzan's* recital. However, with regard to *Modim* this is not sufficient. Expressing one's gratitude to Hashem is such a spiritual experience, and infuses us with such *kedushah* and a feeling of closeness to Him, that we cannot suffice with having the *chazzan* do it for us. We must thank Hashem personally.

It is called *Modim D'Rabbanan* because its text is a composite of the opinions of a number of Talmudic Sages. The first opinion mentioned in the Gemara is that of Rav: "[The congregation says:] 'We gratefully thank You, Hashem, our God, for [the very fact that] we are inspired to give You thanks." *Rashi* interprets this to mean, "[We thank You, Hashem] that You inspired our hearts to cleave to You and give thanks to You." We thank Hashem that He gave us the understanding to recognize His kindness and to express our thanks for all that He has done and continues to do for us.[6]

A wise, God-fearing person finds no shortage of reasons to thank Hashem, every day of his life. Perhaps this is an additional reason why the congregation's response to the *chazzan's* recitation of *Modim* is called *Modim D'Rabbanan*, the Rabbis' *Modim*.

The Four Who Must Thank

Chapter 107 of *Tehillim* speaks of the "four who are required to thank":

---

6. Rav Wolfson noted that it is truly unfortunate that many recite *Modim D'Rabbanan* in a mumble, saying the words quickly without giving thought to what they are saying. The Chofetz Chaim cites an opinion that when saying the *Modim* blessing in *Shemoneh Esrei*, *kavanah* is required just as it is for the first blessing of *Shemoneh Esrei* (*Mishnah Berurah* 101:3).

- seafarers who arrived safely at their destination
- those who have traveled safely through deserts
- those who were released from prison
- sick people who were healed[7]

It is noteworthy that *Tur* finds an allusion to these four in the *Modim* blessing: וְכֹל הַחַיִּים יוֹדוּךָ סֶּלָה, *Everything alive will gratefully acknowledge You.* The word חַיִּים is an acronym for חָבוּשׁ *(imprisoned),* יִסּוּרִים *(suffering, i.e. illness),* יָם *(sea),* and מִדְבָּר *(desert).*[8]

After describing each one's respective salvation, Dovid HaMelech exclaims: יוֹדוּ לַה' חַסְדּוֹ וְנִפְלְאוֹתָיו לִבְנֵי אָדָם, *Let them thank Hashem for His kindness and for His wonders to mankind.* Those who were rescued have an obligation to proclaim Hashem's greatness to mankind and teach them to recognize His providence and goodness.

That chapter concludes with the words *"Whoever is wise let him note these things and comprehend the kindnesses of Hashem."* The words וְיִשְׁמָר אֵלֶּה, *let him note these things,* can be interpreted homiletically: *[Whoever is wise] and will be protected from these things [will comprehend the kindnesses of Hashem].* A wise, God-fearing person who will be protected from the four dangers enumerated in this chapter will find cause to thank Hashem in the daily, hidden miracles that He performs for us.

Based on this psalm, Halachah states that these four are required to recite the *Bircas HaGomel,* a special blessing of thanksgiving, in the presence of a minyan. Ideally, two of those present should be *talmidei chachamim.*[9] Perhaps the basis for this halachah is that, as we have said, it is a wise, God-fearing person who will utilize the occasion of a *Bircas HaGomel* for its intended purpose. He will make everyone aware that great miracles or salvations are an opportunity to ponder *all the daily miracles* that Hashem performs for every one of us, constantly, throughout our lives. When two

7. See Rashi to *Vayikra* 7:12.

8. *Orach Chaim* ch. 219 and cited in *Shulchan Aruch* 219:1.

9. Ibid #3.

such *chachamim* are present, each one reinforces the other's words so that those present will gain a clear perception of the obligation to thank Hashem every day for His unceasing kindness and providence.

For Every Breath

Sefer Tehillim is comprised of prayers and expressions of thanksgiving, the majority being thanksgiving. At the conclusion of 150 chapters of lilting song, prayer, and praise, written with Divine Inspiration, Dovid cannot bring himself to conclude his thanks to Hashem. In the very last verse, he exclaims: כֹּל הַנְּשָׁמָה תְּהַלֵּל יָהּ, *Let all souls praise God!* In a play on words, our Sages expound: עַל כָּל נְשִׁימָה וּנְשִׁימָה תְּהַלֵּל יָהּ, *for every single breath one must praise God.*[10] Every breath of life is reason enough to express our eternal gratitude to Hashem. As we say in *Nishmas:*

> *Were our mouth as full of song as the sea, and our tongue as full of joyous song as its multitude of waves, and our lips as full of praise as the breadth of the heavens, and our eyes as brilliant as the sun and the moon, and our hands as outspread as eagles of the sky and our feet as swift as hinds — we still could not thank You sufficiently ... for even one of the thousand thousand, thousands of thousands and myriad myriads of favors, miracles, and wonders that You performed for our ancestors and for us.*

10. *Bereishis Rabbah* 14:9.

CHAPTER TWENTY-TWO

Returning to This Mundane World

Many *siddurim* cite a custom from the writings of the *Shelah HaKadosh*: At the conclusion of *Shemoneh Esrei* before taking three steps back, one should recite a verse whose opening letter is the first letter of his name and whose concluding letter is the final letter of his name. This is because when a person departs this world and stands before the Heavenly Tribunal he is asked to state his name. If he is wicked, he may forget his name and will be punished for this. To ensure that we will not forget our name, we recite a verse that will help us to remember it.

This demands explanation. If someone is a *rasha*, why should remembering his name save him from punishment? And if someone is *not* a *rasha,* why should he be liable for punishment simply because he forgot his name?

And why is it at the end of *Shemoneh Esrei* that we fulfill this custom?

The Meaning of Names

Dovid HaMelech says, "לְכוּ חֲזוּ מִפְעֲלוֹת ה' אֲשֶׁר שָׂם שַׁמּוֹת בָּאָרֶץ, *Go and see the works of Hashem, Who has wrought devastation in the land.*"[1] The Gemara interprets the verse as if the word שַׁמּוֹת, *devastation,* is pronounced שֵׁמוֹת, *names.* From here, our Sages say, we derive that שְׁמָא גָּרִים, one's name has a profound connection with his destiny.[2]

Every Jew is sent down to this world to accomplish a mission that only he can accomplish. If a Jew lives his life according to the Torah and serves Hashem with sincerity, then Hashem will guide him along the path of life that will allow him to carry out his mission.

In a Jew's Hebrew name, the name he is given at birth, lies hidden his life's mission. It identifies the uniqueness of each particular *neshamah.* Moreover, the name itself charges us with the spiritual energy to accomplish our mission.

The Arizal stated that when choosing a name for their child, parents are endowed with a degree of *ruach hakodesh* (Divine inspiration) so that they will choose the name appropriate for that *neshamah.*[3] If we had the ability to analyze a name according to its combinations of letters, numerical value, etc., we would be able to see how it fits perfectly with that individual's mission.[4]

---

1. *Tehillim* 46:9.

2. *Berachos* 7b. The meaning of the verse according to this interpretation is: *Go and see the workings of Hashem's guidance of each man's destiny, for He arranges that each person be given a name that fits perfectly with his mission in life.*

3. A chassid asked R' Yitzchak Meir of Ger to choose a name for his child. The Rebbe replied, "Why should I deprive you of an opportunity to have *Ruach HaKodesh*? Choose the name yourself."

4. Rav Wolfson added that this is why a new name is sometimes added to the name of

I know of a man who was hospitalized in an unconscious state; doctors were trying to determine whether or not he was comatose. They did this by shouting his name to elicit some response. This was a better test than pricking his skin or some other form of stimulation — for one's name and one's soul are one.

That a *rasha* forgets his name upon coming to the next world indicates that he lived his life on this world in vain. He had gone through life without contemplating the mission inherent in his name, with which he had been entrusted.

In Egypt and in the *Midbar*

In *Parashas Vayigash,* as Yaakov and his family journey to Egypt, they are counted by name.[5] As they descend to a foreign land which would be the place of our first national *galus* (exile), their names point to their mission. Later, in *Parashas Shemos,* after the last of Yaakov's sons has passed away, their names are repeated.[6] For as the *galus* intensified following their deaths, their names reminded the Jewish people of *their* mission, to carry on the legacy of the twelve sons of Yaakov.

In *Parashas Shelach,* where the *Meraglim* (Spies) are about to leave on their mission to scout Eretz Yisrael, they are mentioned by name. Both before and after they are listed the Torah states, "These are the names ..."[7] Moshe called them by name to remind them that in every aspect of life, and specifically in this mission, they needed to view themselves as emissaries of Hashem. With this attitude, they would be endowed with *siyata diShmaya* (Divine assistance) and their mission would end in success.

Tragically, they did not take this message to heart. They saw themselves as emissaries of *the people*, who had approached Moshe

---

someone who is very ill. His illness may indicate that his mission on this world has been completed. The hope is that the additional name will grant him a new mission, and hence additional years.

5. *Bereishis* 46:8-27.

6. *Shemos* 1:-5.

7. *Bamidbar* 13:4,16.

in a chaotic manner to request that spies be sent to scout out the Land. Therefore, the *Meraglim* failed in their mission.

The Two Midwives

The Torah relates how Pharaoh instituted his policy of mass murder in an attempt to thwart the development and independence of the Jewish people.

> *The king of Egypt said to the Hebrew midwives, of whom the name of the first was Shifrah and the name of the second was Puah — and he said, "When you deliver the Hebrew women, and you see them on the birth stool; if it is a son, you are to kill him, and if it is a daughter, she shall live."*[8]

Why is it that the Torah uses the word וַיֹּאמֶר, *and he said,* twice: *The king of Egypt said . . . and he said . . .?*

Our Sages tell us that these midwives were none other than Yocheved, the mother of Moshe Rabbeinu, and Miriam, his sister. Pharaoh knew very well that Yocheved and Miriam would never comply with an order to murder the male babies. How, then, did he expect his evil scheme to succeed?

Sefer Igra D'Kallah[9] offers a fascinating explanation. When someone is called by his Hebrew name, this generates holiness and purity that becomes manifest upon that person and, as we have explained, it reminds the *neshamah* of its calling. Pharaoh knew this, and he was determined to deprive the midwives of this injection of *kedushah*. He would do this by conferring upon them Egyptian names and decreeing that henceforth, they were to be called only by these names. Egypt was a depraved, immoral, idol-worshipping society, and Pharaoh was certain that the midwives' new names would bring impurity upon their souls. Slowly, their attitudes would change and they would eventually be willing to carry out his evil decree.

---

8. *Shemos* 1:15-16.

9. By R' Tzvi Elimelech of Dinov, author of *Sefer Bnei Yissoschor.*

The first verse quoted above can thus be understood: *And the king of Egypt said to the midwives* ***that the name of one should be Shifrah and the name of the second should be Puah.*** Pharaoh summoned them a second time after they had been called by their Egyptian names for a while and, assuming that now they were being influenced by the forces of *tumah* (spiritual impurity), he commanded them to murder the Jewish babies.[10]

However, as the Torah continues, *The midwives feared God and they did not do as the king of Egypt spoke to them* — to change their names. Therefore, their essential purity was untouched and so ... *they caused the boys to live.* And as *Rashi* informs us, not only did they not harm the children, they even took additional risks by providing the infants with food and drink.[11]

Yocheved and Miriam never forgot their names, never abandoned their missions.

The Angel of Esav

The Torah relates how the angel of Esav struggled with Yaakov Avinu. After Yaakov emerged victorious, he said to the angel, *"Please tell me your name,"* to which the angel replied, "לָמָּה זֶּה תִּשְׁאַל לִשְׁמִי", which taken literally means, "Why do you ask my name?"[12] This seems to be a strange response. Yaakov's image is engraved on the Heavenly Throne, and he had just vanquished the angel. Why did the angel not tell Yaakov his name?[13]

The angel of Esav was none other than the Satan. When the angel responded, "לָמָּה זֶּה תִּשְׁאַל לִשְׁמִי, *Why do you ask my name?*"

10. The same explanation is found in *Chasam Sofer al HaTorah.*

11. Another explanation as to why Pharaoh's plan failed is that Hashem influenced Pharaoh to select Egyptian names which in the Hebrew language have a very positive connotation. For, as *Rashi* states, the name Shifra alludes to שֶׁמְּשַׁפֶּרֶת אֶת הַוָּלָד, *that she beautifies the child (at birth)*; and Puah alludes to שֶׁפּוֹעָה וּמְדַבֶּרֶת וְהוֹגָה לַוָּלָד, *that she cries and speaks and coos to the child (in the manner of women who soothe a crying baby).*

12. *Bereishis* 32:30.

13. *Rashi* explains the angel's answer to mean that he does not have a permanent name, for his name changes according to his mission at any given time.

he was saying, *"My name is* לָמָּה זֶּה תִּשְׁאַל לִשְׁמִי*. For my purpose is to make Jews forget their names — that is, to forget their mission in life. When a Jew neglects his Torah study, his davening, and then is momentarily shaken by a fleeting thought of repentance, I come and tell him, 'Why pay attention to your* ***name,*** *your mission? Forget about it and just go on with your routine as if you will be on this world forever!' "*

A Verse of Remembrance

It is true that people can get so caught up in the pressures and vicissitudes of life that they lose sight of their purpose in this world, but this should not be a problem when in the midst of reciting *Shemoneh Esrei.* If a person davens *Shemoneh Esrei* properly, he does so with the cognizance that he is standing before the King of kings. At that time, it is as if he has entered another world and stands fully aware of his true purpose in life. However, when he completes *Shemoneh Esrei* and takes three steps back to return to this mundane world, he is faced with the danger that he will forget his mission in life. Therefore, immediately before taking those three steps, one should recite a verse that will remind him of his name and hence his calling in life. In this way, he will not forget his name after departing this world, for he will have lived his life fully cognizant of his sacred mission.

CHAPTER TWENTY-THREE

Psalm 20: On the Day of Distress[1]

There is a well-known *segulah* (auspicious omen) for this psalm to be recited on behalf of a woman in the throes of childbirth. Our generation finds itself in a similar situation.

Mashiach's arrival is referred to by Yeshayahu HaNavi as a "birth": כִּי יֶלֶד יֻלַּד לָנוּ בֵּן נִתַּן לָנוּ וַתְּהִי הַמִּשְׂרָה עַל שִׁכְמוֹ, *For a child has been born to us, a son has been given to us; and the authority will rest on his shoulder.*[2] Our Sages refer to the difficulties that will precede Mashiach's arrival as חֶבְלֵי מָשִׁיחַ, *the birth pangs of Mashiach.* Just as

1. This psalm is recited each weekday morning (with the exception of certain special occasions such as Rosh Chodesh) as part of *Shacharis*, between *Ashrei* and *Uva L'Tzion.*

2. *Yeshayahu* 9:5.

the time of greatest pain precedes the intense joy of giving birth, so do the *nisyonos* (trials) of *galus* intensify as the glorious days of Mashiach approach. Mashiach's arrival is nearing, and our nation finds itself in very difficult straits.

לַמְנַצֵּחַ מִזְמוֹר לְדָוִד. יַעַנְךָ ה׳ בְּיוֹם צָרָה ...

For the Conductor, a psalm of Dovid.

***Hashem will answer you on the day of distress . . .*[3]**

Certainly we are living through a יוֹם צָרָה, *day of distress*. On a personal level, so many of our brethren are beset with worry over health issues, financial stress, difficulty with raising their children and finding *shidduchim* for them. As a nation, we are filled with concern for the future of Eretz Yisrael and the enemies we face around the world.

Let us not forget that even in recent history, Hashem performed great wonders in rescuing us from the brink of disaster. During the Second World War, the German Army was in Egypt and marching towards Eretz Yisrael. The German general boasted that the next day he would be "drinking coffee in Tel Aviv" but, due to the kindness of Hashem, this did not happen. The Germans never set foot on the Land's holy soil.

We can rest assured that Hashem will not allow the tyrant of Iran and our other enemies to carry out their wicked plans. But we cannot sit back and wait for salvation to come. It is our sacred obligation to use the weapons in our arsenal — Torah, *tefillah*, and *chesed* — to merit that salvation.

A Declaration of Faith

"One who trusts in Hashem will be surrounded by kindness."[4] In this psalm, Dovid demonstrates the rock-firm *bitachon* (trust

3. The common translation is *May Hashem answer you on the day of distress*. Our translation follows Rav Wolfson's interpretation in this essay.

4. *Tehillim* 32:10.

in Hashem) that accompanied him throughout his difficult life. He begins with the words לַמְנַצֵּחַ מִזְמוֹר לְדָוִד, which is commonly translated *For the Conductor, a psalm of Dovid.* The Conductor directed the Levi'im's singing and musical accompaniment in the Beis HaMikdash.

Alternatively, R' Samson Raphael Hirsch relates the word לַמְנַצֵּחַ to נִצָּחוֹן, *triumph.*[5] Dovid dedicated this song to Hashem, the One Who grants triumph to His people. In the midst of the *day of distress*, Dovid already sees a victorious Jewish nation; thus he does not merely recite a psalm, but composes a מִזְמוֹר, *song*, a joyous expression of faith. Dovid declares: יַעַנְךָ ה' בְּיוֹם צָרָה, *Hashem* ***will*** *answer you on the day of distress.* To Dovid, there is no doubt that when we cry out to Hashem, sincerely and passionately, He answers us.

In another psalm, Dovid cries out:

> עַד אָנָה ה' תִּשְׁכָּחֵנִי נֶצַח, עַד אָנָה תַּסְתִּיר אֶת פָּנֶיךָ מִמֶּנִּי? עַד אָנָה אָשִׁית עֵצוֹת בְּנַפְשִׁי, יָגוֹן בִּלְבָבִי יוֹמָם, עַד אָנָה יָרוּם אֹיְבִי עָלָי?
>
> *How long, Hashem, will You endlessly forget me? How long will You hide Your countenance from me? How long must I set schemes within myself? My heart is melancholy even by day; how long will my enemy triumph over me?*[6]

R' Yisrael of Rizhin offers a novel interpretation: *How long, Hashem, will You endlessly forget me? How long will You hide Your countenance from me?* The answer to these questions is: עַד אָנָה אָשִׁית עֵצוֹת בְּנַפְשִׁי, *As long as I believe that I can come up with solutions for my soul.* As long as Jews think that they have their own solution, be it political or otherwise, to the dangers that face them, salvation will not be soon in coming. It is only when they realize that the ***only*** solution is to turn their hearts towards Hashem that salvation will come.[7]

---

5. See R' Hirsch's commentary to the fourth chapter of *Tehillim* where the word לַמְנַצֵּחַ first appears in *Sefer Tehillim.*

6. *Tehillim* 13:2-3.

7. The final mishnah in *Masechta Sotah* tells of the state of the world during *Ikvesa D'Meshicha*. The mishnah concludes: וְעַל מִי יֵשׁ לָנוּ לְהִשָּׁעֵן, עַל אָבִינוּ שֶׁבַּשָּׁמַיִם, *On whom do we*

The God of Yaakov

... יְשַׂגֶּבְךָ שֵׁם אֱלֹהֵי יַעֲקֹב.

... the Name of Yaakov's God shall make you invulnerable.

Yaakov Avinu was granted four blessings.[8] Zohar states that he kept the weakest of these blessings[9] for himself and reserved the other three for the generation that would precede Mashiach's arrival. That generation, says Zohar, will a face a situation which Dovid HaMelech describes in *Hallel*: *"All the nations surround me; in the Name of Hashem, I cut them down! They encircle me, they also surround me; in the Name of Hashem, I cut them down!"*[10] This is how we find ourselves now, surrounded by enemies who seek to destroy us. But through the power of Yaakov's blessings, we will be transformed from the generation of *Ikvesa D'Meshicha* (the Footsteps of Mashiach) to the generation of *Geulah* (Redemption).

As we have discussed elsewhere, Yaakov is the embodiment of *bitachon.* His life was filled with tragedy and travail. He fled a bloodthirsty Esav, spent 22 years in the house of the scheming Lavan, suffered the abduction of Dinah and the sale of Yosef. And then, toward the end of his life, he was commanded to leave Eretz Yisrael and live his remaining years in Egypt. Never did his trust in Hashem waver. In fact, soon after the episode of Dinah, Yaakov

---

have to rely? On our Father in Heaven. Rav Wolfson interpreted this to mean that the *galus* will end when Jews will recognize clearly that no one can save them from their predicament other than their Father in Heaven.

8. When Yaakov posed as his brother Esav, he was given the blessing that begins וְיִתֶּן לְךָ הָאֱלֹהִים מִטַּל הַשָּׁמַיִם ..., *And may God give you of the dew of the heavens ...* (*Bereishis* 27:28); before Yaakov departed for Padan Aram, the Torah states, וַיִּקְרָא יִצְחָק אֶל יַעֲקֹב וַיְבָרֶךְ אֹתוֹ, *So Yitzchak summoned Yaakov and blessed him* (ibid 28:1)*;* the angel of Esav blessed Yaakov after losing the struggle with him (ibid. 32:30); and later, when Hashem conferred the name Yisrael upon Yaakov, He blessed him (ibid. 35:9).

9. Yitzchak's blessing to him before he departed for Padan Aram.

10. *Tehillim* 118:10-11.

told his family, "*. . . let us go up to Beis El; I will make there an altar to God Who answered me in my time of distress . . . .*"[11]

And so, as we pray for Hashem's mercy and imminent rescue, we invoke the merit of Yaakov Avinu.

יִשְׁלַח עֶזְרְךָ מִקֹּדֶשׁ וּמִצִּיּוֹן יִסְעָדֶךָּ.

He will dispatch your help from the place of holiness, and support you from Zion.

Though we find ourselves in the Diaspora, our salvation comes from Zion, and specifically the site of the Beis HaMikdash. That place was revealed to Yaakov as the Gateway to Heaven, the place from which all our tefillos, wherever they are uttered, ascend.

The Poor Man's Offering

יִזְכֹּר כָּל מִנְחֹתֶךָ וְעוֹלָתְךָ יְדַשְּׁנֶה סֶלָה.

He will remember your minchah offerings and consider your olah offerings generous, Selah.

A *minchah* is an offering of flour that is usually brought by a poor person who cannot afford to bring an animal or even a bird as a *korban.* Though it is small and inexpensive, the poor man's *korban* is very precious to Hashem, so much so that it is considered as if he offered his very soul on the Altar.[12]

Our generation, in comparison to earlier generations, is like a poor man who has little to offer. We cannot hope to attain the levels of Torah, tefillah, and chesed of the *tzaddikim* of yesteryear of whom we read and whose lives inspire us. But this should not be cause for despair. Just as Hashem greatly valued the poor man's *minchah,* so too does He greatly value our sincere efforts in *avodas Hashem.*

---

11. *Bereishis* 35:3.

12. See *Rashi* to *Vayikra* 2:1.

In this verse, Dovid likens the *minchah* to an expensive *olah* offering; the word יְדַשְּׁנֶה is related to וְדָשֵׁן, *and grow fat,*[13] indicating an animal offering of the highest quality. As we have mentioned elsewhere, the fact that we continue to serve Hashem with love and strive to remain a pure and holy people, even in a world so decadent and depraved, is exceedingly precious in Heaven. Therefore, we can remain confident that יִתֶּן לְךָ כִלְבָבֶךָ וְכָל עֲצָתְךָ יְמַלֵּא, *He will grant you your heart's desires and fulfill your every plan.*

A Time to Sing

נְרַנְּנָה בִּישׁוּעָתֶךָ וּבְשֵׁם אֱלֹהֵינוּ נִדְגֹּל יְמַלֵּא ה׳ כָּל מִשְׁאֲלוֹתֶיךָ.
Let us sing for joy at your salvation and raise our banner in the name of our God, Hashem shall fulfill all your requests.

We are a unique people. Times are very difficult, and every person's heart is burdened by worry, yet we find it within ourselves to truly rejoice that we are a nation of Hashem. On Simchas Torah we reach elevated spiritual heights as we celebrate with Hashem and His Torah, and we do the same on other occasions. In this verse, Dovid proclaims that we sing with joy even as we are experiencing trials and tribulations because we know that all is for the good, and ultimately, Hashem will improve our situation.

The Baal Shem Tov offers an original interpretation of יְמַלֵּא ה׳ כָּל מִשְׁאֲלוֹתֶיךָ. Following our first war with Amalek, Moshe Rabbeinu said:

> כִּי יָד עַל כֵּס יָהּ מִלְחָמָה לַה׳ בַּעֲמָלֵק מִדֹּר דֹּר.
> *For there is a hand on the throne of God: Hashem maintains a war against Amalek from generation to generation.*[14]

13. *Devarim* 31:20.
14. *Shemos* 17:16.

The Hebrew word for *throne* is usually spelled כִּסֵּא, but here it is spelled כֵּס; the name of Hashem is usually spelled י־ה־ו־ה but here it is spelled יָהּ. Our Sages comment: *"HaKadosh Baruch Hu swore that His Name is not whole and His Throne is not whole until the name of Amalek is completely eradicated."*[15]

In our verse, says the Baal Shem Tov, Dovid describes how the Jewish people place their concern for Hashem's honor ahead of their own suffering. Their primary reason for praying for salvation is that as long as this *galus* continues and Amalek exists, Hashem's glory remains concealed, as represented by the incomplete spelling of His Name. And our primary tefillah, represented by the words כָּל מִשְׁאֲלוֹתֶךָ *(all your requests),* is that יְמַלֵּא ה׳, the Name of Hashem shall once again be complete, when Mashiach will arrive and His glory will fill the earth.

Our Survival Is Ensured

עַתָּה יָדַעְתִּי כִּי הוֹשִׁיעַ ה׳ מְשִׁיחוֹ יַעֲנֵהוּ מִשְּׁמֵי קָדְשׁוֹ ...
Now I know that Hashem has saved His anointed one; He will answer him from His sacred heaven ...

We are confident that ultimately salvation will come, because our bond with Hashem is eternal and He will never forsake us. Furthermore, even in recent times, our people have merited Hashem's miraculous rescue from a tense, dangerous situation. Dovid therefore declares that not only do I *believe* that Hashem will save us, I *know* that this is so.

בִּגְבֻרוֹת יֵשַׁע יְמִינוֹ ...
With the mighty deliverance of His right arm ...

The term גְּבֻרוֹת represents the power of Hashem's *Middas HaDin* (Attribute of Judgment). יְמִינוֹ, *His right arm,* represents

15. *Rashi* ad loc. citing *Midrash Tanchuma.*

His *Middas HaChesed* (Attribute of Kindness). Even when the Jewish people have sinned, resulting in the arousal of the *Middas HaDin* towards them, Hashem finds ways for the judgments to be "sweetened" by the *Middas HaChesed* so that ultimately they are saved.

Arising From Our Fall

אֵלֶּה בָרֶכֶב וְאֵלֶּה בַסּוּסִים וַאֲנַחְנוּ בְּשֵׁם ה׳ אֱלֹהֵינוּ נַזְכִּיר.

Some with chariots and some with horses, but we — in the Name of Hashem, our God — call out.

Today's "horses" are tanks, drones, and laser-guided missiles. Nations of the world place their faith in the weapons created by modern technology, but we know that the outcome of war is entirely in Hashem's hands.

הֵמָּה כָּרְעוּ וְנָפָלוּ וַאֲנַחְנוּ קַּמְנוּ וַנִּתְעוֹדָד.

They slumped and fell, but we arose and were invigorated.

When our enemies slump in defeat, they fall, broken and shattered. When the Jewish people falls, God forbid, it is only temporary. וַאֲנַחְנוּ קַּמְנוּ, *But we arose* after having fallen, because when we do fall it is Hashem's way of motivating us to mend our ways, to strengthen our *avodas Hashem*. The word וַנִּתְעוֹדָד is related to the word עוֹד, *still,* representing the eternity of the Jewish people.

The prophet Michah says: אַל תִּשְׂמְחִי אֹיַבְתִּי לִי כִּי נָפַלְתִּי קָמְתִּי כִּי אֵשֵׁב בַּחֹשֶׁךְ ה׳ אוֹר לִי, *Rejoice not over me, my enemy, for though I have fallen, I have risen; though I sit in darkness, Hashem is a light for me.*[16]

---

16. *Michah* 7:8. *Midrash Shochar Tov* (*Tehillim* 5) comments, "Had I not fallen, I would not have arisen; had I not sat in darkness, Hashem would not have been a light for me."

The Final Sigh

ה' הוֹשִׁיעָה הַמֶּלֶךְ יַעֲנֵנוּ בְיוֹם קָרְאֵנוּ.
Hashem save! The King will answer us on the day we call.

Zohar states that the 70 words in this psalm correspond to the 70 אֲנָחוֹת, *sighs,* of a woman in the throes of childbirth. We are nearing the arrival of Mashiach, and it may well be that we are in the midst of the 70th sigh represented by the psalm's final word, קָרְאֵנוּ, *we call.* Let us call out to Hashem with heartfelt tefillah, and through this we will merit the *Geulah*, may it come speedily and in our time.

CHAPTER TWENTY-FOUR

Psalm 92: A Song for the Day of Shabbos

The daily song that the Levi'im recited in the Beis HaMikdash was as follows: On the first day of the week they would say ... On the second day ... On Shabbos they would say: "A psalm, a song for the day of Shabbos." A psalm, a song for the time to come, to the day that will be entirely Shabbos and contentment for the eternal life (*Mishnah Tamid* 7:4).

Psalm 92 is recited on Friday night as part of *Kabbalas Shabbos;* on Shabbos day as part of *Pesukei D'Zimrah;* and as the *Shir shel*

Yom (daily song as sung by the Levi'im). *Shulchan Aruch* states that for someone who recites *Kabbalas Shabbos* before sunset, his recital of Psalm 92 constitutes acceptance of Shabbos and he must then cease all forbidden labors.[1]

According to Midrash,[2] this psalm was recited by Adam. Adam ate from the Tree of Knowledge late Friday afternoon, and as Shabbos arrived death was decreed upon him. The Shabbos came forward to serve as Adam's advocate. "*Ribbono shel Olam*," the Shabbos said, "during the six days of creation, no man was punished with death. Must such judgment begin today? Is this my sanctity? Is this my blessing?" Hashem accepted the Shabbos' plea and Adam was spared.

Adam then begin to sing, "A psalm, a song for the day of Shabbos ..." Said the Shabbos, "You are praising me? Let us both praise the Holy One. *It is good to praise Hashem ...*[3]

A total of ten great personalities contributed to the writing of *Sefer Tehillim*, Adam among them.[4] However, as *Alshich* explains, every word of *Sefer Tehillim* is attributed to Dovid.[5]

---

1. *Orach Chaim* 261:4. Today, when *Lechah Dodi* is part of *Kabbalas Shabbos*, saying the words בּוֹאִי כַלָּה *(enter, O [Shabbos] bride)* constitutes acceptance of Shabbos. For a woman, candle-lighting itself constitutes acceptance of Shabbos.

2. *Yalkut Shimoni.*

3. According to another Midrash, after Kayin killed Hevel he encountered his father Adam, who asked him, "How did the Heavenly tribunal judge you?" Kayin replied, "I repented and my punishment was lightened." Adam then exclaimed, "I did not realize that the power of repentance is so great!"

Immediately, Adam composed this psalm, in which he declared: *It is good to praise Hashem ... (Bereishis Rabbah* 22:13).

The Manchester Rosh Yeshivah, R' Yehudah Zev Segal, explained that when Adam saw the power of repentance, he took this lesson and applied it to Shabbos, whose essence inspires *teshuvah me'ahavah*, repentance out of love, a most exalted form of *teshuvah*. Thus was he inspired to sing this psalm in honor of Shabbos (*Inspiration and Insight on the Torah*, published by ArtScroll/Mesorah).

4. The ten are: Dovid, Adam, Malkitzedek, Avraham, Moshe, Shlomo, Assaf, and the three sons of Korach (*Rashi* to *Tehillim* 1:1. There are other opinions as to the ten who comprise this count).

5. Psalm 72 concludes: כָּלּוּ תְפִלּוֹת דָּוִד בֶּן יִשָׁי, *The prayers of David son of Yishai are ended.* The Gemara (*Pesachim* 117a) interprets the word כָּלּוּ (*they are ended*) as if it read כָּל אֵלּוּ, *All these ([psalms are] the prayers of Dovid son of Yishai*). See *Hagahos Yaavetz* ad loc.

At Sinai, every Jew was granted his unique portion in Torah, the *chiddushim* (original insights) that are his to propound. *Sefer Tehillim* was Dovid's to reveal, but at various points in history before Dovid's *neshamah* descended to this world, certain individuals were permitted to reveal psalms that in essence belonged to the "sweet singer of Israel," Dovid HaMelech. In the case of Adam, his elation at being saved in Shabbos' merit inspired him to reveal this song of Dovid.[6]

As we have already mentioned,[7] when we recite chapters of *Tehillim* Dovid sings along with us from his place in Heaven, and in his merit our supplication gains entry before the Heavenly Throne.

A Day of Contentment

From a simple reading of the words of this psalm, it seems to have no connection at all to Shabbos. As we see from the mishnah in *Masechta Tamid* cited above, the "Shabbos" to which this psalm refers is not the seventh day, our Shabbos, but to the seventh millennium.

At the end of six millennia, the world as we know it will cease to exist.[8] The "song for the Shabbos day" refers to the seventh millennium, for "day" in this context refers to a thousand years, as the verse states: *"For a thousand years in Your eyes are like a day."*[9] During this period, there will be a cessation of physical activity and only the righteous will exist. It will be a time of utter contentment.

We recite this psalm on Shabbos because Shabbos is מֵעֵין עוֹלָם הַבָּא, *a semblance of the World to Come.* Shabbos is a day of מְנוּחָה,

6. As we have mentioned elsewhere, Zohar states that Dovid and Adam were the same *neshamah*. The name אָדָם is an acronym for אָדָם, דָּוִד, מָשִׁיחַ.

7. See essay on *Pesukei D'Zimrah*.

8. This change will occur sometime after Mashiach's arrival which will hopefully be well before the end of the sixth millennium.

9. *Tehillim* 90:4.

a word often mistakenly translated as *rest.* Someone who views Shabbos as primarily a day to catch up on his sleep and enjoy a well-earned day of rest has no concept of what Shabbos truly is. The correct translation of מְנוּחָה is *contentment.*[10]

On the words *God completed on the seventh day* Rashi states: "What was the world lacking? *Menuchah.* Shabbos came — *menuchah* came. The work was completed and finished."[11] With the onset of the first Shabbos, creation was completed. Nothing was lacking. It was a perfect world. And so as creation entered the seventh day, it was enveloped in an aura of contentment.

As our Sages teach, when Shabbos arrives, a Jew should experience a feeling of utter contentment; he should banish all mundane thoughts from his mind, as if all his weekday activities have been completed and need no further contemplation.[12] He should focus his thoughts on the opportunity that this holy day presents, to renew one's closeness with Hashem and tap into the day's heightened spirituality.

Seven Days, Seven Notes

The seven days of the week correspond to the seven *Sefiros,* the Heavenly attributes of Hashem through which He conducts the affairs of this world. On Friday night we recite Psalm 29 in which we mention the seven קוֹלוֹת, *voices,* which also correspond to the seven *Sefiros.* These correspond to the seven notes of the musical scale.

In our discussion of the psalms of *Pesukei D'Zimrah,* we noted that all of creation is one magnificent symphony singing *shirah* to

---

10. In *Megillas Rus,* Naomi encouraged her widowed daughters-in-law to return home and marry, saying: יִתֵּן ה' לָכֶם וּמְצֶאןָ מְנוּחָה אִשָּׁה בֵּית אִישָׁהּ, *May Hashem grant you that you should find contentment, each in the home of her husband (Rus* 1:9).

11. *Bereishis* 2:2.

12. "When Shabbos comes, it should seem to you as if all your work is done so that you will not give any thought to forbidden work" (*Rashi* to *Shemos* 20:9).

Hashem. There is another symphony in this world, the symphony of Jewish history. If one looks at Jewish history, he is amazed at how Hashem has ensured not only our survival but also that Torah will never become forgotten by the Jewish people.[13] For example, in recent history, as the destruction of European Jewry was taking place, Eretz Yisrael and the United States were already developing as great Torah centers.

As much as we *can* recognize the guiding hand of Hashem in history, there is much that we do not understand, both on personal and communal levels. We cannot know, for example, why the Holocaust was decreed and why so many righteous souls perished at that time. After Mashiach's arrival, the veil of history will be lifted and everything will become clear.

This, as we shall see, is the theme of the Song of the Day of Shabbos. In the world's present state, we cannot fathom the Divine plan. Even Moshe Rabbeinu was told by Hashem, *"You will see My back, but My face may not be seen."*[14] Hashem was saying: "I will show you the reason for past happenings ("My back") but I will not explain the reasons for present occurrences or that which will transpire in the future."

But in the glorious era of Mashiach, we will recognize the true beauty of the symphony of history. In the meantime, we live with the *emunah* that all that Hashem does is for the good, and that some day we will clearly perceive how this is so.

On Shabbos, a semblance of the World to Come, our elevated souls experience a taste of the future, and we recite this psalm joyously and with renewed faith.

---

13. *"For it [the Torah] shall not become forgotten from the mouths of his children"* (*Devarim* 31:21; see *Rashi*).

14. *Shemos* 33:23.

A Time to Thank and Admit

טוֹב לְהֹדוֹת לַה׳ וּלְזַמֵּר לְשִׁמְךָ עֶלְיוֹן.
It is good to thank Hashem and to give praise to Your Name, O exalted One.

The word לְהֹדוֹת means both *to thank* and *to admit.* In the future, we will understand how all the happenings of *galus*, difficult though they were, all led to a perfect conclusion. At that time, we will thank Hashem for what He did and admit that indeed, it was all for the good. In the words of Yeshayahu Hanavi, *"Then, on that day, you will say, 'I thank You, Hashem, for having been angry with me.'"*[15]

We also acknowledge that the *Ribbono shel Olam* is עֶלְיוֹן, *exalted.* We recognize that it is impossible for a mere mortal to fully comprehend the ways of Hashem, Who, from His vantage point on High, sees the entire sweep of history before Him and bridges the past with the present and future.

In Times of Light and Darkness

לְהַגִּיד בַּבֹּקֶר חַסְדֶּךָ וֶאֱמוּנָתְךָ בַּלֵּילוֹת.
To relate Your kindness in the dawn and Your faith in the nights.

Dawn refers to the tranquil periods in exile, when our people flourished in their lands and Torah scholars were revered even among the non-Jewish populace. At such times, it was easy to recognize Hashem's kindness and offer praise for it. *Night* refers to the dark periods when our people were scorned and persecuted. Such times require a Jew to reach deeply into his reservoir of faith and believe that all is for the good.

---

15. *Yeshayahu* 12:1.

עֲלֵי עָשׂוֹר וַעֲלֵי נָבֶל עֲלֵי הִגָּיוֹן בְּכִנּוֹר.
Upon ten-stringed instrument and lyre,
in meditation upon the harp.

The symphony of history is produced by a variety of "instruments" of varying sounds, some more pleasant, some less so. They require our הִגָּיוֹן, *meditation,* to internalize and truly feel what we know in the deepest recesses of our souls: *"The Rock — perfect is His work, for all His paths are justice; a God of faith without iniquity, righteous and fair is He."*[16]

R' Nachman of Breslov would say that every Jew's life is a *niggun* (tune).[17] Some parts of the *niggun* are happy, some are mournful. So too, every day in history, every year, decade, century, and millennium, plays its song. Think into the song and recognize that it is all part of Hashem's master plan.

Great Deeds, Profound Thoughts

כִּי שִׂמַּחְתַּנִי ה׳ בְּפָעֳלֶךָ בְּמַעֲשֵׂי יָדֶיךָ אֲרַנֵּן.
For You have gladdened me, Hashem, with Your deeds;
at the works of Your hands I sing glad song.

I rejoice in the knowledge that whatever transpires, whether of major or minor importance, is פָּעֳלֶךָ, *Your deed*, Hashem. I sing with the knowledge that all that transpires is מַעֲשֵׂי יָדֶיךָ, *the work of Your hands.* How wonderful it is to possess an *emunah* that is strong and pure, to believe with perfect faith that what happens to me, to my people, and to the world as a whole is being carefully orchestrated from Above. How comforting it is to know that the Master of the Universe involves Himself in my personal life on a constant basis, guiding my every step. And with this knowledge, I am prepared to face whatever tests life may bring.

16. *Devarim* 32:4.

17. Rav Wolfson quoted his *rebbi*, R' Shraga Feivel Mendlowitz, who said that R' Nachman of Breslov was the "poet of Chassidus."

מַה גָּדְלוּ מַעֲשֶׂיךָ ה׳ מְאֹד עָמְקוּ מַחְשְׁבֹתֶיךָ.
How great are Your deeds, Hashem; exceedingly profound are Your thoughts.

Someone asked the Chazon Ish to explain why the Holocaust happened. The *gaon* responded with a parable of someone who entered a tailor shop for the first time in his life and found the tailer cutting pieces of various shapes from a beautiful piece of silk. The visitor was aghast. "Why are you ruining such beautiful material?" he demanded. He did not realize that the tailor would soon fashion the pieces into a beautiful garment.

So it is with the workings of history. *How great are Your deeds, Hashem; exceedingly profound are Your thoughts.* Hashem is the "tailor" and we are the ignorant visitor who cannot possibly comprehend how all His deeds and thoughts will result in a glorious conclusion.

אִישׁ בַּעַר לֹא יֵדָע וּכְסִיל לֹא יָבִין אֶת זֹאת.
A boor cannot know, nor can a fool understand this.

An אִישׁ, *human being,* is in essence a בַּעַר, *boor,* when it comes to understanding the ways of Hashem. A כְּסִיל, *fool,* does not understand this. There are people who are considered intellectuals, men of great wisdom, who foolishly reject out of hand anything that their minds cannot comprehend. They refuse to recognize that when it comes to comprehending the deep, unfathomable ways of Hashem, the most brilliant individual is nothing more than an ignorant boor.

The Rise and Fall of the Wicked

בִּפְרֹחַ רְשָׁעִים כְּמוֹ עֵשֶׂב וַיָּצִיצוּ כָּל פֹּעֲלֵי אָוֶן ...
When the wicked bloom like grass and all the doers of iniquity blossom ...

Among the many mistakes non-believers make is their lack of understanding that the purpose of the wicked's "blossoming" is לְהִשָּׁמְדָם עֲדֵי עַד, *to destroy them until eternity.*

Does man truly think he can comprehend the ways of Heaven? How can he not recognize that "וְאַתָּה מָרוֹם לְעֹלָם ה׳, *You remain exalted forever, Hashem*"? Hashem's ways are beyond our comprehension.

Those who do recognize this have faith that ultimately כִּי הִנֵּה אֹיְבֶיךָ ה׳ כִּי הִנֵּה אֹיְבֶיךָ יֹאבֵדוּ יִתְפָּרְדוּ כָּל פֹּעֲלֵי אָוֶן, *For behold! — Your enemies, Hashem, for behold! — Your enemies shall perish, dispersed shall be all doers of iniquity.* This will surely come to pass at the End of Days, a time that is swiftly approaching. At that time, the glory of the Jewish people will shine once more.

וַתָּרֶם כִּרְאֵים קַרְנִי בַּלֹּתִי בְּשֶׁמֶן רַעֲנָן.
As exalted as a re'eim's shall be my pride,
I will be saturated with ever-fresh oil.

The *re'eim* has beautiful, tall horns, a symbol of the pride that the Jewish nation will experience with Mashiach's arrival. They will be like one who is *saturated with ever-fresh oil,* in a state of utter euphoria and contentment.

וַתַּבֵּט עֵינִי בְּשׁוּרָי בַּקָּמִים עָלַי מְרֵעִים תִּשְׁמַעְנָה אָזְנָי.
My eyes have seen my vigilant foes;
when those who would harm me rise up against me,
my ears have heard their doom.

We will witness the downfall of our enemies, of those who seek to annihilate us.

Of Grass and Trees

צַדִּיק כַּתָּמָר יִפְרָח כְּאֶרֶז בַּלְּבָנוֹן יִשְׂגֶּה.

A righteous man will flourish like a date palm, like a cedar in the Lebanon he will grow tall.

Above, the wicked were likened to grass, which is an unusual type of vegetation. It grows very quickly, almost as soon as it is planted, but when not watered adequately, it can quickly turn brown, then white, and even wither away. By contrast, it can take years for a date tree or cedar to fully develop, but once it has grown it can remain strong and healthy for many, many years.

The wicked appear at times to be blessed with meteoric success, achieving their diabolical goals in a relatively short time. Often, they fall as quickly as they rise, as was the case with Haman. The *tzaddik*, by contrast, spends a lifetime on self-improvement, climbing the rungs of the spiritual ladder carefully, one at a time. His hard-earned achievements remain with him forever, and even when he stumbles, he garners his inner strength to correct his mistake and maintain or surpass his previous level.

There is another message in the comparison between the withering grass and the strong, erect palm and cedar trees. There is a well-known story of a group of concentration camp inmates who, in defiance of their liberators, joined hands and sang, *"Mir velen zei iberleben* (We will outlive them)." The German officer asked one of the prisoners, "Do you truly believe that?" to which the Jew replied, "Absolutely." The officer shook his head and said, "I am afraid the *Fuhrer* is wrong. We will never win over you people."

One of the incredible, indisputable facts of world history is that the mocked, oppressed, downtrodden Jewish nation has outlived the many mighty empires that persecuted and exiled it. The Egyptian empire is no more, and the same is true of the Babylonian, Persian, Greek, and Roman empires.

When the Inquisition tortured and killed countless of our brethren, Spain was a mighty world empire; today it is a weak country. But the Jewish people live on. We have been witness to incredible *siyata diShmaya* that made it possible to rebuild the world of Torah that had been so decimated during the Second World War.

We are the ever-productive date tree, the tall and mighty cedar tree. Our future is ensured by the grace of our Father in Heaven.

Fruit-Bearing and Tall

The *Baal Haflaah* offers another insight into the *tzaddik* being compared to a date palm and a cedar. A date palm does not grow tall precisely because much of its inner strength is utilized to produce fruits. A cedar does not bear fruit, and therefore is able to grow tall. A *tzaddik* gives of his time and energy to transmit the Torah to *talmidim.* He would much prefer to closet himself in his room and devote his days and nights to learning Hashem's Torah and rising above this mundane world as he draws ever closer to Hashem. But because he knows that it is Hashem's desire that he "produce fruit" and inculcate the next generation with Torah wisdom and the Torah way of life, he is willing to sacrifice his own personal growth.

In truth, it is not a sacrifice at all. In his own spiritual ascent, he will grow tall like a cedar. The Chasam Sofer writes that when a *talmid chacham* gives of his time to teach others *l'shem Shamayim* (for the sake of Heaven), he can rest assured that his efforts in his own *avodas Hashem* will be blessed from Above and he will "grow tall," achieving levels that he may have thought were unattainable.

Planted in the House of Hashem

What is the secret of *tzaddikim's* success? They are שְׁתוּלִים בְּבֵית ה' בְּחַצְרוֹת אֱלֹהֵינוּ יַפְרִיחוּ, *planted in the house of Hashem, in the courtyards of our God they will flourish.*

Our Sages teach that when Yaakov and Esav were in their mother's womb, they both sought to "run out" at different times. Esav sought to run out whenever Rivkah passed a place of idolatry, while Yaakov sought to run out whenever she passed the beis midrash of Shem or Ever. The question is asked: Why would Yaakov want to leave in order to enter the beis midrash? Our Sages teach that inside the mother's womb, an angel teaches the unborn child the Torah in its entirety. What was Yaakov lacking in this sublime beis midrash that made him want to leave for the beis midrash outside?

The answer is that he wanted to leave the bad environment he was in: the company of his brother Esav. Even if a Heavenly angel serves as one's *rebbi*, he can be ruined by the poisonous influence of a bad friend. A *tzaddik's* spiritual success is predicated on his being firmly planted in the house of Hashem, away from the lures and influences of a decadent society.

We are an ancient people; our history since the birth of Avraham spans almost 4,000 years. Nevertheless, we have lost none of our vitality. And in the יוֹם שֶׁכּוּלּוֹ שַׁבָּת, *Day that is entirely Shabbos, tzaddikim* will attain yet greater levels. עוֹד יְנוּבוּן בְּשֵׂיבָה דְּשֵׁנִים וְרַעֲנַנִּים יִהְיוּ, *They will still be fruitful in old age, vigorous and fresh they will be.*

And at that time, with utmost clarity and understanding they will proclaim כִּי יָשָׁר ה׳ צוּרִי וְלֹא עַוְלָתָה בּוֹ, *that Hashem is just, my Rock and in Whom there is no wrong.*

CHAPTER TWENTY-FIVE

Maariv — the Tefillah of Yaakov

The Gemara tells us that our forefathers, Avraham, Yitzchak, and Yaakov, established the three daily tefillos. Avraham established *Shacharis*; Yitzchak established *Minchah*; and Yaakov established *Maariv*.[1] The Gemara concludes that the Sages also drew a parallel between the daily tefillos and the Beis HaMikdash service. *Shacharis* corresponds to the morning *Tamid* sacrifice; *Minchah* corresponds to the afternoon *Tamid* sacrifice; and *Maariv* corresponds to the limbs and fats of sacrifices that were burned on the Altar during the night, after the sacrificial blood was applied by day.

---

1. *Berachos* 26b.

Elsewhere, R' Shimon bar Yochai teaches that the ideal time for burning the limbs and fats is by day, to the point that the limbs and fats of a *Korban Tamid, Mussaf,* or *Pesach* that was slaughtered on Shabbos should be burned on Shabbos if at all possible, rather than on Motzaei Shabbos.[2] Thus, the burning of the fats and limbs at night was a *bedi'eved,* after the fact, allowance.

Yaakov, says the Midrash, was the בְּחִיר שֶׁבָּאָבוֹת, *the most esteemed among the Patriarchs.*[3] Zohar extolls the uniqueness of *Maariv* and how it brings about *tikkunim* (spiritual rectifications) that the world had not previously known.[4] It seems strange that this great tefillah, established by the greatest of the *Avos,* should correspond to something that, rather than being an integral part of the daily *avodah,* was a *bedi'eved.*

The Gemara rules that, as opposed to *Shacharis* and *Minchah* which are obligatory, *Maariv* is a *reshus*, a voluntary tefillah. (Nevertheless, the Jewish people have since accepted *Maariv* as a *chovah*, obligation, and it must be recited.)[5] This, too, demands an explanation. Why should Yaakov's tefillah be any less important than that of Avraham or Yitzchak?

The Time of Yaakov's Prayer

There is something else about *Maariv* that demands explanation. The Torah says regarding Yaakov's journey from his father's house to the house of Lavan: *"And Yaakov departed from Be'er Sheva and went to Charan. He encountered the place ..."*[6] The Gemara comments:

> *Upon reaching Charan, Yaakov said to himself: "How could I have passed the place where my fathers prayed and not have prayed there myself?" As soon as he set his mind*

2. *Pesachim* 68b.

3. *Bereishis Rabbah* 76:1.

4. *Zohar*, vol. I, 72b.

5. *Rambam, Hilchos Tefillah* 1:6; see also *Mishnah Berurah* 237:1.

6. *Bereishis* 28:10-11.

to return [to that spot], the ground miraculously contracted and immediately "he encountered the place."

When he finished praying, he sought to return to Charan, but HaKadosh Baruch Hu declared, "This righteous man has come to My lodging place. Shall he depart without spending a night?" Immediately the sun [miraculously] set [early, forcing Yaakov to spend the night there].[7]

Yaakov's tefillah at that time was the *Maariv* prayer that he established. As *Tosafos* notes,[8] Yaakov prayed during daylight hours. Only after he completed his prayer did Hashem cause the sun to set early so that he would be forced to spend the night there. Yet, says *Tosafos*, according to the majority opinion, *Maariv* should not be recited until the onset of night.[9]

Interestingly, *Shulchan Aruch* rules that on Friday evening, it is proper to recite *Maariv* earlier than on a weekday, any time after *plag haminchah*, which is 1-1/4 hours before nightfall.[10] *Magen Avraham* explains that, as mentioned above, *Maariv* corresponds to the limbs and fats of that day's sacrifices that were burned at night. On Shabbos, it was forbidden to burn sacrifices that had been offered on Friday. Therefore, it is proper on Friday evening to recite *Maariv* during daylight, while it was still permissible to burn the limbs and fats.

Furthermore, Zohar states that although on weekdays *Maariv* is not obligatory, the *Maariv* of Shabbos is obligatory.[11]

It is obvious that there is more to *Maariv* than meets the eye.

The House of the God of Yaakov

The Gemara states:[12]

---

7. *Chullin* 91b.

8. *Berachos* 26b ד"ה יעקב תקן תפילת ערבית.

9. I.e. when three medium stars are visible.

10. *Orach Chaim* 267:2.

11. See also *Shaarei Teshuvah* to *Shulchan Aruch* 268:2.

12. *Pesachim* 88a.

R' Elazar said: What is the meaning of that which is written, "Many nations will come and say, 'Come, let us go up to the mountain of Hashem, to the House of the God of Yaakov'"?[13] *Is the Beis HaMikdash only the House of the God of Yaakov and not the God of Avraham and Yitzchak?*

Rather, the verse teaches that the site of the Beis HaMikdash is not like the description found in connection with Avraham, concerning whom that place is referred to as "mountain," as it is written, "On the mountain Hashem is seen."[14] *And it is not like the description found in connection with Yitzchak, concerning whom that place is referred to as a "field," as it is written, "Yitzchak went out to pray in the field."*[15] *Rather, it is like the description found in connection with Yaakov, who referred to the site of the Beis HaMikdash as a "house," as it is written, "He named that place the House of God."*[16]

Maharsha explains that each of the three descriptions cited by the Midrash corresponds to a different Beis HaMikdash. Avraham's "mountain" corresponds to the First Beis HaMikdash, which the *Shechinah* watched over like a guard strategically placed atop a mountain. However, this protection was not permanent, as eventually this Beis HaMikdash was destroyed. Thus did Yirmiyahu HaNavi say, "For *Mount* Tzion which lies desolate."[17]

The "field" of Yitzchak represents the Second Beis HaMikdash, in which the *Shechinah* was manifest to a lesser degree.[18] This Beis HaMikdash was also destroyed, as is alluded to in the verse "Zion will be plowed over like a *field.*"[19]

---

13. *Yeshayahu* 2:3.

14. *Bereishis* 22:14.

15. Ibid. 24:63. Yitzchak was not praying at the site of the Beis HaMikdash. However, he was directing his heart toward that site (as required by Halachah). In so doing, he perceived the site as a field *(Ben Yehoyada).*

16. Ibid. 28:19.

17. *Eichah* 5:18.

18. Several miracles that occurred regularly in the First Beis HaMikdash did not occur in the second.

19. *Yirmiyahu* 26:18.

The "house" of Yaakov symbolizes the Third Beis HaMikdash, may it be built speedily and in our time. Hashem caused the sun to set early, forcing Yaakov to spend the night there, as one does in a house, for it will be permanent, never to be destroyed.

The preface to *Sefer Yam shel Shlomo*[20] states that every Torah scholar propounds *chiddushei Torah* (original Torah insights) in accordance with the uniqueness of his *neshamah* and its Heavenly roots. Similarly, we may suggest that the tefillos that the *Avos* established were rooted in their respective perception of the place where the *Shechinah* would dwell. Avraham's *Tefillas Shacharis* corresponds to the First Beis HaMikdash, Yitzchak's *Tefillas Minchah* corresponds to the Second Beis HaMikdash, and Yaakov's *Tefillas Maariv* corresponds to the Third Beis HaMikdash.

The Third Beis HaMikdash will descend from Heaven complete, and the level to which the *Shechinah* will manifest itself there will surpass even that of the First Beis HaMikdash. In our present state, we are far removed from any understanding of or connection to the spiritual aura that will shine forth from that holy edifice. And just as we are removed from that aura, so are we removed from the full essence of the tefillah that corresponds to that House of Hashem. Therefore, our Sages rule that until Mashiach's arrival, the tefillah of *Maariv* should remain voluntary. They could not obligate us in something from which our souls are presently distant.

Light vs. Darkness

In *Tanach,* as well as in the writings of our Sages, clarity is represented by day, and obscurity is symbolized by night.[21] Because we are able to fully connect to the essence of *Shacharis* and *Minchah*, we recite them during daylight hours. Regarding *Maariv,*

20. By the *Maharshal,* R' Shlomo Luria.

21. For example, the Torah states, *"If the sun shone upon him"* (*Shemos* 22:2), which our Sages interpret to mean,"If it is as clear to you as day."

however, our comprehension is still obscured, and therefore we recite it at night.

Yaakov Avinu *did* relate to *Maariv's* full meaning and depth. After all, he referred to the Third Beis HaMikdash with the term *bayis* (house), he spent the night on that holy spot, and there he dreamt a prophetic vision. At that time, Hashem showed Yaakov the future Beis HaMikdash in all its splendor. Yaakov, the one who established *Tefillas Maariv,* surely comprehended its full essence. Therefore, he recited this tefillah when it was still day.

As we have already mentioned, *Shacharis* and *Minchah* correspond to the *Korban Tamid* that was brought twice daily, morning and afternoon. More specifically, they correspond to the *zerikas hadam* (application of blood) of these offerings upon the *Mizbei'ach* (Altar), the primary service of any offering. *Zerikas hadam* served as an atonement for the sins of the offering's owner, which in the case of the *Korban Tamid* was the entire Jewish people.

Shacharis and *Minchah* also correspond, as we have said, to the First and Second Batei Mikdash, respectively, when the *yetzer hara* induced man to sin and there was a need for atonement. Thus, *Shacharis* and *Minchah* effect atonement for the individual and for the Jewish people as a whole.

Maariv, on the other hand, corresponds to the burning of the fats and limbs which in contrast to the blood is not essential for the offering to be valid and thus for the owner to gain atonement. Rather, their burning effects a רֵיחַ נִיחוֹחַ, *satisfying aroma*, for Hashem. As our Sages put it, Hashem is pleased by their burning, for "I have spoken and My will has been done."[22] And *Maariv,* as we have said, corresponds to the Third Beis HaMikdash, when the *yetzer hara* and its allures will cease to exist. As the Gemara states:

> *"And I will distance the 'hidden one' from you"*[23] — This refers to the *yetzer hara* which is hidden and lurks in man's heart. *"And I will banish him to an arid and*

22. *Rashi* to *Vayikra* 1:9.

23. *Yoel* 2:20.

> *desolate land"* — to a place where there are no people for him to incite. *"His face to the first sea"* — for he [the *yetzer hara*] laid his eyes on the First Beis HaMikdash and destroyed it, and killed the *talmidei chachamim* who were in it. *"And his end to the last sea"* — for he laid his eyes on the Second Beis HaMikdash and destroyed it.[24]

By contrast, at the time of the Final Redemption, as the Gemara there states, Hashem will destroy the *yetzer hara* and we will no longer sin. At that time the blood of offerings will not be needed as an atonement. Rather, it will serve the same purpose as the fats and limbs served — as a source of satisfaction, as it were, to Hashem.

The *nachas ruach* (pleasure) that the offerings of earlier times brought Hashem was somewhat tainted by the sins that required atonement. This was symbolized by the fact that the limbs and fats could be burned at night, a time of darkness and confusion. But in the future, when we will bring our *korbanos* in utter purity and atonement will not be necessary, the *nachas ruach* that Hashem will derive from the *korbanos* will be complete. It is possible that at that time the limbs and fats will be offered only by day, a time of light and clarity. It is also possible that at that time, we will recite *Tefillas Maariv* specifically before dark, as Yaakov Avinu did.[25]

Shabbos — A Semblance of the World to Come

Even today, in the darkness of this difficult *galus*, there is a time each week when our souls are transported to a place in the realm of the future, a day that is *me'ein Olam Haba*, a semblance of the World to Come, a day of intense spiritual light. Shabbos, in the words of Midrash, is a day "in which darkness does not serve. Regarding each day of Creation it is written, *'And it was evening*

24. *Succah* 52a.

25. In doing so we will be following the opinion of R' Yehudah, who says that *Maariv* may be recited after *plag haminchah* (1-1/4 hours before dark; see *Berachos* 26a).

and it was morning'; however, regarding Shabbos it does not say *'And it was evening.'* "[26]

This is why on Shabbos we do not wish one another "Good night," but rather, "Good Shabbos."

Shabbos is a day when our souls feel a connection to the Beis HaMikdash of the future. In the special paragraph that we add to *Bircas HaMazon* on Shabbos we pray, *"And show us, Hashem, our God, the consolation of Zion, Your city, and the rebuilding of Jerusalem, City of Your holiness ...."* In the Shabbos *zemiros* we sing: *"Those who love Hashem, who long for the building of His holy temple, on the Shabbos day rejoice and be glad ...."*

Yaakov Avinu has a special connection to Shabbos. Another Midrash states:

> *R' Yochanan said in the name of R' Yose ben Chalafta: Avraham, regarding whom the observance of Shabbos is not mentioned [in the Torah], inherited the world [i.e. Eretz Yisrael] with distinct borders, as it is written, "Arise, walk about the land through its length and breadth, for to you I will give it."*[27] *But regarding Yaakov observance of Shabbos* is *mentioned, as it is written, "and he encamped before the city,"*[28] *meaning that he entered [the area on Friday afternoon] as the sunlight was becoming dim and established [Shabbos] boundaries for himself when it was still day.*[29] *Therefore, he inherited this world without limit, as it is written,*[30] *"Your offspring shall be like the dust of the earth and you shall burst forth westward, eastward, northward, and southward."*[31]

---

26. *Midrash Shochar Tov* to *Tehillim* ch. 19.

27. *Bereishis* 13:17.

28. Ibid. 33:18.

29. He placed an *eruv techumin* which allowed him and his people to walk 2,000 *amos* on Shabbos from that spot in every direction (*Maharzu*; see *Ramban* ad loc.).

30. *Bereishis* 28:14.

31. *Bereishis Rabbah* 11:7.

Thus does the Gemara state:[32]

> *Whoever delights in the Shabbos is granted a boundless heritage, as it says, "... then you shall be granted pleasure with Hashem, and I shall mount you astride the heights of the world; and I will provide you the heritage of your forefather Yaakov,"*[33] *... like the heritage of Yaakov, regarding whom it is written, "And you shall burst forth westward ...."*

When a Jew experiences Shabbos the way in which it is intended, he merits a taste of what Yaakov experienced as his *neshamah* soared in prayer at the site of the House of Hashem. Therefore, *Shulchan Aruch* states that it is proper to daven *Maariv* earlier than usual on Friday evening. As we have mentioned, *Magen Avraham* explains that the limbs and fats of the offerings, to which *Maariv* corresponds, had to be burned before the onset of Shabbos, while it was still day. In light of what we have said, there is additional reason to recite the *Maariv* of Shabbos during daylight hours. The light of Shabbos is borrowed from a future time, a time of spiritual bliss and utter clarity. Therefore, the *Maariv* of Shabbos may be recited during daylight hours, just as Yaakov prayed when it was still light.

Above, we quoted Zohar which states that although *Maariv* is a *reshus* (voluntary prayer — see above), on Friday evening it is a *chovah* (obligatory prayer). As we have explained, in the time of Mashiach we will recite *Maariv* as Yaakov did, with a proper perception and clarity, and therefore, it will be a *chovah* just as *Shacharis* and *Minchah* are now. For this very reason even today, in the darkness of *galus*, the light of Shabbos allows us to daven *Maariv* on a level that makes it a *chovah*.

32. *Shabbos* 118a-b.

33. *Yeshayahu* 58:14.

Sanctifying Through Prayer

In citing the opinion of Zohar regarding *Maariv* of Friday evening, the Viener Rav, R' Yonason Steif,[34] offers an explanation: On Shabbos eve, there is a mitzvah of *Kiddush* which can be fulfilled with the recitation of the *Maariv Shemoneh Esrei* (in which the verses of *"Vayechulu"* are said). *Maariv* is thereby obligatory so that through it the mitzvah of *Kiddush* is fulfilled.

At first glance, this seems difficult. Why must we fulfill our *Kiddush* obligation through *Maariv* when, in any case, there is a Rabbinic obligation to recite *Kiddush* over a cup of wine?[35]

Our understanding of the uniqueness of the Shabbos *Maariv* resolves this. This is a tefillah of the future, of the *Yom Shekulo Shabbos* (the Day of Everlasting Shabbos). When a Jew sanctifies the day of Shabbos by reciting the *Maariv* of Shabbos, it awakens a desire in Heaven to hasten the Redemption, when the Third Beis HaMikdash, the House of Yaakov, will descend from Above. The *Maariv* of Shabbos is the choicest of tefillos, established by the בְּחִיר שֶׁבְּאָבוֹת, *the most esteemed among the Patriarchs.*

And every time we daven *Maariv,* even on a weekday, we are privileged to utter a prayer whose essence we cannot perceive, for it belongs to the glorious days of Mashiach, may he come speedily and in our time.

34. In his *Sefer Chadashim Gam Yeshanim.*

35. See *Magen Avraham* to *Orach Chaim* 271:1.

PART THREE

Gateways *to* Heaven

Tefillah and Eretz Yisrael's Holy Cities

CHAPTER TWENTY-SIX

Facing Jerusalem, With Humility

"This day Hashem, your God, commands you to perform these decrees and the statutes"[1] *— This is the intent of "Come! Let us prostrate ourselves and bow, let us kneel before God, our Maker."*[2] *Now, is not "prostrating" included in "bowing" and "bowing" included in "prostrating"? What are "prostrate . . . bow . . . kneel" coming to teach us?*

Moshe saw through Divine Inspiration that the Beis HaMikdash was destined to be destroyed and the [mitzvah of] bikkurim would cease. So he arose and established for the Jewish people that they should pray three times each day.

1. *Devarim* 26:16.
2. *Tehillim* 95:6.

(This is alluded to in the three words "prostrate . . . bow . . . kneel.")[3]

This Midrash is quite puzzling. The Torah commands that the *bikkurim,* first ripened fruits of the seven species with which Eretz Yisrael has been especially blessed, be brought to the Beis HaMikdash and given to the Kohen, as the farmer's expression of gratitude for all the good that Hashem has bestowed upon him.[4] The Midrash seems to be informing us that the three daily tefillos are a substitute for this mitzvah.

However, this seems to be contradicted by the Gemara which teaches that the three daily tefillos were enacted by Avraham, Yitzchak, and Yaakov respectively, and that they correspond to the daily communal sacrifices brought upon the *Mizbei'ach*!

In fact, there is no contradiction at all.

A Land of Torah

Before we resolve the above, another question must be asked. One of the verses regarding *bikkurim* states: וְשָׂמַחְתָּ בְּכָל הַטּוֹב, *You shall rejoice with all the goodness [that Hashem, your God, has given to you].*[5] *Ohr HaChaim* sees the word הַטּוֹב as alluding to the teaching אֵין טוֹב אֶלָּא תּוֹרָה, *Only Torah is truly good.*[6]

Why is this alluded to in the mitzvah of *bikkurim* as opposed to any other mitzvah?

In *Sefer Yehoshua,* as the Jews went about their conquest of Eretz Yisrael, Calev ben Yefuneh found himself unable to vanquish the city of Kiryas Sefer. He declared that whoever would be able to conquer it would earn the right to marry his daughter, Achsah. The city was then conquered by Calev's half-brother, Asniel ben Kenaz.[7]

---

3. *Midrash Tanchuma, Parashas Ki Savo.*
4. See *Devarim* ch. 26.
5. *Devarim* 26:11.
6. *Avos* 6:3.
7. *Yehoshua* 15:15-17.

The Gemara[8] states that "Kiryas Sefer" is actually a reference to the 300 laws that were forgotten during the mourning period following Moshe Rabbeinu's passing. Calev was saying that whoever would restore these forgotten laws through his deductive reasoning [בְּפִלְפּוּלוֹ] could marry his daughter. Asniel accomplished this.

The obvious question is, how does this fit with the plain meaning of the verse, which says that a city needed to be conquered?

Sefer Arvei Nachal explains that the plain meaning and the Gemara's explanation complement each other. The holy land of Eretz Yisrael is comparable to a geographical *sefer Torah*. Each part of the land corresponds to a specific mitzvah. The 300 forgotten laws corresponded to the city of Kiryas Sefer. It was precisely because these laws had been forgotten that it became impossible to conquer that city. Calev knew that whoever would restore those laws through his Torah reasoning would be able to conquer the city.

In a similar vein, the name יִשְׂרָאֵל forms the initial letters of יֵשׁ שִׁשִּׁים רִבּוֹא אוֹתִיּוֹת לַתּוֹרָה, *There are 600,000 letters in the Torah.*[9] All Jewish souls are encompassed within the 600,000 souls that left Egypt, and each one of those souls was rooted in a specific letter in the Torah. And that letter corresponds to the portion in Eretz Yisrael which that soul was allotted.

Regarding the apportioning of the Land, the Torah states: אִישׁ לְפִי פְקֻדָיו יֻתַּן נַחֲלָתוֹ, which in its plain meaning is translated as *Each man according to his count shall his inheritance be given.*[10] The word פְקֻדָיו can also be interpreted as relating to פִּקּוּדֵי ה' יְשָׁרִים מְשַׂמְּחֵי לֵב, *The commandments of Hashem are upright, gladdening the heart,*[11] in which case the verse would mean, *Each man according to his portion of Torah shall his inheritance be given.* The word is also related to תַּפְקִיד, *mission*. A prime mission of a Jew on this world is

8. *Temurah* 16a.

9. *Zohar Chadash* to *Shir HaShirim.*

10. *Bamidbar* 26:54.

11. *Tehillim* 19:9.

to study and reveal his portion of Torah, and for that he requires his specific portion in the Land.

The Torah enjoins us, *You shall not move back the boundary of your fellow which the early ones marked out, in your inheritance that you shall inherit ...*[12] Why is there a specific prohibition against pushing back someone's boundary in Eretz Yisrael? Is this not simply a variation on the general prohibition against stealing? The answer is that to rob someone of his Divinely allotted portion of Eretz Yisrael is to deny him his portion in Torah.

The Torah states: **אָרוּר מַסִּיג גְּבוּל רֵעֵהוּ**, *Cursed is one who moves back the boundary of his fellow.*[13] When rearranged, the initial letters of these words spell גְּמָרָא, the Oral Law of which every Jew is granted his portion to acquire as a *kinyan nefesh,* an acquisition of the soul. The end letters spell גּוֹרָל, *lottery.* Eretz Yisrael was divided through a Divinely controlled lottery.[14] In any lottery, the results are beyond human understanding. We cannot begin to fathom why this person wins and that one loses. Similarly, why each *neshamah* is rooted in its specific portion of the Land is beyond human comprehension.

This is why we are required to mention the gift of Torah in the second blessing of *Bircas HaMazon,* the blessing in which we thank Hashem for the gift of Eretz Yisrael.

When a Jew brings his *bikkurim,* the precious products of his portion in Eretz Yisrael, he is offering to Hashem the fruits of his Torah learning in a literal sense.

The Need for Humility

Our Sages make clear that to make Torah a *kinyan nefesh* (i.e. bound up with one's soul), one must be truly humble. Torah is likened to water, which naturally flows from a higher elevation to

12. *Devarim* 19:14.
13. Ibid. 27:17.
14. *Bamidbar* 26:55.

a lower place.[15] Torah will attach itself to someone who recognizes that his inborn talents are nothing more than a Divine gift to be used in Hashem's service, and that without Hashem's constant help, success in learning or in any other endeavor is impossible.

The same is true of acquiring the gift of Eretz Yisrael. A person can live in Eretz Yisrael and not feel an intense love for the Land and the spiritual uplift that it should bring. Such feeling is possible only with humility, as Dovid HaMelech says, *"But the humble shall inherit the land."*[16] Without humility, one can live in Eretz Yisrael for years and not feel a spiritual connection to it.

When Yehoshua and Calev refuted the evil report of the Spies, they said, "טוֹבָה הָאָרֶץ מְאֹד מְאֹד, *the land is very, very good.*"[17] *Tzaddikim* have interpreted: the Land is good for those who fulfill the teaching מְאֹד מְאֹד הֱוֵי שְׁפַל רוּחַ, *Be exceedingly humble.*[18]

The mitzvah of *bikkurim* represents humility and self-negation before Hashem. The farmer brings the beautiful, first-ripened fruits for which he toiled long and hard to the Beis HaMikdash, prostrates himself before Hashem, and acknowledges that all that Hashem has granted the Jewish people, from the days of our forefathers, is only thanks to Him. He expresses his gratitude and, as *Rashi* says, acknowledges that he is not כְּפוּי טוֹב, *unappreciative.*[19]

Parashas Ki Savo opens with the mitzvah of *bikkurim*. The previous *parashah, Ki Seitzei,* concludes with the mitzvah to eradicate the nation of Amalek. These mitzvos are juxtaposed because Amalek represents the height of arrogance and lack of appreciation. The word עֲמָלֵק has the same *gematria* as רָם (*high and mighty* — 240).

In the beautiful liturgical piece that we recite on the night of Purim following the reading of the Megillah, we say of Amalek's descendant, Haman, "He did not remember Shaul's compassion,

15. *Taanis* 7a.

16. *Tehillim* 37:11.

17. *Bamidbar* 14:7.

18. *Avos* 4:4.

19. *Rashi* to *Devarim* 26:3.

that through his pity on Agag the foe was born."[20] In plotting the annihilation of the Jewish people, Haman chose to forget that he was born only through the mercy of Mordechai's ancestor, King Shaul, who allowed Haman's ancestor King Agag of Amalek to live long enough to leave behind offspring.

Amalek is called רֵאשִׁית, the first among the gentile nations, because it viewed itself as such.[21] *Bikkurim* is also called רֵאשִׁית, first fruits; the farmer presents his רֵאשִׁית before the רֵאשִׁית הַכֹּל, First and Only God, and humbly declares, "Everything is Yours."

When the farmer presents the Land's seven species of blessed fruits to Hashem, he is humbly declaring that the gift of Eretz Yisrael, and the gift of Torah which is so intimately connected to the Land's holy soil, are both his only by the grace of the One Above.

With Our Hearts Towards Jerusalem

Halachah teaches that when one davens, he should concentrate his thoughts towards Eretz Yisrael, as it is written: "... *and they will pray to You by way of their land* ..."[22] He should also concentrate his thoughts towards Jerusalem and the Beis HaMikdash and picture himself as if he were standing in the *Kodesh HaKodashim*, the holiest place on earth, in front of the *Aron* where Hashem's Presence rested.[23]

The Baal Shem Tov taught[24] that where a person's thoughts are is where, in essence, he is at that given moment.[25] It is the same

20. See *Shumuel I* 15:9.

21. There is a tradition from the Vilna Gaon that the German nation descends from Amalek. In the years leading to the Second World War, the Germans declared themselves "the Master Race."

22. *Melachim I* 8:48.

23. *Mishnah Berurah* 94:7.

24. Cited in *Toldos Yaakov Yosef, Parashas Chayei Sarah.*

25. The Avnei Nezer brings halachic support for this from a law regarding *eruvei techumim*: If one is walking on the road as Shabbos approaches and spots a tree in the distance, he can declare the area beneath that tree his "place of residence" for that Shabbos

when we stand before Hashem reciting *Shemoneh Esrei.* By directing our hearts towards the *Kodesh HaKodashim* it is as if we are standing in that holiest of places at that moment. This is another incredible aspect of tefillah.

That we direct our hearts towards Jerusalem and the *Kodesh HaKodashim* is crucial for our tefillah to gain acceptance on High. For as Yaakov Avinu said upon awakening from his dream at the site of the future Beis HaMikdash, *"This is none other than the abode of God and this is the gateway to the Heavens!"*[26] As *Rashi* explains, the site upon which the Beis HaMikdash would later be built is the place from where all prayers ascend to the Heavens. When we direct our hearts to Jerusalem, it is as if we are there and our tefillos can ascend Heavenward.

However, as we have seen, one cannot merit the gift of Eretz Yisrael if he lacks the *middah* of *anavah* (humility). Only with true humility can we merit that when we focus on Jerusalem and the *Kodesh HaKodashim* it is as if we truly are there.

Furthermore, the Baal Shem Tov taught that when a person is unworthy of entering the Heavenly gates of prayer, he will find himself confounded by all sorts of foreign thoughts so that his tefillos will be devoid of any spiritual power.[27] This is because passionate, heartfelt tefillah is a *Gan Eden* on this world. The Torah tells us that when Adam was banished from *Gan Eden*, sword-bearing angels stood guard at its entrance. When someone is unworthy of entering the *Gan Eden* that is tefillah, foreign thoughts ensure that though his lips utter the words, he will not experience the spiritual pleasure and uplift that proper tefillah brings.

---

although he would not reach the spot until Shabbos actually began (*Mishnah Eruvin* 4:7). This will allow him to walk 2,000 *amos* in all directions from the tree. We see that a person's thought that he wishes to be at a certain spot gives him the halachic status of actually being at that spot at that given moment.

26. *Bereishis* 28:17.

27. Of course, there are times when foreign thoughts are the person's own doing, for he makes little or no effort to put aside whatever pressing matter is on his mind.

This is what happens to someone who lacks humility. On the other hand, when someone *does* possess humility, when he experiences true *bitul hayeish*, self-negation before Hashem, the angels of destruction pay no attention to him. Since he views himself as nothing more than a minuscule being who is wholly dependent on his Creator, they view him the same way. In this way, he is able to daven with a clear mind and his tefillos ascend to their intended destination.

Encompassing Souls

Our forefathers, Avraham, Yitzchak, and Yaakov, encompassed within themselves all the *neshamos* of future generations. In this way, they established the tefillos of *Shacharis, Minchah,* and *Maariv* and bequeathed to us their awesome power of tefillah.

Moshe Rabbeinu also encompassed within himself all of *Klal Yisrael.* As *Rashi* states, "Moshe is equivalent to the entire Jewish people."[28] Moshe represents the epitome of humility for, as our Sages teach,[29] his humility was even greater than that of Avraham who said, *"I am dust and ashes."*[30] Moshe and Aharon said, *"And what are we?"*[31] And the Torah bears witness, *"Now the man Moshe was exceedingly humble, more than any man on the face of the earth."*[32]

Moshe composed the 11 chapters of *Tehillim* beginning with *Tefillah L'Moshe*[33] and concluding with *Mizmor L'Sodah*, a humble expression of thanksgiving to Hashem. In chapter 95, Moshe says: בֹּאוּ נִשְׁתַּחֲוֶה וְנִכְרָעָה נִבְרְכָה לִפְנֵי ה' עֹשֵׂנוּ, *Come! — let us prostrate ourselves and bow, let us kneel before Hashem, our Maker.*

28. *Rashi* to *Shemos* 18:1 citing *Mechilta.*
29. *Chullin* 89a.
30. *Bereishis* 14:24.
31. *Chullin* 89a.
32. *Bamidbar* 12:3.
33. *Tehillim* ch. 90.

The words נִשְׁתַּחֲוֶה וְנִכְרָעָה נִבְרְכָה (*let us prostrate ourselves and bow, let us kneel*) have the same *gematria* as that which the Torah says regarding *bikkurim*: וְהִשְׁתַּחֲוִיתָ לִפְנֵי ה' אֱלֹהֶיךָ (*and you shall prostrate yourself before Hashem, your God* — 1,397).

Moshe saw that the Beis HaMikdash would be destroyed and *bikkurim*, with its inherent message of humility, would cease. He therefore instituted that we bow humbly during tefillah. This is not a mere added quality in prayer; it was absolutely essential in order that our tefillos be able to reach Eretz Yisrael and ascend from the "gateway to the Heavens."

It was fitting that Moshe, who personified humility, should be the one to institute this. He taught us that through humility, we can direct our thoughts during tefillah toward Eretz Yisrael and the site of the *Kodash HaKodashim* — and in this way, it is as if we are there.

This is the meaning of "Moshe established for the Jewish people that they should pray three times each day." Our tefillos can only be effective and ascend Heavenward by way of Eretz Yisrael. Moshe's enactment that we should *"prostrate ... bow ...* and *kneel"* when we daven ensures that our tefillos would achieve their goal even when physically we are not in our precious Land.

CHAPTER TWENTY-SEVEN

Jerusalem and Chevron

My Beloved, recall for my merit the shekels that [Avraham gave] Ephron that the Patriarch weighed for the Cave of Machpeilah; consider the shekels that [Dovid] paid the Yevusi [to purchase the Temple Mount], whose sacrifices still the Heavenly wrath (from the Yotzros of Parashas Shekalim).

Our holy forefathers, Avraham, Yitzchak, and Yaakov, encompassed within their lofty *neshamos* the souls of all their future offspring. When they left this world, the roles were reversed; in every generation for all time, every Jew has within his or her soul a spark of Avraham, Yitzchak, and Yaakov.

Tikkunei Zohar states that every person is an *olam katan,* a miniature world.[1] Whatever is found in this world is found, in a sense, within everyone's soul. Within the heart of every Jew is a Me'aras HaMachpeilah (the Tomb of the Patriarchs), and that is where the sanctity and essence of the *Avos* is to be found.

The literal meaning of Me'aras HaMachpeilah is "the double cave." The *Avos* are interred below ground level in a cave that is hidden below or behind another cave.[2] Similarly, the essence of the *Avos* is deep within the recesses of one's heart, so deep that it cannot be perceived. But it is there.

Avraham, Yitzchak, and Yaakov established the three daily tefillos.[3] When we daven, the *Avos* daven with us. It is for this reason that our Sages made mention of the *Avos* in the opening blessing of *Shemoneh Esrei*; in this way, we connect to them and access their spark that is hidden within the Machpeilah of our soul.

Gateway to Gan Eden

The Midrash and later writings extol the uniqueness of the Me'aras HaMachpeilah. The entrance to Gan Eden is found there, and it is there where the *Avos* continue to pray to this very day. As the Gemara relates in the name of Eliyahu HaNavi, if Avraham, Yitzchak, and Yaakov would be permitted to pray at the same time, the power of their simultaneous prayers would bring Mashiach — before the world was ready for his arrival.[4]

---

1. *Tikkunei Zohar* 130b.
2. See *Eruvin* 53a.
3. *Berachos* 26b.
4. *Bava Metzia* 85b. Zohar states that if mankind would know of the esteem in which Yaakov Avinu is held in Heaven, they would kiss the earth within a 12-*mil* radius around the Cave of Machpeilah.

Ramban writes that upon his arrival in Eretz Yisrael, he made his way to Jerusalem and prayed at the Kosel HaMaaravi. From there he journeyed to the Cave of Machpeilah "to kiss the burial place of my forefathers."

Yalkut Reuveni[5] states that all tefillos pass through the Me'aras HaMachpeilah before ascending to Heaven. This would seem to contradict the teaching of our Sages, which is accepted as halachah, that the site of the Beis HaMikdash is the "gateway to Heaven" from where our tefillos ascend, and it is toward that direction that we turn when we pray *Shemoneh Esrei*.[6]

Zohar[7] writes that the cave is called Machpeilah ("Double") because it is a "double" of Jerusalem. If this is so, and if our tefillos *do* in fact ascend from there as well, then it would seem proper to face Chevron as we pray. Why must we face Jerusalem?

Similar but Different

Jerusalem and Chevron, the Har HaBayis (Temple Mount) and the Me'aras HaMachpeilah, have much in common, and at the same time are opposites. The Har HaBayis is the place on this earth of *giluy Shechinah*, the revelation of Hashem's Presence. There, during the First Beis HaMikdash era, there were ten constant miracles. What made this precious spot a place fit for the *Shechinah*? It was the tefillos of Avraham, Yitzchak, and Yaakov, who all prayed at the future site of the Beis HaMikdash.[8] During the Three Festivals, the Jewish people would ascend the Temple Mount to bask in the *Shechinah's* Presence and be influenced by the spiritual qualities of the Patriarch associated with that particular Yom Tov.[9]

The Me'aras HaMachpeilah, by contrast, is not a place of revelation. To the contrary, the spiritual radiance of the *Avos* is hidden there, deep within its subterranean burial place. The Beis HaMikdash, perched high atop a mountain, was the place where

5. Citing *Sefer Megaleh Amukos*.

6. See *Bereishis* 28:17 with *Rashi*.

7. Vol. I, 121b.

8. See *Targum Onkelos* to *Bereishis* 22:14; *Midrash Aggadah* to *Bereishis* 24:63, and *Rashi* to *Bereishis* 26:11.

9. Pesach is associated with Avraham, Shavuos with Yitzchak, and Succos with Yaakov.

the *Avos* prayed in their lifetime. The Me'aras HaMachpeilah is the place where they were laid to rest when their mission on this world was completed.

It would seem, then, that Jerusalem is a place where we experience contact with the Divine, while the sanctity of Chevron, though it surely exists, is removed from us. In truth, this is not so.

To our misfortune the Beis HaMikdash was destroyed, and when that happened, the *Shechinah* departed from that sacred spot, as it is written, *"Gone from the daughter of Zion is all her splendor."*[10]

The Me'aras HaMachpeilah, however, is impervious to destruction. *Churban* is possible only where there once was revelation, Divine service, open miracles. When these cease to be, *churban* has taken place. The Me'aras HaMachpeilah, by contrast, *always was* a place of *hester* (concealment). The burial place of the *Avos* represents our connection to Hashem even in *galus*, in a time of *hester panim* (Divine concealment).

Yes, the *Shechinah* departed from the Har HaBayis, but it did not abandon us. It accompanied us throughout our exile, wherever Providence sent us. Nevuchadnezzar and Titus thought they could sever our connection with our Father in Heaven. In fact, they could only destroy the *place* where that connection was revealed; but the connection is eternal. The Me'aras HaMachpeilah represents our connection to Hashem even in a time of *churban*.

חוּרְבָּן has the same letters as חֶבְרוֹן, and חֶבְרוֹן represents חִבּוּר, *connection*. Even when the *Shechinah* has departed from its sacred House, Chevron comes and proclaims that we are still Hashem's beloved, chosen nation.

The exact burial spot of the *Avos* is hidden from us; even when we daven at the Me'aras HaMachpeilah, we do not know exactly where the entrance to the cave of their interment lies — but

10. *Eichah* 1:6. A degree of its Presence remains eternally at the Kosel HaMaaravi, the Western Wall of the Temple Mount.

we know it is there, somewhere. And there in that cave, their radiance continues to glow, though we cannot see it. While our enemies rejoiced and celebrated their success in the *Churban* they brought about, Chevron bore witness that a time will yet come when God's Presence will once again be revealed to all. Then the nations of the world will realize that throughout this long and difficult *galus*, Hashem was with us every step of the way.

Cave Within a Cave

In *Parashas Vayeilech,* the Torah speaks about the difficulties that will befall the Jewish people at the End of Days, before Mashiach's arrival. Hashem informs us, וְאָנֹכִי הַסְתֵּר אַסְתִּיר פָּנַי בַּיּוֹם הַהוּא, *But I will utterly conceal My face on that day.*[11] Our Sages interpret the double usage הַסְתֵּר אַסְתִּיר to mean הֶסְתֵּר בְּתוֹךְ הֶסְתֵּר, *a concealment within a concealment.* In the period of *Ikvesa D'Meshicha* events will be so confusing, so difficult to comprehend, that only a true *maamin* (believer) will be able to perceive that indeed, it is Hashem Who is orchestrating all that is happening. For Hashem will conceal Himself beneath layers and layers of apparent cause and effect.[12]

This too is what the Me'aras HaMachpeilah, with its double cave, symbolizes. Though Hashem may utterly conceal His Presence from us, we remain bound to Him through our *Avos* and through the power of tefillah that they bequeathed to us.

This is what Zohar means in referring to Chevron as Jerusalem's "double." These two holy places complement one another. Chevron teaches us that even when the physical Beis HaMikdash lies in ruins, our attachment to the *Shechinah* still remains. As the Maggid of Kozhnitz writes, only the material Beis HaMikdash of stone was destroyed. Its spiritual counterpart remains intact and our connection to it remains intact as well.

---

11. *Devarim* 31:18.

12. Certainly, we are living in such a time.

The place that is called Chevron represents the fact that our relationship with Hashem is not dependent on any given place. Jerusalem, on the other hand, is the place where the *Shechinah* reveals itself on this earth. This is why throughout *Chumash*, Jerusalem is referred to as הַמָּקוֹם, *the place*. It is the place of revelation. This is why we face Jerusalem when we daven, and not Chevron, the place of concealment.

The Me'aras HaMachpeilah and the Har HaBayis are two most precious possessions of the Jewish nation, purchased with love by Avraham Avinu and Dovid HaMelech, respectively. It is not coincidental that the account of *Akeidas Yitzchak*, which took place on the future site of the Beis HaMikdash, and Avraham's purchase of the Me'aras HaMachpeilah are juxtaposed in the Torah. Both are places of intense connection between the Jewish people and their Father in Heaven.[13]

Cradle of *Emunah*

When Calev ben Yefuneh feared that he might be drawn after the evil plans of his fellow *Meraglim* (Spies), he went to the Me'aras HaMachpeilah and prostrated himself in prayer at the tomb of our holy ancestors. The Cave of Machpeilah is the cradle of *emunah* (faith in God), for it was discovered and purchased by, and is the burial place of, Avraham Avinu. Of Avraham we say every day, "You found his heart faithful before You." Therefore, when Calev felt that his *emunah* needed strengthening, he went to the Me'aras HaMachpeilah and prayed.

So, my dear reader, precious member of the Jewish people, remember that there is a Har HaBayis in Jerusalem and a Me'aras HaMachpeilah in Chevron; and there is a Har HaBayis and Me'aras HaMachpeilah that lie within your heart. In a time of spiritual clarity and light, when you feel a closeness with the

13. *Daas Zekeinim* writes that the word הַמֹּרִיָּה, the name given to the Temple Mount in *Parashas HaAkeidah*, has the same *gematria* as חֶבְרוֹן (266).

Ribbono shel Olam, you are ascending the Temple Mount within you, where the radiance of the *Avos* glows and your eyes perceive all that is good.

However, there are also times when one's heart seems closed and one's mind is confused; when the heavens are darkened by clouds and one sees only darkness. At such times, you may find that Torah study brings you no joy and your davening is devoid of passion.

Your *mikdash* appears to have been destroyed.

Do not lose hope.

If you cannot ascend your Har HaBayis, then descend to your Me'aras HaMachpeilah. As Calev did when he was faced with the test of the *Meraglim*, prostrate yourself before the graves of the *Avos* that are hidden within the deepest recesses of your heart — daven with faith, even if your davening lacks feeling. Study Torah even if at present you are not experiencing the ecstasy that it should bring. Remember that the Machpeilah within your heart can never be destroyed. Fulfill the words of Yeshayahu HaNavi, *"I shall await Hashem Who has concealed His Face from the House of Yaakov."*[14]

Strengthen your *emunah*, encourage and fortify yourself, until Heaven will have mercy on you, for ultimately, your tefillos will be answered. Then the glory of Hashem will be revealed to you once more and your *mikdash* will be resurrected.

---

14. *Yeshayahu* 8:17.

CHAPTER TWENTY-EIGHT

Beis Lechem and Kever Rochel

The Midrash states:

What did our forefather Yaakov see that impelled him to bury Rochel on the road to Ephras [Beis Lechem]?

He saw that the exiles were destined to pass by there, so he buried her there so that she would plead for mercy for her children, as it is written, "A voice is heard on high, wailing, bitter weeping, Rochel weeps for her children; she refuses to be consoled for her children, for they are gone. Thus said Hashem: Restrain your voice from weeping and your eyes from tears; for there is reward for your accomplishment — the word of Hashem — and they will return

> *from the enemy's land. There is hope for your future — the word of Hashem — and your children will return to their border."*[1]

Maharal[2] explains that the entire Jewish people is considered Rochel's offspring, as it is written, *"Is Ephraim My favorite son or a delightful child, that whenever I speak of him I remember him more and more?"*[3] Though Ephraim was a son of Yosef and a grandson of Rochel, in this verse the name refers to the entire Jewish people.

In the Talmud we find that a wife and mother is referred to as a *bayis,* home, for she is the one who maintains its smooth functioning and is the family's unifying force.[4] Just as the house itself is the place that brings together all the family's members and all its possessions, so it is with the wife and mother. Though Yaakov Avinu had four wives, Rochel was the עֲקֶרֶת הַבַּיִת, the mainstay of his home.[5] As such, Rochel has the power to bring together her dispersed to children, no matter where they have been dispersed in this long and difficult exile.

A *derech*, road, is an open path leading in different directions; thus it represents *pizur*, dispersion, in contrast to a *bayis* which unites. Had Rochel been buried in a cave, a walled structure, like the Patriarchs and other Matriarchs, she would have been apart from her scattered children in exile and thus would have lacked the power to reunite and return them to their homeland. It was for their sake that Yaakov buried her on the road to Beis Lechem, so that she would be with them in their dispersion and bear within her the latent power to reunite them when the moment of redemption would arrive. And there on the road she beseeches the Heavens for mercy on their behalf until the time when her

---

1. *Yirmiyahu* 31:14-16.
2. *Netzach Yisrael* ch. 1.
3. *Yirmiyahu* 31:19.
4. R' Yose would refer to his wife as his *"bayis"* for this reason (*Shabbos* 118b).
5. *Bereishis Rabbah* 71:2.

prayers will be answered and her children will return to their precious land.

Therefore, Hashem tells her, "*Restrain your voice from weeping and your eyes from tears; for there is reward for your accomplishment — and they will return from the enemy's land.*" It will be in the merit of Rochel's tefillos and her power as a *mekabetz* (gatherer) and *me'ached* (unifier) that we will return, hopefully soon, from this *galus*.

Rochel's Merit

> *O Hashem, remember unto Dovid all his suffering. How he swore to Hashem and vowed to the Strong One of Yaakov: "If I enter the tent of my home, if I go upon the bed that is spread for me, if I allow sleep to my eyes, slumber to my eyelids; before I find a place for Hashem, resting places for the Strong One of Yaakov."*[6]

Dovid HaMelech did not merit to build the Beis HaMikdash; this privilege was granted his son Shlomo. However, Dovid prayed that he should merit to determine the exact spot upon which Hashem's House should be built, that Heaven would show him the blueprint for the Beis HaMikdash and its vessels, and that he would be permitted to prepare its materials. This tefillah was answered.

Where did he utter this tefillah? Dovid continues, הִנֵּה שְׁמַעֲנוּהָ בְאֶפְרָתָה ..., *Behold! We heard of it in Efras* ... Efras, says the Torah, is another name for Beis Lechem, the burial place of Rochel Imeinu (our Mother).[7] It was in Rochel's merit that Dovid's tefillah was answered.

Zohar teaches that our Mother Leah represents דִּינָא קַשְׁיָא, *strict judgment,* while Rochel represents דִּינָא רַפְיָא, *soft judgment.* With regard to Rosh Hashanah, the first day is one of דִּינָא קַשְׁיָא while

6. *Tehillim* 132:1-4.

7. *Bereishis* 35:18.

the second is one of דִּינָא רַפְיָא. A Jew should pray, therefore, that he be judged on the second day.

Sefer Yetzirah states that we find parallels in נֶפֶשׁ, *soul*; מָקוֹם, *place*; and זְמַן, *time*.[8] For example, the Kohen Gadol is the holiest *soul*; the *Kodesh HaKodashim* is the holiest *place*; and Yom Kippur is the holiest *day*. Similarly, Kever Rochel is, of course, the *place* of Rochel Imeinu, while the second day of Rosh Hashanah is the *day* of Rochel. It is on that day when we read in the *haftarah*: "*A voice is heard on high, wailing, bitter weeping, Rochel weeps for her children ... Restrain your voice from weeping and your eyes from tears ...*"

The above words were uttered by Yirmiyahu HaNavi, the prophet who, more than any other, lamented the Destruction. And yet, nowhere do we find such comforting words as here, when Yirmiyahu invokes the merit of our Mother Rochel. When one visits Kever Rochel, it is proper to recite this *haftarah*, which is dipped in the honey of Rosh Hashanah and, in fact, is sweeter than honey.

When one prays at Kever Rochel, on any day of the year, it is in a sense as if he is praying on the second day of Rosh Hashanah, a day when the *middas hadin*, the Attribute of Judgment, is of a lenient nature. It is a most auspicious place to pray for our people's salvation and to recite the tefillah of Dovid that the Beis HaMikdash be built.

City of Reconciliation

In *Tanach* we find a schism between Yehudah and Yosef. When Yosef related his dreams to his brothers, they accused him of trying to usurp the monarchy, which belonged to Yehudah, and claim it as his own. This schism was never fully healed; it peaked after the death of Shlomo HaMelech when Yeravam ben Navat of *shevet Ephraim* (Yosef's son) led the breakaway kingdom of the

8. This concept is also discussed in "*Shema* and Its Introductory Blessings" (ch. 18).

Ten Tribes while Rechavam, Shlomo's son, led the kingdom of Yehudah and Binyamin.

Once in our history, an incident occurred that alluded to the days of Mashiach, when this schism will finally end. *Parashas Vayigash* opens with the words ... וַיִּגַּשׁ אֵלָיו יְהוּדָה, *Then Yehudah approached him [Yosef] ...*[9] which resulted in the revelation of "אֲנִי יוֹסֵף, *I am Yosef.*"[10] The Midrash comments:

> *"And Yehudah approached" — This alludes to that which is written, "Behold, days are coming — the word of Hashem — when the plowman will meet the reaper, and the treader of grapes [will meet] the one who carries the seed; the mountains will drip juice and all the hills will melt."*[11] *The "plowman" — this is Yehudah; "the reaper" — this is Yosef, who carries the seed.*[12]

And Yeshayahu HaNavi prophesies: *"The jealousy of Ephraim will stop and the oppressors of Yehudah shall be cut off; Ephraim will not be jealous of Yehudah and Yehudah will not harass Ephraim."*[13] The reconciliation of Yehudah and Yosef is alluded to in the *gematria* of וַיִּגַּשׁ אֵלָיו יְהוּדָה, which is equal to דָּוִיד בֶּן יִשַׁי (396).[14]

The city of Beis Lechem represents this reconciliation. It is the city from which the family of Dovid originated, as we say in the Friday night prayer of *Lechah Dodi*: עַל יַד בֶּן יִשַׁי בֵּית הַלַּחְמִי, *Through the son of [Dovid] ben Yishai of Beis Lechem.* It was there that Boaz married Rus, and Shmuel anointed Dovid. The city's other name, Ephras, alludes to Ephraim, as *Targum* states regarding the description of Shmuel's father, Elkanah, as an *Ephrasi* — *"[He heralded] from the mountains of Ephraim."* The name Beis

9. *Bereishis* 4:18.

10. Ibid. 45:3.

11. *Amos* 9:13.

12. *Bereishis Rabbah* 93:5.

13. *Yeshayahu* 11:13.

14. The name Dovid is sometimes spelled דָּוִיד; see, for example, *Divrei HaYamim I* 29:10 which we recite each morning in *Pesukei D'Zimrah*.

Lechem alludes to Yosef, for it can be translated as "Two *Lechem* (Breads)."[15] The word לֶחֶם times 2 has the same *gematria* as יוֹסֵף (156).

May we soon witness this reconciliation, when Rochel's tears will cease as her tefillos and those of her children — the entire Jewish nation — will be answered with the coming of Mashiach, speedily and in our time.

15. The letter *beis* is the second in the Hebrew alphabet.

CHAPTER TWENTY-NINE

Planted on the Mountain of Hashem[1]

תְּבִאֵמוֹ וְתִטָּעֵמוֹ בְּהַר נַחֲלָתְךָ ... ה׳ יִמְלֹךְ לְעֹלָם וָעֶד.

You will bring them and implant them on the mountain of Your heritage . . . Hashem shall reign for all eternity![2]

These concluding verses of the *Shiras HaYam* (Song at the Sea) speak of the days of Mashiach, when all of Eretz Yisrael will attain the holiness of Jerusalem and all of Jerusalem will be like the Beis HaMikdash in days of old.[3]

1. For a better understanding of *Shiras HaYam*, one should study the verses in *Sefer Shemos* ch. 15 with the major commentaries. This *shmuess* focuses on a single verse in the *shirah*. The *Shirah's* importance as part of the daily tefillah is discussed in ch. 17.

2. *Shemos* 15:17,18.

3. See *Shir HaShirim Rabbah* 7:5.

"You shall bring them and implant them . . ." The word וְתִטָּעֵמוֹ, *and implant them,* seems redundant. As we shall see, it is not redundant at all.

A Song That Inspires

אָז יָשִׁיר מֹשֶׁה וּבְנֵי יִשְׂרָאֵל אֶת הַשִּׁירָה הַזֹּאת . . .
Then, Moshe and Bnei Yisrael sang this song . . .[4]

Sfas Emes writes that the word יָשִׁיר means *caused to sing.* The Jews' Song at the Sea awakened within each component of creation its respective song to Hashem. For, as delineated in *Perek Shirah*, each component gives praise to Hashem in its own unique way.

This is especially true of trees, which the Torah refers to as שִׂיחַ הַשָּׂדֶה, *trees of the field.*[5] The term שִׂיחַ also means *prayer*, as in וַיֵּצֵא יִצְחָק לָשׂוּחַ בַּשָּׂדֶה, *Yitzchak went out to pray in the field.*[6] Thus, the very essence of trees is their expression of praise to their Creator. In *Perek Shirah,* we are taught that the song of the trees is expressed in the verse **אָז** יְרַנְּנוּ עֲצֵי הַיָּעַר, מִלִּפְנֵי ה' כִּי בָא לִשְׁפּוֹט אֶת הָאָרֶץ, ***Then*** *all the trees of the forest will sing with joy, before Hashem — for He will have come to judge the earth.*[7] In the world as we know it, the song of the trees is hidden from man. In Messianic times, their song will be revealed to all. And what brought forth this song? **אָז** יָשִׁיר מֹשֶׁה וּבְנֵי יִשְׂרָאֵל.

There is a profound connection between man and trees, as the Torah states, כִּי הָאָדָם עֵץ הַשָּׂדֶה, *for man is the tree of the field.*[8] This is particularly true of the Jewish people, as we find in *Shir*

4. *Shemos* 15:1.
5. *Bereishis* 2:5.
6. Ibid. 24:63. See commentary of R' Samson Raphael Hirsch.
7. *Divrei HaYamim I* 16:33.
8. See *Devarim* 20:19 with Ibn Ezra.

HaShirim: *"The fig tree has formed its first figs ... the vines in blossom ...;"*[9] *"Such is your stature, likened to a palm tree."*[10] All these verses refer to the Jewish people.

Barren Trees

The Gemara states: "All the barren trees that are in Eretz Yisrael are destined to bear fruit ..."[11]

At the time of Creation, all trees were to be fruit-bearing, as it is written, *"Let the earth sprout forth ... trees of earth yielding fruit ..."*[12] However, after Adam and Chavah ate from the Tree of Knowledge and the earth was cursed, it lost some of its productive capabilities and a large percentage of trees remained barren. In the End of Days when the world will attain its perfection and the sin of Adam will have been rectified, the earth will regain its full strength and all trees will bear fruit.

Just as there are fruit trees and barren trees in our world, so too are there Jews who are productive and Jews whose lives are barren, devoid of spiritual quality. In our days, to our misfortune, the vast majority of Jews in this world are "barren trees," estranged from their rich heritage and devoid of Torah and mitzvah observance.

In our exposition of *Baruch She'amar*, we mentioned that at times, there are *kitrugim*, Heavenly indictments, which threaten to deny mankind the mercy that it needs. However, if it is decreed that animal life be the beneficiary of Hashem's mercy, then once the Divine compassion begins to flow, it can benefit mankind as well.

In a similar vein, we can pray that the innocent trees, which did not sin and were weakened on account of man, be restored to their original strength through the coming of Mashiach when the

---

9. *Shir HaShirim* 2:13

10. Ibid. 7:8.

11. *Kesubos* 112b. The Gemara derives this from a verse.

12. *Bereishis* 1:11.

world will attain its perfection. When that day comes, the "barren trees" among us, the lost *neshamos* of our people, will return to Hashem and bear the fruit of Torah, tefillah, and good deeds.

Perhaps Dovid alludes to this sort of prayer when he says:

> פָּנָה אֶל תְּפִלַּת הָעַרְעָר, וְלֹא בָזָה אֶת תְּפִלָּתָם. תִּכָּתֶב זֹאת לְדוֹר אַחֲרוֹן ...,
> *He turned to the prayer of the barren tree,*[13] *and has not despised their prayer. Let this be recorded for the last generation ...*[14]

Apples of Gold

Scriptures refers to the Beis HaMikdash as לְבָנוֹן, *forest.*[15] The Gemara explains:

> *Just as the forest blooms, so too the Beis HaMikdash blooms. At the time that Shlomo [HaMelech] built the Beis HaMikdash, he planted in it all kinds of fine trees of gold, and they [miraculously] brought forth fruit in their appointed time. And when the wind would blow on them, their fruits would fall off ... and in the future, the Holy One, blessed is He, will restore them to us.*[16]

In the world as we know it, inanimate objects cannot reproduce. However, the Beis Hamikdash was the location of the אֶבֶן שְׁתִיָּה, *foundation stone*, the rock that was the first part of the earth to be created and around which Hashem formed the rest of the

---

13. See *Radak* and *Ibn Ezra* who relate עַרְעָר to עֲרִירִי, *childless* or *barren.*

14. *Tehillim* 102:18-19. Rav Wolfson reflected that 15 Shevat (known as ט"ו בִּשְׁבָט), the new year for trees, is an especially auspicious day for such prayer. He found an allusion to this: The *gematria* of וְעֵץ הַשָּׂדֶה יִתֵּן פִּרְיוֹ (*and the tree of the field will give its fruit — Vayikra* 26:4) is equal to חֲמִשָּׁה עָשָׂר בִּשְׁבָט (1,236).

Ashkenazic custom is to partake of a variety of fruits on 15 Shevat (see *Mishnah Berurah* 131:31). Rav Wolfson commented that when reciting the blessing of בּוֹרֵא פְּרִי הָעֵץ *(Who creates the fruit of trees)* on that day, one should have in mind, "Please, *Ribbono shel Olam,* create fruits even for those trees that are presently barren" — a prayer for the coming of Mashiach, when all trees and all Jewish souls will "bear fruit."

15. *Melachim I* 7:2.

16. *Yoma* 39b.

world.[17] Thus at that spot inanimate earth was able to expand and become an entire world.

In the world in which we live, embassies of a foreign country enjoy a unique status, as they are considered like the territory of the country they represent. In a similar sense, the Beis HaMikdash, though it was a structure on this earth, was in fact from another world that is beyond the limitations of our earthly existence. It retained the quality of the אֶבֶן שְׁתִיָּה, so that trees made of inanimate gold could produce fruits.

As we have already mentioned, in the End of Days all of Jerusalem will have the status of the Beis HaMikdash. Golden trees lining the streets of the holy city will bear fruit. And certainly *real* trees, though they now are barren, will bear beautiful fruits.

Barren trees of another type will also bear fruit at that time. *"And it will be on that day, that a great shofar will be blown, and then will come those lost in the land of Assyria and those cast away in the land of Egypt; and they shall bow to Hashem on the holy mountain in Jerusalem."*[18]

This is the meaning of the word וְתִטָּעֵמוֹ, *and implant,* in *Shiras HaYam.* We yearn for the day when the entire Jewish people will be firmly planted on the mountain of Hashem, and all its trees, without exception, will bear precious golden fruits of Torah, tefillah, and good deeds.

17. *Yoma* 54b.

18. *Yeshayahu* 18:3.

CHAPTER THIRTY

Soul of Faith, City of Faith

In the first and most important blessing of *Shemoneh Esrei,*[1] we invoke the merit of our *Avos* (Patriarchs), and in particular Avraham Avinu. The blessing concludes, *"Blessed are You, Hashem, Shield of Avraham."*

R' Yitzchak Meir of Ger (the *Chiddushei HaRim*) offered a novel interpretation of this *berachah.* In every *neshamah* there is

1. As we have noted elsewhere, one must focus on the meaning of the words for at least the first blessing of *Shemoneh Esrei;* otherwise, according to the strict letter of the law, he must repeat *Shemoneh Esrei* (*Shulchan Aruch, Orach Chaim* 101:1). However, as *Rema* writes, already in his time the custom was not to repeat *Shemoneh Esrei,* for it is quite possible that the second time the person will again not have proper *kavanah,* and his repetition will have been for naught.

a spark of Avraham Avinu that burns with the fire of Avraham's pure *emunah*. Hashem "shields" this spark so that it can never be extinguished. It may lie dormant for years in a *neshamah* that has strayed, but it will never be snuffed out. The day will yet come when that spark will be fanned into a roaring flame.

A Soul of Faith

R' Tzadok HaKohen of Lublin writes that if we wish to know the personification of a given spiritual concept, we should see where it first appears in the Torah. *Emunah* is first mentioned in the Torah regarding Avraham: וְהֶאֱמִן בַּה', *And he trusted in Hashem.*[2] At the age of 3, Avraham recognized his Creator and blazed a path of service to Hashem in a world steeped in idolatry. Avraham, the *rosh l'maaminim*, the guiding light of those who faithfully follow Hashem, personifies *emunah*. This is alluded to in the name אַבְרָהָם, for the *gematria* of its letters when spelled out [אַלֶף, בֵּית, רֵישׁ, הֵא, מֵם][3] is equal to וּמָצָאתָ אֶת לְבָבוֹ נֶאֱמָן (*and You found his [Avraham's] heart faithful*[4] — 1,119).

At the conclusion of the chapter of Creation, the Torah states: אֵלֶּה תוֹלְדוֹת הַשָּׁמַיִם וְהָאָרֶץ בְּהִבָּרְאָם, *These are the products of the heaven and the earth when they were created.*[5] The Midrash rearranges the letters of בְּהִבָּרְאָם to spell בְּאַבְרָהָם and comments: *"In the merit of Avraham [were heaven and earth created]."*[6] Creation was considered incomplete until Avraham appeared. He was the first of a new kind of human being, for he developed within himself a pure *emunah* that became a part of his very essence and bequeathed it to his progeny in their "spiritual genes."[7]

Each morning we recite these verses:

---

2. *Bereishis* 15:6.

3. This is a system of *gematria* utilizing the מִלּוּי הָאוֹתִיּוֹת *(full spelling of each letter)*.

4. From *Nechemiah* 9:8, recited each morning in *Pesukei D'Zimrah*.

5. *Bereishis* 2:4.

6. *Bereishis Rabbah* 12:9.

7. See "In the Merit of Our Forefathers" (ch. 20).

You made the heavens, the most exalted heavens and all their legion, the earth and all that is upon it, the seas and all that is in them, and You give them all life; and the heavenly legions bow to You. You are Hashem, the God, You selected Avram and brought him out of Ur Kasdim, and changed his name to Avraham. You found his heart faithful to You ...[8]

At first glance it might seem difficult to understand the connection between Hashem's making the heavens and the earth and His taking Avraham out of Ur Kasdim. However, according to the above, these two concepts are in fact one. For as the Midrash says, the purpose of creating heaven and earth was that there should be an Avraham Avinu, the Patriach of a nation of *emunah*. With the arrival of Avraham, creation was complete.

City of Faith

As we have mentioned elsewhere in this volume, *Sefer HaYetzirah* states that there are spiritual concepts that find parallel expression in *makom,* place; *zman*, time*;* and *nefesh*, soul.[9]

Avraham, as we have explained, is the soul of *emunah*.

What Avraham is in *nefesh,* Jerusalem is in *makom.* Jerusalem is the world's spiritual center point, the place from which all Divine blessing, both spiritual and material, flows. It is the location of the אֶבֶן שְׁתִיָּה, *foundation stone*, the rock that was the first part of the earth to be created and around which Hashem formed the rest of the world.[10]

The entire Torah revolves around the mitzvah of *emunah*, pure, unshakable faith in the only and only God. *Ramban* does not count the first of the Ten Commandments, *"I am Hashem, your God ..."* as one of the 613 mitzvos because it is the foundation

---

8. *Nechemiah* 9:6-8.

9. See, for example, "Beis Lechem and Kever Rochel" (ch. 28).

10. *Yoma* 54b.

upon which all the mitzvos are based. Without *emunah,* we have nothing.[11] And just as the entire Torah revolves around *emunah,* the entire world revolves around Jerusalem. It follows, then, that Jerusalem corresponds to the mitzvah of *emunah.*

The Gemara states:[12]

> *Jerusalem was destroyed only because faith had disappeared from it, as it is written, "Walk about the streets of Jerusalem, see now and know, and seek in its plazas; if you will find a man, if there is one who dispenses justice and seeks emunah, then I will forgive her."*[13]

In his *Sefer Mevakesh Emunah* R' Aharon Roth[14] explains that the term עֹשֶׂה מִשְׁפָּט, *dispenses justice,* refers to the strengthening of one's *bitachon,* trust in Hashem, which is the practical outgrowth of *emunah.*[15] Because Jerusalem, as the world's spiritual fulcrum, is the place that embodies *emunah,* it could remain standing only as long as its people lived with faith and trust in Hashem. When there could not be found a man of faith in the city of faith, it had to be destroyed.

To the Land That I Will Show You

After Avraham demonstrated his faith at Ur Kasdim and emerged alive from a fiery furnace, Hashem commanded him:

> לֶךְ לְךָ מֵאַרְצְךָ וּמִמּוֹלַדְתְּךָ וּמִבֵּית אָבִיךָ אֶל הָאָרֶץ אֲשֶׁר אַרְאֶךָּ.
> *Go for yourself from your land, from your birthplace, and from your father's house to the land that I will show you.*[16]

11. And as we have noted elsewhere, the prophet Chavakuk teaches that one mitzvah is the foundation of the entire Torah: *"And a tzaddik lives by his faith"* (*Chavakuk* 2:4).

12. *Shabbos* 119b.

13. *Yirmiyahu* 5:1.

14. Famed chassidic leader and author of *Sefer Shomer Emunim.*

15. As *Ramban* puts it, *emunah* is the "tree" and *bitachon* is its "fruit." For example, a person demonstrates *bitachon* when he is scrupulously honest in his business dealings. The fact that he possesses such *bitachon* is indicative of his exalted level of *emunah.*

16. *Bereishis* 12:1.

Avraham heeded Hashem's command and journeyed with his wife and household to the Land of Canaan. Avraham entered the land and soon after *was told* by Hashem, "I will give this land to your descendants." However, we do not find that Hashem directed Avraham to the land, as the words "to the land *that I will show you*" would seem to indicate.

We find the opposite situation regarding *Akeidas Yitzchak.* There, Hashem told Avraham regarding Yitzchak, "Please take your son ... to the land of Moriah; bring him there as an offering upon one of the mountains *which I will tell you.*"[17]

However, we do not find that Hashem verbally *told* Avraham where the *Akeidah* would take place. Rather, as Midrash states, Avraham was *shown* a cloud hovering over the future Temple Mount, and that was how he knew that this was the desired place.

Chasam Sofer explains that when Hashem initially told Avraham to go to "the land that I will show you," he was referring specifically to Jerusalem. It was only when Avraham saw the cloud hovering over the Temple Mount at the time of the *Akeidah* that the words "*Go ... to the land that I will show you*" was fulfilled. And when the Torah states regarding the *Akeidah*, "So Avraham ... went to the place of which God had spoken to him,"[18] it refers to this very command with which *Parashas Lech Lecha* begins.

As the Torah relates, after entering the Land, *"Avraham journeyed on, journeying steadily toward the south.*"[19] Rashi comments that Avraham was traveling toward Jerusalem. Jerusalem, the *makom ha'emunah* (place of faith), was the ultimate destination for Avraham, *ish ha'emunah* (the man of faith).

To that verse Zohar comments, "[Avraham was ascending] in exalted levels of complete faith, and was informed that it [i.e *emunah*] would never leave his descendants." The *gematria* of

17. Ibid. 22:2.

18. Ibid 22:3.

19. Ibid 12:9.

the word יְרוּשָׁלַיִם, usually spelled in Scripture without the second י, equals that of וַיַּאֲמִינוּ בַּי־ה־וָה וּבְמֹשֶׁה עַבְדּוֹ *(And they had faith in Hashem and in Moshe, His servant*[20] — 586).

The *gematria* of לֶךְ לְךָ מֵאַרְצְךָ וּמִמּוֹלַדְתְּךָ וּמִבֵּית אָבִיךָ *([Hashem said to Avram]: Go for yourself from your land, from your birthplace, and from your father's house)* equals that of עֹשֶׂה מִשְׁפָּט מְבַקֵּשׁ אֱמוּנָה וְאֶסְלַח לָהּ *([Walk about the streets of Jerusalem . . . and seek] one who dispenses justice and seeks emunah, then I will forgive her* — 1,488*)*.

The Kosel HaMaaravi

Zohar refers to the Kosel HaMaaravi (Western Wall) as "the peak of *emunah*."[21] *Sefer Yismach Moshe*[22] writes that the Jewish people's existence throughout the millennia of exile has been possible only because the Divine Presence still rests at the site of the Beis HaMikdash, though in a diminished sense. As Zohar states, "The *Shechinah* has never left the Kosel HaMaaravi.[23] And similarly, our continued existence has been possible only through our *emunah* which emanates from the spark of faith that Avraham has bequeathed to each and every one of us and which Hashem eternally shields, so that it will never be extinguished.

20. *Shemos* 14:31.

21. Zohar, vol. II, p. 5b.

22. *Haftarah* to *Parashas Pekudei.*

23. Ibid.

PART FOUR

ELUL *and the* DAYS *of* AWE

CHAPTER THIRTY-ONE

Elul — A Time for Purity

אַחַת שָׁאַלְתִּי מֵאֵת ה׳ אוֹתָהּ אֲבַקֵּשׁ שִׁבְתִּי בְּבֵית ה׳
כָּל יְמֵי חַיַּי לַחֲזוֹת בְּנֹעַם ה׳ וּלְבַקֵּר בְּהֵיכָלוֹ.

***One thing I ask of Hashem, that shall I seek: That I dwell in the House of Hashem all the days of my life; to behold the sweetness of Hashem and to contemplate His sanctuary.*[1]**

In its plain meaning, the phrase לַחֲזוֹת בְּנֹעַם ה׳, *to behold the sweetness of Hashem,* is Dovid's prayer that he should merit to experience the sweetness, the pleasure, of an intimate relationship with Hashem. *Chasam Sofer,* however, understands

1. *Tehillim* 27:4.

the phrase differently. Dovid expresses the hope that Hashem will take pleasure *in him*, that Hashem, as it were, will "derive *nachas*" from Dovid's spiritual efforts.

Twice daily, from Rosh Chodesh Elul until Shemini Atzeres, we recite "*L'Dovid, Hashem,*"[2] in which this tefillah is expressed.

The word אֱלוּל is found in the initial letters of אֲנִי לְדוֹדִי וְדוֹדִי לִי, *I am my Beloved's and my Beloved is mine.*[3] This description of the relationship between a *chasan* and *kallah* represents the relationship between Hashem and His beloved people. The month of Elul is a time of Divine favor and mercy, when Hashem looks towards us with love and awaits our efforts to draw closer to Him through *teshuvah* and introspection. It is a time when we strive to deepen our relationship with Him, and when we hope that Hashem will "derive *nachas*" from our efforts.

The Month of Yosef

Tur[4] writes that the 12 months of the Jewish calendar correspond to the 12 *Shevatim* (Tribes).[5] The *Arizal* taught that additionally, there is a parallel between the first seven months of the year, beginning with Nissan, and the *Shivah Ro'im* (Seven Shepherds), the seven great souls of Jewish history — Avraham, Yitzchak, Yaakov, Moshe, Aharon, Yosef, and Dovid. The sixth month, Elul, corresponds to Yosef.

The *Shivah Ro'im* also correspond to the seven *Sefiros,* the Heavenly Emanations, attributes of Hashem through which He conducts the affairs of this world and which we, on our level of understanding, should strive to emulate.[6]

---

2. *Tehillim* ch. 27.

3. *Shir HaShirim* 6:4.

4. *Orach Chaim* ch. 417.

5. According to *Yaavetz,* the parallel between the months (beginning with Nissan) and the *shevatim* follows the order of birth of the sons of Yaakov (with Reuven being first). According to the *Arizal,* it follows the order of the encampment in the *Midbar* (where Yehudah led the way).

6. See "*Ahavas Yisrael* and Tefillah" (ch. 5) in this volume.

Yosef, the sixth Shepherd, corresponds to the attribute of *yesod* (lit. foundation), which represents purity in deed and thought. Yosef is associated with this *middah* because of the great spiritual struggle he overcame involving the wife of Potiphar.[7] It is because of his perseverance in this area that he is known as Yosef *HaTzaddik* (the Righteous).

Embodiment of Purity

In fact, Yosef's association with *taharah,* purity, precedes the episode with Potiphar's wife. The Torah states that Yaakov had particular love for Yosef כִּי בֶן זְקֻנִים הוּא לוֹ.[8] *Targum Onkelos* understands the word זְקֻנִים to mean בַּר חַכִּים, *a wise son,* for, as *Rashi* explains, whatever Yaakov learned in the yeshivos of Shem and Ever he taught to Yosef.

Baal HaTurim adds that the word זְקֻנִים is an acronym for five of the six orders of the Mishnah: **ז**ְרָעִים, **קָ**דָשִׁים, **נָ**שִׁים, **יְ**שׁוּעוֹת (נְזִיקִין),[9] **מ**וֹעֵד.

But what of the sixth order, טַהֲרוֹת, the laws of ritual purity? Why would Yaakov teach Yosef all but this body of *Torah Sheb'al Peh*?

Regarding Avraham Avinu we are taught: "Hashem gave Avraham two kidneys that were like two sages. They gave him understanding, advised him, and taught him wisdom the entire night."[10] By seeking and discovering Hashem on his own, Avraham merited such a *dveikus* (attachment to the Divine) that all of Torah became revealed to him without his having been taught it.

Yosef HaTzaddik, through his lifelong efforts to maintain utmost purity in word, deed, and thought, merited this sort of revelation of *Seder Taharos*. He did not need to be taught the laws of purity.

7. See *Bereishis* ch. 39.

8. Ibid. 37:3.

9. The Gemara (*Shabbos* 31a) uses יְשׁוּעוֹת as an alternative name for *Seder Nezikin.*

10. *Avos d'Rav Nassan* 33:1.

Covenant of Kedushah

The moral purity that Yosef HaTzaddik represents is referred to in Torah writings as *shemiras habris*, guarding of the covenant of *bris milah. Rashi*[11] writes that when Yosef revealed himself to his brothers, he made known that he was circumcised as proof that he was, indeed, their brother. *Zohar* elaborates: The brothers wondered, "Yosef, how did you merit to rule over Egypt?" Yosef "showed them that he was circumcised"; he told them that it was in the merit of maintaining his moral purity that he ascended the throne as viceroy of Egypt.

The effect that *shemiras habris* has on all aspects of one's *avodas Hashem* is profound. For example, in its merit one experiences a radiance, a spiritual elevation and joy. on Shabbos. He perceives the day for what it is: a semblance of the World to Come.

The Torah states: **מִי יַעֲלֶה לָּנוּ הַשָּׁמַיְמָה** ...?, *Who will ascend for us to Heaven ...?*[12] Zohar notes that the initial letters of these words spell מִילָה, while the end letters form י־ה־ו־ה. *Shemiras habris* is the primary requirement one needs to ascend the ladder of spiritual growth.

Hashem enjoins us repeatedly to be a holy, pure people: קְדשִׁים תִּהְיוּ, *You shall be holy;*[13] וְלֹא תָתוּרוּ אַחֲרֵי לְבַבְכֶם וְאַחֲרֵי עֵינֵיכֶם ... וִהְיִיתֶם קְדשִׁים לֵאלֹהֵיכֶם, *You shall not spy after your heart and after your eyes ... so that you will be holy to your God.*[14] A Jew must stand guard over his eyes and heart and in so doing protect his inherent *kedushah*.

This requires *yiras Shamayim* (awe of Hashem), which can be acquired only by learning *sifrei mussar,* such as *Mesilas Yesharim, Chovos HaLevavos, Orchos Tzaddikim,* or specific *sifrei chassidus* that can be classified as *sifrei mussar.*

---

11. *Bereishis* 45:4, citing Midrash.
12. *Devarim* 30:12.
13. *Vayikra* 19:2.
14. *Bamidbar* 15:39.

Seeing From Afar

The Mishnah states:

> *There is no difference between [the laws of the Mishkan at] Shiloh and [those pertaining to the Beis HaMikdash in] Jerusalem, except that in Shiloh one was permitted to eat kodashim kalim and maaser sheini anywhere within view [of Shiloh], but in Jerusalem [one was only permitted to do so] within the walls.*[15]

The *kedushah* (sanctity) of Jerusalem (as it pertains to *korbanos* and ritual purity) is eternal, while that of Shiloh is not. Nevertheless, the Mishkan in Shiloh had one advantage over the Beis HaMikdash in Jerusalem: If one was outside Shiloh's walls but could still see the city, it was as if he was in the city in regard to eating the above-mentioned sacred foods.

Shiloh was in the territory of Ephraim, son of Yosef. Because Yosef overcame the most difficult tests in keeping his eyes pure, having his city of Shiloh in one's range of vision was like actually being there.[16]

Regarding the words הַדּוּדָאִים נָתְנוּ רֵיחַ, *The violets emit a fragrance,*[17] the Gemara expounds, "This refers to young Jewish men who have not tasted the taste of sin."[18] We see that maintaining moral purity is associated with רֵיחַ, sense of smell.

Elsewhere the Gemara relates:

> *R' Chiya bar Avin said in the name of R' Yehoshua ben Korcha: An elderly man told me, "Once, I went to Shiloh and I smelled the fragrance of the ketores (incense) from between its walls."*[19]

---

15. *Mishnah Megillah* 1:11.
16. See *Zevachim* 118b.
17. *Shir HaShirim* 7:14.
18. *Eruvin* 21b.
19. *Yoma* 39b.

This fragrance was a residue of the *ketores* which Shiloh's walls had absorbed when the Mishkan had stood there nearly a thousand years earlier! This miraculous power of fragrance was unique to Shiloh, a city of Ephraim, in the merit of the purity of Yosef HaTzaddik.

In the phrase הַדּוּדָאִים נָתְנוּ רֵיחַ, the word דּוּדָאִים alludes to אֲנִי לְדוֹדִי וְדוֹדִי לִי, the month of Elul, the month when the love between Hashem and His people is most manifest. It is a month most auspicious for cleansing one's *neshamah* from spiritual impurity. When the Gemara speaks of "young Jewish men who have not tasted the taste of sin," this also includes those who sinned but have cleansed themselves through *teshuvah*.

Taharah, spiritual purity, must precede *kedushah*, sanctity. One cannot enter the holy confines of the Beis HaMikdash without first purifying himself through immersion in a *mikveh.* Elul is the month of *taharah,* spiritual purity, that must precede our entrance into the *kedushah* of the month of Tishrei. רֹאשׁ הַשָּׁנָה has the same *gematria* as בֵּית הַמִּקְדָּשׁ (861).

The *Baal HaTanya* writes that in Elul, Hashem is likened to a מֶלֶךְ בַּשָּׂדֶה, a king who has left his palace for the fields to stroll among his people. He is easily accessible to all. In Elul, the *Ribbono shel Olam* is walking among us, as it were, eagerly awaiting our return. He calls out to us, "Open for Me an entrance as tiny as the point of a needle, and I, in turn, shall open for you an entrance as wide as the entrance of a hall."[20]

Let us make the most of the precious month of Elul so that we can enter Rosh Hashanah with a pure heart.

---

20. *Shir HaShirim Rabbah* 5:3.

CHAPTER THIRTY-TWO

Elul — A Time to Seek Refuge

As the Mishnah teaches, on Rosh Hashanah "all who walk the earth pass before Him like sheep."[1] On that day, *tzaddikim* merit a favorable judgment while *beinonim*, those whose merits and sins are counterbalanced, have until Yom Kippur to achieve the necessary level of *teshuvah.*[2] For *tzaddikim* the 30 days of Elul are sufficient, while *beinonim* need the additional 10 days from Rosh Hashanah until Yom Kippur.

Zohar teaches that there is yet another judgment that commences on Hoshana Rabbah and concludes on the following

1. *Mishnah Rosh Hashanah* 1:2.

2. *Rosh Hashanah* 16b.

day, Shemini Atzeres.[3] Thus, someone who has not repented sufficiently to merit favor on Yom Kippur still has an opportunity during the joyous days of Succos to accomplish this.

The author of *Bas Ayin,*[4] quoting the *Arizal,* writes that for those who have engaged in *teshuvah* during the 52 days from Rosh Chodesh Elul until Shemini Atzeres but have not yet achieved a favorable judgment, there is still time until the last day of Chanukah, known as Zos Chanukah,[5] to gain atonement. This is alluded to in the verse בְּזֹאת יְכֻפַּר עֲוֹן יַעֲקֹב (lit. *Through this* — zos — *shall Yaakov's sin be atoned*),[6] which *Bas Ayin* interprets as: *On Zos Chanukah, the sins of Yaakov [i.e. the Jewish People] shall be atoned.*

A Remarkable Allusion

The four periods of *teshuvah* we have enumerated are alluded to in the *parshiyos* that are read during the month of Elul and into the new year.

Parashas Vayeilech has 30 verses, alluding to the 30 days of Elul that are sufficient for *tzaddikim* to be inscribed in the Book of Life on Rosh Hashanah.

Parashas Nitzavim has 40 verses, alluding to the 40 days from Rosh Chodesh Elul until Yom Kippur, when hopefully those of average merit will be inscribed and sealed in the Book of Life.

Parashas Haazinu contains 52 verses, alluding to the 52-day period from Rosh Chodesh Elul until Shemini Atzeres.

The combined total of the above *parshiyos* is 122 verses. This alludes to the 122 days from Rosh Chodesh Elul until Zos Chanukah. Perhaps this allusion is less obvious, in contrast to the other three, to indicate that requiring so much additional time is far from an optimum solution for one who sincerely engages

3. See *Zohar, Parashas Tzav* 31b.

4. He was a disciple of the Baal Shem Tov.

5. The 8th day of Chanukah is known by this name because the Torah reading for that day states (twice): זֹאת חֲנֻכַּת הַמִּזְבֵּחַ (*Bamidbar* 7:84,88).

6. *Yeshayahu* 27:9.

in *teshuvah*. Woe to the one who after experiencing the uplifting days of Elul, Rosh Hashanah, *Aseres Yemei Teshuvah* (Ten Days of Repentance), Yom Kippur, Succos, and Shemini Atzeres, still requires more time to achieve a favorable judgment.

If we go back one more *parashah*, we find that *Parashas Ki Savo* contains exactly 122 verses! It would seem, then, that combining the verses of *Nitzavim, Vayeilech,* and *Haazinu* is unnecessary.

However, this is not so. *Parashas Ki Savo* contains the *Tochachah* (Admonitions), the 98 frightening punishments that are foretold if the Jewish people sin and are unworthy of remaining in their precious Land. The Gemara teaches that we read *Ki Savo* before Rosh Hashanah כְּדֵי שֶׁתִּכְלֶה הַשָּׁנָה וְקִלְלוֹתֶיהָ, *so that the year may end along with its curses.*[7] The 122 verses of *Ki Savo* allude to the beginning days *of the year that is ending.* As the year draws to a close, and one reflects on those happenings that were not pleasant, on those dreams that remained unfulfilled, he must ask himself: "How did I utilize the precious *teshuvah* period of the year gone by? Was my Elul what it could have been? And what of my Aseres Yemei Teshuvah and Succos? Did I take advantage of the days between Shemini Atzeres and the conclusion of Chanukah to effect real improvement in my *avodas Hashem*?"

Hopefully, such introspection will ensure that the coming Elul and the days that follow will be utilized properly.

A "City of Refuge"

In the previous essay, we cited the famous allusion to the month of Elul in the initial letters of **א**ֲנִי **ל**ְדוֹדִי **ו**ְדוֹדִי **ל**ִי, *I am my Beloved's and my Beloved is mine.*[8] There is another allusion, taught by the Arizal.[9] The Torah states:

---

7. *Megillah* 31b.

8. *Shir HaShirim* 6:4.

9. Cited in *Kitzur Shulchan Aruch* 128:1.

וַאֲשֶׁר לֹא צָדָה וְהָאֱלֹהִים אִנָּה לְיָדוֹ וְשַׂמְתִּי לְךָ מָקוֹם אֲשֶׁר יָנוּס שָׁמָּה.

But one who did not lie in wait and God brought about to his hand, I shall provide a place to which he shall flee.[10]

This refers to one who has killed unintentionally. He is sent to the *ir miklat*, city of refuge, where he is safe from the *goel hadam* (lit. redeemer of blood), the relative of the victim who is permitted to kill the murderer should he venture outside the *ir miklat*.[11]

The initial letters of **א**ִנָּה **ל**ְיָדוֹ **וְ**שַׂמְתִּי **ל**ְךָ spell אֱלוּל. The Arizal is teaching us that Elul, and the Aseres Yemei Teshuvah that follow, are a "city of refuge" to which one can flee from the *yetzer hara* and return to Hashem with a full heart.

Place of Hashem's Sovereignty

The Torah states that there were six primary cities of refuge and 42 additional ones. In the writings of holy *sefarim,* we find that these 48 cities, all of which were inhabited by Kohanim and Leviim, were, in a spiritual sense, an extension of Jerusalem. Jerusalem is the place of *malchus Shamayim* (the sovereignty of Heaven) on this world, and by extension, the *miklat* cities too were places where Hashem's sovereignty in this world was better perceived. This would have a positive effect on the murderer who had fled there.[12]

There is, in fact, an *"ir miklat"* in the Torah itself. The Gemara states that if someone feels himself being overpowered by the *"goel hadam"* — his *yetzer hara* — he should toil in Torah study. If this is not sufficient, then he should recite the *Shema*.[13]

---

10. *Shemos* 21:13.

11. The laws pertaining to the *ir miklat* are discussed in detail in *Bamidbar* ch. 35 and *Devarim* ch.19.

12. *Sefer HaChinuch* (mitzvah 408) writes: "Their [the Leviim's] land was chosen as a place of refuge for all who killed unintentionally, more than the lands of the other *shevatim* (tribes), in the hope that their land's sanctity would atone for them."

13. *Berachos* 5a.

There are 48 words in the first portion of *Shema. Tzaddikim* teach that the six letters of the verse *"Shema Yisrael . . ."* correspond to the six primary *miklat* cities, while the remaining 42 words correspond to the others. If the *yetzer hara* seeks to destroy a person, he should accept upon himself *ol malchus Shamayim* by reciting *Shema.*

Three Parallels

As we have seen in previous essays,[14] there are parallels in *makom*, place; *nefesh,* soul; and *zman,* time. In *Sefer Arvei Nachal's* famous example, the *Kodesh HaKodashim* is the holiest place on earth; the Kohen Gadol is the holiest soul; and Yom Kippur is the holiest day. On the day of Yom Kippur, all three come together when the Kohen Gadol enters the *Kodesh HaKodashim* to perform the day's special service.

The 48 *arei miklat* are the *places* of refuge on this world.

As we have seen, the period from Rosh Chodesh Elul until Yom Kippur is the *zman,* time, of refuge. The month of Elul leads us into Rosh Hashanah, the day of *kabbalas ol malchus Shamayim,* when in unison we cry out *"HaMelech!"* ("The King!") and accept Hashem's sovereignty upon ourselves. The conclusion of *Kiddush* of Rosh Hashanah and the central blessing of *Shemoneh Esrei* is, *"Blessed are You, Hashem, King over all the world . . ."*

Who is the *nefesh* of refuge?

Rambam writes that one who denies belief in the coming of Mashiach denies belief in the Torah itself, for in three places in the Torah, the future Redemption is mentioned. The last of the three, says *Rambam,* is in *Parashas Shoftim*, in the chapter of the *arei miklat.* There the Torah writes that at the time of the Redemption, the borders of Eretz Yisrael will expand and there will be an additional three primary *miklat* cities. In *Rambam's* words:

> *. . . regarding the cities of refuge it says, "When Hashem will broaden your boundary . . . then you shall add three*

14. See, for example, "*Shema* and Its Introductory Blessings" (ch. 18).

more cities ...."[15] *This has never happened, and Hashem did not command it for naught.*[16]

Melech HaMashiach will be the one to set aside these three cities. In so doing he will bring the observance of the 613 mitzvos to completion. For of all the mitzvos in the Torah, only this mitzvah, the setting aside of the remaining *miklat* cities, has not yet been accomplished.

All Jewish *neshamos* are encompassed within the 600,000 souls that left Egypt, and they correspond to the 600,000 letters of the Torah.[17] Additionally, every Jewish soul is rooted in a particular mitzvah in the Torah. It seems that Mashiach is the *nefesh* of the *arei miklat.*

On Simchas Torah, the *"Chasan Torah"* is honored with completing the Torah reading of the entire *Chumash.* Mashiach is the *"Chasan Torah"* of the Jewish people. He will bring the fulfillment of the Torah to completion. He will be the *nefesh* of refuge, saving the Jewish people from its enemies, both physical and spiritual.

Mashiach will rescue us from the *yetzer hara's* clutches and will make Hashem's sovereignty recognized throughout the world.

What is *kabbalas ol Malchus Shamayim*? It means to make oneself *batel* (nullified) before Hashem, to dedicate one's very essence, desires, and aspirations to Him. As we pray every morning in *Birchos HaShachar*: וְכוֹף אֶת יִצְרֵנוּ לְהִשְׁתַּעְבֶּד לָךְ, *and compel our evil inclination to be subservient to You.* This is *kabbalas ol Malchus Shamayim.*

The Role of the King

One of the 613 mitzvos is: שׂוֹם תָּשִׂים עָלֶיךָ מֶלֶךְ, *You must put a king over you.*[18] The Gemara expounds the double expression שׂוֹם תָּשִׂים to teach, שֶׁתְּהֵא אֵימָתוֹ עָלֶיךָ, *that his awe must be upon*

15. *Devarim* 19:8-9.

16. *Rambam, Hilchos Melachim* 11:2.

17. See "*Ahavas Yisrael* and Tefillah" (ch. 5).

18. *Devarim* 17:15.

you.[19] In its basic interpretation, this means that one must fear the Jewish king. However, one can also interpret it to mean that אֵימָתוֹ, *his yiras Shamayim,* should be manifest upon you. As opposed to kings of other nations, who often rule harshly with impunity and arrogance, viewing themselves as the ultimate power, the Jewish king is specifically commanded "*... so that he will learn to fear Hashem, his God, to observe all the mitzvos of this Torah ....*"[20] A Jewish king should be a *tzaddik*, whose great level of *yiras Shamayim* influences all his subjects.

The *gematria* of וְיָסַפְתָּ לְךָ עוֹד שָׁלֹשׁ *(Then you shall add three more [cities])* is equal to that of שׂוֹם תָּשִׂים עָלֶיךָ מֶלֶךְ (*You must put a king over you* — 1,316).

Moshe Rabbeinu was the first Jewish king. The verse *"He became king over Yeshurun ..."*[21] is a reference to Moshe.[22] Zohar states that Mashiach will possess the soul of Moshe.[23]

Moshe was the first to designate *miklat* cities. *"Then Moshe set aside three cities on the bank of the Jordan."*[24] Moshe began this mitzvah and Mashiach will complete it. יַבְדִּיל מֹשֶׁה שָׁלֹשׁ עָרִים *(Moshe separated three cities)* has the same *gematria* as מִקֶּרֶב אַחֶיךָ תָּשִׂים עָלֶיךָ מֶלֶךְ (*from amongst your brothers you shall place upon you a king* — 1,351).

Immediately following the verses that speak of Moshe's designating the *miklat* cities, the Torah states: *This is the Torah [i.e. teaching] that Moshe placed before Bnei Yisrael.*[25] From this juxtaposition our Sages derive that Torah study itself is a *miklat,* a source of refuge, from harm.[26]

---

19. *Kiddushin* 32b.

20. *Devarim* 17:19.

21. Ibid. 33:5.

22. See *Ibn Ezra.*

23. An allusion to this, says Zohar, is the verse מַה שֶּׁהָיָה הוּא שֶׁיִּהְיֶה, *Whatever has been is what will be* (*Koheles* 1:9). The initial letters of מַה שֶּׁהָיָה הוּא spell מֹשֶׁה, a hint that the original redeemer, Moshe, will be the redeemer in the future.

24. *Devarim* 4:41.

25. Ibid. v. 44.

26. *Makkos* 10a.

How do we "seek refuge" in Elul? Through increased Torah study, by studying works of *mussar* that will lead to increased *yiras Shamayim*. We engage in *teshuvah, tefillah,* and *tzedakah*. The literal translation of *teshuvah* is *return*. We return to our spiritual roots by bringing our *neshamos* back to their original state of purity and reuniting ourselves with the *Ribbono shel Olam*.

The Way of a Son

There is another means by which we "seek refuge" from the *yetzer hara* in Elul. The Gemara relates:

> *R' Pinchas ben Yair was once traveling to carry out the ransoming of captives. He encountered the Ginai River and said to it, "Ginai, split your waters for me so that I may cross through you." The river replied, "You are going to perform the will of your Maker, and I [by flowing] am going to perform the will of my Maker. You might accomplish and you might not accomplish [for your efforts to redeem the captives may fail], but I will surely accomplish [His will. Therefore, it is best that I not split for your sake]."*
>
> *R' Pinchas ben Yair replied, "If you do not split, I decree that water should never again flow through you!" The river then split for him.*[27]

Why did the river split? It challenged R' Pinchas ben Yair with a solid argument, to which R' Pinchas did not directly respond.

R' Yeshayah of Kuzhmir explained that R' Pinchas did not have to respond, because the river's argument was no argument at all. *Precisely because* the success of R' Pinchas' mission was in doubt was he deserving of the river moving aside. His mission of *pidyon shevuyim* surely involved danger and was one of *mesiras nefesh* (self-sacrifice). Why did R' Pinchas ben Yair undertake such a mission when its success was doubtful? Because the love of

27. *Chullin* 7a.

a son for his father or mother impels him to undertake deeds for their benefit that others would never attempt. It was R' Pinchas ben Yair's burning love for Hashem and His people that impelled him to make the attempt to *possibly* carry out His will despite the risks involved. This was much greater than the river's fulfillment of Hashem's will, for its success is guaranteed.

As we mentioned in the previous essay, Elul is a time when Hashem looks towards us like a Father, with an abundance of love and mercy. It is incumbent upon us to respond in kind, in the way of a son who seeks to extend himself on behalf of his beloved father. This is why we arise earlier than usual to recite *Selichos*. We strive to daven with even greater *kavanah* and increase our *tzedakah*-giving. We are showing the *Ribbono shel Olam* that we are His children and are extending ourselves in order to draw closer to Him. When we reach out in this way, Hashem responds in kind and welcomes us back with open arms.

CHAPTER THIRTY-THREE

Rosh Hashanah — A New Breath of Life

R*ambam* writes:

Although the shofar-blowing of Rosh Hashanah is a Scriptural decree [and must be observed whether or not one understands the reason for it], there is a רֶמֶז *(allusion) in it, as if the shofar were saying, "Awake, sleepers, from your sleep! Arise, slumberers, from your slumber! Examine your deeds! Return [to Hashem] through teshuvah! Remember your Creator! ... Peer into your souls, improve your ways and deeds."*[1]

1. *Rambam, Hilchos Teshuvah* 3:4.

As is well known, *Rambam's* wording of his *Yad HaChazakah* is exceptionally precise. Shofar is not the only mitzvah regarding which he cites a *remez,* allusion.[2] Yet, only here does he use the words אַף עַל פִּי ... שֶׁגְּזֵרַת הַכָּתוּב רֶמֶז יֵשׁ **בּוֹ**, *Though ... it is a Scriptural decree, there is an allusion **in it**.* The wording implies that the *remez* is in the Torah itself.

There is something about the mitzvah of shofar as it appears in the Torah that demands explanation. In the latter part of *Parashas Emor* we find the *parashas hamo'adim,*[3] which includes the five Scriptural *yomim tovim* and the special mitzvos associated with them. There, Rosh Hashanah is referred to as a day of **זִכְרוֹן** תְּרוּעָה, ***recalling** the sounding of the* shofar.[4] These words, זִכְרוֹן תְּרוּעָה, are used in *Kiddush* and *Shemoneh Esrei* when Rosh Hashanah falls on Shabbos and we do not sound the shofar. On a day when the shofar is blown, we use the words יוֹם תְּרוּעָה *(a day of the sounding of the shofar),* which are from *Parashas Pinchas.*[5] There, the Torah lists the various animals brought as part of the *Korban Mussaf* of Shabbos and Yom Tov. That is where the Torah refers to Rosh Hashanah as יוֹם תְּרוּעָה and which *poskim* cite as the source of the mitzvah of shofar.[6]

Why is the mitzvah's primary mention not in *Parashas Emor,* together with the mitzvos of the other *mo'adim*?

Man's "Re-creation"

Talmud Yerushalmi notes something unusual about the Torah's terminology for the *Korban Mussaf* of Rosh Hashanah. Regarding the other *yamim tovim* the Torah says וְהִקְרַבְתֶּם עֹלָה, *You shall **offer** a [Korban] Olah*. However, regarding the *Mussaf* of Rosh Hashanah the Torah states: וַעֲשִׂיתֶם עֹלָה, *And you shall **make** an Olah.*[7]

2. See, for example, *Rambam, Hilchos Mikvaos,* 11:12.
3. *Vayikra* ch. 23.
4. Ibid. v. 24.
5. *Bamidbar* 29:1.
6. See *Rambam, Hilchos Shofar* 1:1.
7. *Bamidbar* 29:2.

R' Yosei said: Regarding the other korbanos it says וְהִקְרַבְתֶּם*, whereas here it says* וַעֲשִׂיתֶם*. Said HaKadosh Baruch Hu to [Bnei] Yisrael: "Because you came before Me for judgment on Rosh Hashanah and emerged in peace, I consider it as if you were created as a new creation."*[8]

There is a fundamental difference between the Jewish calendar and the secular one. Secular holidays are a commemoration of events that once happened. The holiday has no intrinsic significance, as can be seen from the fact that many holidays are not connected to a specific calendar date but to a Monday that will allow for a "long weekend."

The Jewish calendar can be likened to a rolodex directory containing hundreds of names and phone numbers. The information is always there, but only when the wheel is turned does one see a specific name and address.[9]

Each date in the Jewish calendar — especially the *yamim tovim* — represents Divine emanations of spiritual blessing that are unique to it alone. On Pesach there are emanations of *cheirus*, freedom, which provide every Jew with a unique opportunity to break free of the earthly desires that impede our *avodas Hashem*. On Shavuos we return to the spiritual emanations that were present at the Giving of the Torah, and we have a special opportunity to attach ourselves to Torah and its study.

The six days of Creation began on 25 Elul. Rosh Hashanah is the anniversary of Adam's creation.[10] On that day, as the Torah describes it, וַיִּפַּח בְּאַפָּיו נִשְׁמַת חַיִּים וַיְהִי הָאָדָם לְנֶפֶשׁ חַיָּה, *He [Hashem] blew into his nostrils the soul of life, and man became a living spirit.*[11]

---

8. *Yerushalmi Rosh Hashanah* 4:8.

9. Another metaphor is that of a train traveling from place to place. The stations are always there, but only at certain times does the train arrive at a specific station.

10. In *Tefillas Mussaf* of Rosh Hashanah we say: זֶה הַיּוֹם תְּחִלַּת מַעֲשֶׂיךָ, *This day is the anniversary of the start of Your handiwork.* It was only when Adam was created that Hashem's mission for the universe was fulfilled.

11. *Bereishis* 2:7.

Each year on Rosh Hashanah, the *baal tokei'a*, as representative of the entire congregation, blows into the shofar. This is not a mere physical act. The mitzvah of *tekias shofar* must be accompanied by heartfelt *teshuvah,* a sincere desire to begin anew in one's commitment to serve Hashem. When the *baal tokei'a* blows into the shofar, it comes not just from his lips but from the depths of his soul. It is a *tekiah* of *teshuvah*, of regret for past misdeeds, and a desire to attach oneself to Hashem and His Torah as never before.

And Hashem reciprocates, as it were. As He did to Adam, He blows into us a new Godly light, and we become like one born anew. This is the power of the mitzvah of shofar.

"Awake, Sleepers, From Your Sleep!"

We can now understand *Rambam's* teaching that a *remez,* allusion, is to be found in the mitzvah of shofar as it is stated in the Torah. As we have seen, the words וַעֲשִׂיתֶם עֹלָה teach us that on Rosh Hashanah when we "emerge from judgment in peace" it is as if we have been recreated. How does this occur? Through the mitzvah of shofar. This is why the mitzvah of shofar appears in the preceding verse: יוֹם תְּרוּעָה יִהְיֶה לָכֶם. Rosh Hashanah is a day of mutual "blowing" — from ourselves to Hashem, and from Hashem to us.

And so, as *Rambam* writes, the shofar calls out to us to utilize the moment and begin anew: *"Awake, sleepers, from your sleep! Arise, slumberers, from your slumber! Examine your deeds! Return [to Hashem] through teshuvah!"*

As we prepare for the great mitzvah of shofar, we must realize that we are preparing for a new *brias haolam* (creation of the world) and the *Ribbono shel Olam* is calling to us through the shofar: *"Whatever your life has been like until now has come to an end — now is a new beginning! Improve your ways! Arise from your slumber! Do not be like those who are mired in their material, earthly existence. Blow the shofar from the depths of your heart with sincere regret, with a renewed acceptance of Torah and with a complete teshuvah. In this way, you will be making yourself into a new creation as I blow into you a new neshamah."*

"Where Are You?"

On that very first day of Adam's existence, he and Chavah sinned by eating from the Tree of Knowledge. Adam and Chavah went to hide when they heard the sound of Hashem approaching. Opening His dialogue with Adam in a calming way, Hashem asked him, "אַיֶּכָּה, *Where are you*?"[12] The *Baal HaTanya*[13] sees a deeper meaning to this word:

> *Adam, where are you in this world? What has happened to you? How could you have fallen so quickly from the exalted level you had previously enjoyed?*

Every year on this day, Hashem calls to each of us with the same question. It is for us to respond by asking ourselves, "Indeed, where am I? Have I improved since the last Rosh Hashanah? Am I giving significant attention to fulfilling my purpose in this world?"

Seven Times Seven

The *siddur* of the *Baal Tanya* writes regarding Rosh Hashanah: "After the reading of the Torah, one should prepare himself for the blowing of the shofar and recite [the chapter of *Tehillim* that opens with] לַמְנַצֵּחַ לִבְנֵי קֹרַח מִזְמוֹר."[14] The wording implies that this chapter of *Tehillim*, which we recite seven times, is a form of preparation for the great mitzvah of *tekias shofar*. How is this so?

The *mekubalim* note that the name אֱלֹהִים appears in this chapter seven times; by reciting the chapter seven times we invoke this Name of God 49 times.

12. *Bereishis* 3:9.

13. See also *Aderes Eliyahu.*

14. *Tehillim* ch. 47.

There is a deep connection between Rosh Hashanah and the Yom Tov of Shavuos, when the Torah was received at Sinai. Shavuos is on the 50th day from when the *Sefirah* count begins; Rosh Hashanah is the 50th day from 11 Av, which begins the seven weeks of *nechamah* (consolation) following Tishah B'Av.[15]

R' Saadiah Gaon enumerates 10 allusions in the mitzvah of shofar, one of them being the shofar blast that was heard at Sinai when we accepted the Torah. The shofar of Rosh Hashanah reminds us to renew the commitment we made at that time.

In the *Tefillas Mussaf* of Rosh Hashanah, the blessing of *Shofaros* focuses on the Giving of the Torah:

> *You were revealed in Your cloud of glory to Your holy people to speak with them ... the entire universe shuddered before You ... during Your revelation, our King, on Mount Sinai to teach Your people Torah and mitzvos ....*

The three verses of *Shofaros* from the Torah are all from the chapter of *Matan Torah.* For Rosh Hashanah, besides being a day of judgment and general renewal, is also a day akin to Shavuos as a time to accept the Torah anew.

One who failed to utilize Shavuos to strengthen his attachment to Torah has a "second chance" on Rosh Hashanah. Reciting לַמְנַצֵּחַ לִבְנֵי קֹרַח מִזְמוֹר seven times and invoking the Name אֱלֹהִים 49 times reminds us to use the 50th day of this period, the awesome day of Rosh Hashanah, to dedicate ourselves anew to the study and observance of Hashem's holy Torah.

---

15. The burning of the Beis HaMikdash occurred primarily on 10 Av, which is why the laws of mourning are in force until noon of that day. We fast on the Ninth of Av because that is when the fires were set and the Beis HaMikdash began to burn.

The connection between Rosh Hashanah and Shavuos is even deeper. Both are related to the concept of *Yovel,* which, in its most basic definition, refers to the 50th year of the agricultural cycle, when the land of Eretz Yisrael lies fallow (as it does during *Shemittah*) and all Jewish slaves are freed. These slaves, whose spirituality had been diminished during their years of slavery — as evident from the fact that they are permitted to marry a Caananite maidservant — return to their "roots" upon gaining their freedom on *Yovel.* Rosh Hashanah and Shavuos which, as we have seen, both relate to the number 50, are days that are most auspicious for one to return to his spiritual roots and begin anew.

CHAPTER THIRTY-FOUR

Rosh Hashanah — Shemoneh Esrei Insights

Ascending the Mountain

שִׂמְחָה לְאַרְצֶךָ וְשָׂשׂוֹן לְעִירֶךָ.

[Grant] gladness to Your land and joy to Your city.

The focus of much of the Rosh Hashanah davening, and in particular the third blessing of *Shemoneh Esrei*, is our yearning for Mashiach and the rebuilding of the Beis HaMikdash. As we have mentioned previously, there are parallels in *nefesh* (soul), *makom* (place), and *zman* (time). The parallel of Rosh Hashanah, the day which encompasses the entire year, is the site of the Beis HaMikdash, the place of the אֶבֶן שְׁתִיָּה (foundation stone), with which Creation of the earth began.

ראֹשׁ הַשָּׁנָה has the same *gematria as* בֵּית הַמִּקְדָּשׁ (861).

Prior to Rosh Hashanah, we read *Parashas Ki Savo,* which opens with the mitzvah of *bikkurim.* In the time of the Beis HaMikdash a farmer would ascend to Jerusalem and bring to the Beis HaMikdash his first ripened fruits of the seven species with which the Land is blessed.

Rosh Hashanah, the day of renewal when Hashem breathes new spiritual life into each of us, is most opportune for freeing ourselves from the bonds of the *yetzer hara.* We should ascend to the "Beis HaMikdash" by tapping into the awesome sanctity and blessing inherent in Rosh Hashanah. We should offer ourselves as *"bikkurim"* to Hashem as we begin anew.

This concept is alluded to in the verses of *mitzvas bikkurim*:

And it will be when you will come to the Land ... you shall take the first of every fruit ... and go to the place that Hashem, your God, will choose to make His Name rest there.[1] As we have explained, when a Jew makes a commitment on Rosh Hashanah to renew his attachment to Hashem and His Torah, it is likened to one who ascends the Temple Mount with his *bikkurim.*

You shall prostrate yourself before Hashem, our God. At the Beis HaMikdash, upon the stone floor of the Courtyard, Jews would prostrate themselves before Hashem. In *galus,* on Rosh Hashanah, the counterpart to the Beis HaMikdash in time, we lower ourselves to the floor to bow before Hashem.[2]

You shall rejoice with all the goodness that Hashem, your God, has give you. If we utilize Rosh Hashanah as we should and truly begin anew, we will rejoice as we receive the blessings and goodness that the new year will bring.

---

1. *Devarim* 26:1,2.

2. We also bow in this way on Yom Kippur when we recite the Temple service of that awesome day.

Rejoice With Trembling

אַתָּה בְחַרְתָּנוּ מִכָּל הָעַמִּים ... וְקֵרַבְתָּנוּ מַלְכֵּנוּ לַעֲבוֹדָתֶךָ ...
You have chosen us from all the peoples ...
You drew us close, our King, to Your service ...

As the Day of Judgment, Rosh Hashanah is a day that evokes *yirah,* awe of Hashem. As we say in the *Unesenah Tokef* prayer: *Let us now relate the power of this day's holiness, for it is awesome and frightening.*

However, there is another, little-known aspect to Rosh Hashanah. In the verse in *Maariv* recited on the eve of Rosh Hashanah, Dovid HaMelech declares:

> תִּקְעוּ בַחֹדֶשׁ שׁוֹפָר בַּכֶּסֶה לְיוֹם חַגֵּנוּ.
> *Blow a shofar at the moon's renewal, when [the moon] is covered on this festive day.*[3]

Just as the moon is covered on Rosh Hashanah, so too is an aspect of the day concealed. As we have seen in the previous essay, on Rosh Hashanah Hashem "breathes" new life into us and grants us the opportunity to renew our attachment to Him and His Torah. It is a day when He seeks to draw us close to Him, a day that, like the challah and apple of our *seudos,* is "dipped in honey."[4]

The *gematria* of וְקֵרַבְתָּנוּ מַלְכֵּנוּ *(You drew us close, our King)* is equal to that of תִּשְׁרֵי (910). The *gematria* of אַב הָרַחֲמִים *(Merciful Father)* is equal to דְּבַשׁ (*honey* — 306).

The verses of *mitzvas bikkurim* discussed above open with the word וְהָיָה, *And it will be [when you will come to the Land].* The Midrash tells us that the word וַיְהִי, *and it was,* denotes *tzaar*, pain,

3. *Tehillim* 81:4.

4. Rav Wolfson often remarks that the tefillos of Rosh Hashanah, particularly the *Mussaf Shemoneh Esrei,* are "dipped in honey" and that *tzaddikim* of earlier generations "could not pull themselves away" from the words of the *Shemoneh Esrei.*

while וְהָיָה denotes *simchah,* joy.[5] *Sefer Yismach Moshe* explains that וַיְהִי refers to the past, and when one thinks of his personal past, he is often saddened by his spiritual failings. However, וְהָיָה refers to the future, and when one looks to the future with a sincere desire to improve, he becomes filled with joy.

There is a kabbalistic principle that every month in the Jewish calendar is related to the Name י-ה-ו-ה, each month with a different arrangement of the letters. The order of the letters for each month is derived from the words in a specific verse.

The Name arrangement for the month of Tishrei is derived from the words וַיִּרְאוּ אֹתָהּ שָׂרֵי פַרְעֹה (*When the officers of Pharaoh saw her [Sarah]*).[6] The end letters of these words spell וְהָיָה, which when rearranged spell the Name of Hashem. The month of Elul is a time to cry over our past sins. Zohar states that the verse *She shall weep for her father and mother for a full month*[7] alludes to Elul. Rosh Hashanah, however, is a day when we accept upon ourselves Hashem's sovereignty with renewed commitment and resolve to make the coming year one of real spiritual change. This is cause for joy, and indeed, the Baal Shem Tov and his disciples would find the balance between the awe that the Day of Judgment evokes and the joy that should be experienced as Hashem draws us close and welcomes our sincere desire to change.

The Source of His Love

וְגַם אֶת נֹחַ בְּאַהֲבָה זָכַרְתָּ ...

Moreover, You remembered Noach with love ...

In the blessings of *Zichronos* (Remembrance), the first of the 10 special verses is from the episode of Noach and the Flood. We introduce it by saying:

5. *Vayikra Rabbah* 11:8.

6. *Bereishis* 12:15.

7. *Devarim* 21:13.

Moreover, You remembered Noach with love and recalled him with words of salvation and mercy, when You brought the waters of the Flood to destroy all living flesh ... his remembrance comes before You, Hashem, our God, to make his offspring as abundant as the dust of the world and his descendants as the sand by the sea.

What is the meaning of this "remembrance"? Did not Hashem promise Noach before he even built the Ark that he and his family would survive the Flood? And what is the connection between this remembrance and our tefillos on Rosh Hashanah? Finally, where in the Torah do we see that this remembrance was with "love," as we say in this blessing?

When Hashem commanded Noach to build the Ark, it was intended as a means of returning the world to its original state. The world first lost its perfection with the sin of Adam and Chavah and then in later generations it declined to an astonishing degree. Hashem has made the world in a way that man's actions impact all of creation. In Noach's times civilization had become so morally corrupt that the animals and even plant life were affected. The world could not be allowed to exist in this state.

Noach, as the Torah testifies, was a perfect *tzaddik,* and those aspects of creation that were connected to his spiritual roots were still pure and wholesome. Whatever was allowed into the Ark was, in a sense, a part of Noach's "mini-world" even before entry, and therefore was unaffected by the prevailing *tumah* (spiritual defilement). The Ark's self-contained world was, at the outset, one of perfection.

The world outside the Ark would be destroyed by way of the Flood; with the physical destruction, the *tumah* would be wiped away as well. After the flood, Noach and his family were to begin anew in a world that had returned to its original, pristine state.

But inside the Ark, something happened that would change everything. Cham, son of Noach, sinned.[8] Once again, a perfect

8. See *Sanhedrin* 108b.

world was rendered imperfect. With Cham's sin, Noach and his family were in danger of being destroyed. For they had been permitted to survive with the understanding that their new world would not be one of spiritual failings, but what point was there in beginning a new civilization that ultimately would end in the same dismal failure as before? It was not for this that Hashem had promised Noach and his family that they would survive.

In what merit did Noach and his family survive after Cham's sin? The *Ribbono shel Olam* saw that from Shem, Noach's son, would one day be born Avraham Avinu, a perfect *tzaddik*, who would transmit to his offspring that indestructible spark of purity that made him unique in his generation. Hashem knew that in the End of Days with the coming of Mashiach, this spark in every Jewish soul would be ignited, so that the entire Jewish people, and with them the entire world, would be restored to the state of perfection that existed before Adam had sinned.

You remembered Noach with love .... The remembrance of אַבְרָהָם אוֹהֲבוֹ, *Avraham, His beloved,*[9] came before Him, and in Avraham's merit, Noach and his family were saved. Hashem promised Avraham, *I will make your offspring as the dust of the earth so that if one can count the dust of the earth, then your offspring too can be counted.*[10] This blessing is alluded to when we say in *Tefillas Mussaf, ... his [Noach's] remembrance comes before You, Hashem, our God, to make his offspring as abundant as the dust of the world and his descendants as the sand by the sea.*

It is to this remembrance, of Avraham and his precious offspring — the Jewish nation — that we allude in the blessing of *Zichronos*, when we recall how Noach and his family were saved.

9. From the Friday night *zemiros*. In *Sefer Yeshayahu* (41:8), Hashem refers to him as אַבְרָהָם אוֹהֲבִי.

10. *Bereishis* 13:16.

CHAPTER THIRTY-FIVE

Yom Kippur — A Mikveh in Time

The concluding *mishnah* of *Masechta Yoma*, the tractate dealing with the holy day of Yom Kippur, ends with the famous words of Rabi Akiva:

Praiseworthy are you, Yisrael! Before Whom do you purify yourselves? Who purifies you? Your Father in Heaven, as is said, "And I will sprinkle pure water upon you, and you shall be cleansed";[1] *and it also says, "The mikveh of Yisrael is Hashem."*[2] *Just as a mikveh purifies the contaminated, so does HaKadosh Baruch Hu purify Yisrael.*[3]

1. *Yechezkel* 36:25.
2. *Yirmiyahu* 17:13.
3. *Mishnah Yoma* 8:9.

The concluding words of a final mishnah are like the concluding line of a *shtar* (legal document); it encapsulates the entire *masechta.* In the Torah, a *mikveh* is a gathering of rain water measuring 40 *sa'ah* or more that is halachically fit for ritual immersion.[4] *Sefer Bnei Yissoschor* states that each of the 40 days beginning with Rosh Chodesh Elul represent 1 *sa'ah* of a *mikveh.* On Yom Kippur, the 40th *sa'ah* is added and the *"mikveh"* is complete. On the day of Yom Kippur, the *Ribbono shel Olam,* through the awesome sanctity that He has granted this day, cleanses us of our sins; *the mikveh of Yisrael is Hashem.*[5]

As stated above, Yom Kippur is the climax of a 40-day period of *teshuvah* that begins with the first day of Rosh Chodesh Elul. As we shall see, the number 40 is significant, especially as it relates to the power inherent in this day.

The Indestructible Spark

Our Sages teach that it takes 40 days for *yetziras havlad,* the formation of a human fetus.[6] We know that for willfully transgressing a *lo sa'aseh* (negative commandment) involving an action, one is liable to receive *malkos* (lashes) in *beis din.* "... *The judges shall cast him down and strike him ... Forty shall he strike him* ..."[7] *Ramban* explains that the 40 lashes correspond to the 40 days of *yetziras havlad* which the sinner forfeited through his transgression (and which is atoned for through this punishment).

---

4. The literal meaning of *mikveh* is *gathering of water.* In the chapter of Creation, the Torah states: וּלְמִקְוֵה הַמַּיִם קָרָא יַמִּים, *and to the gathering of waters He called "Seas."* (*Bereishis* 1:10).

5. *Rema,* citing *Rambam,* states: "Yom Kippur atones only for penitents who believe in its [the day's power of] atonement; but for one who is scornful of it and thinks in his heart, 'What does Yom Kippur accomplish for me?' it will not atone" (*Orach Chaim* 607:6).

6. See *Rashi* to *Bereishis* 7:4. The Gemara states that for 40 days from the moment of conception, parents can pray for the child to be a boy or a girl (*Berachos* 60a).

7. *Devarim* 25:3.

Ramban's words demand explanation, for as is well known, though the Torah uses the number 40, the sinner, in fact, receives only *39 malkos*![8]

We know that every person has *bechirah*, free will, to choose between good and evil. However, there is a chamber in every Jew's heart that is impervious to sin; evil simply cannot affect the essential purity and Godliness of that aspect of the *neshamah*. Dovid HaMelech alludes to this in the words וְעוֹד מְעַט וְאֵין רָשָׁע, which can be translated as *There is a little bit where there is no wicked one.*[9]

The human heart is the seat of passion and desire. It and its spiritual counterpart are formed during the 40 days of *yetziras havlad*. On one of those 40 days, we are given that part of the heart which is an inheritance from Avraham Avinu. It is a spark of holiness, infused with Avraham's pure, unshakable *emunah* in Hashem. It is indestructible and, as we have said, impervious to sin. It is this spark that makes it possible for even the most wayward sinner to return to his roots through *teshuvah*.

This, says R' Yitzchak Meir of Ger, is the meaning of the conclusion of *Shemoneh Esrei's* opening blessing: *[Blessed are You, Hashem,] Shield of Avraham*. Hashem "shields" and preserves the spark of Avraham in every one of us so that it is never snuffed out.[10]

Coerced, but Willing

The above adds insight to a fascinating statement of *Rambam*. The Torah states that a *korban* must be offered לִרְצוֹנוֹ, *in accordance*

---

8. The Torah states: *"and he shall strike him, before him, according to his wickedness, by a count* [בְּמִסְפָּר]*."* The next verse begins, אַרְבָּעִים יַכֶּנּוּ, *Forty shall he strike him*. Our Sages expound these verses as if they read בְּמִסְפָּר אַרְבָּעִים יַכֶּנּוּ, *By a number which leads to forty [i.e. thirty-nine] shall he strike him* (*Makkos* 22b).

9. *Tehillim* 37:10.

10. This thought is the focus of "Soul of Faith, City of Faith" (ch. 30).

with his [the owner's] will.[11] However, from the word יַקְרִיב אוֹתוֹ, *he shall bring it,* the Sages derive that if the owner refuses to fulfill his vow, we force him to do so. The obvious question is: How is this *in accordance with his will*? The resolution to this apparent contradiction is כּוֹפִין אוֹתוֹ עַד שֶׁיֹּאמַר "רוֹצֶה אֲנִי", *They force him until he says, "I am willing."*[12] *Rambam* explains:

> *[In essence, every Jew] wants to be a[n observant member of Klal] Yisrael, perform the mitzvos, and distance himself from transgression. It is his evil inclination that pulls him in the opposite direction. However, when he is flogged [by beis din's agent] until his evil inclination is weakened and then he says, "I am willing ..." this is ... in accordance with his [essential] will.*[13]

Rambam means that even when a Jew stubbornly refuses to fulfill his obligations as he succumbs to the dictates of his *yetzer hara,* there is still that unsullied spark in the depths of his heart, the spark of Avraham Avinu, that *does* want to fulfill Hashem's will. That spark is like a stove's pilot light that has the power to ignite a huge flame. When *beis din* employs physical coercion upon the Jew who has thus far refused to fulfill his vow, his evil inclination is weakened and from the depths of his soul that spark of purity cries out, "רוֹצֶה אֲנִי, *I am willing!"*

We can now understand the *Ramban* quoted above regarding *malkos.* The *malkos* that a sinner receives does correspond to the *kochos hanefesh* (spiritual attributes) that are formed over a 40-day period. However, there is one aspect of his soul, one small spark, with which he did not sin. It is the spark of Avraham Avinu, the spark that cries out "רוֹצֶה אֲנִי!" — "I want to fulfill Hashem's will, I do not want to sin!" The sin that was committed did not reach this aspect of his soul. Therefore, he receives not 40 but 39 lashes.

---

11. *Vayikra* 1:3.

12. *Rashi* ad loc. from *Rosh Hashanah* 6a.

13. *Hilchos Gerushin* 2:20. *Maharal* (in his *Gur Aryeh* commentary on the Torah) applies *Rambam's* words to this law regarding *korbanos.*

The Day of the Indestructible Spark

The 40 days of *teshuvah* from Rosh Chodesh Elul until Yom Kippur correspond to the 40 days of *yetziras havlad* in which the *kochos hanefesh* are formed. Yom Kippur corresponds to the spark that sin cannot reach. It is a day, says the Gemara, on which the Satan has no power.[14] Yom Kippur is the day when the *neshamah* cries out "!רוֹצֶה אֲנִי." The *gematria* of יוֹם כִּפּוּר is equal to רוֹצֶה אֲנִי (362).

On Yom Kippur a Jew makes contact with that chamber in his heart, that nucleus of *tzidkus* (righteousness), that remains eternally pure, his inheritance from his forefather Avraham.

On all other days of the year no one, not even a Heavenly angel, was permitted entry into the *Kodesh HaKodashim* (Holy of Holies), the holiest place on earth where Hashem's Presence was most manifest. On Yom Kippur, the Kohen Gadol, as representative of the entire Jewish nation, was permitted entry into this chamber.

Every Yom Kippur, each one of us enters his own personal *"Kodesh HaKodashim."* The Midrash teaches that in every Jewish heart there is a Beis HaMikdash, and in that holy edifice there is a *Kodesh HaKodashim.* This is the place in one's heart in which the spark of Avraham Avinu resides. Neither the Satan nor any other angel can gain entry to this holy chamber; it is a place where only one's *yetzer tov*, good inclination, can be found.

Any Jew who engages in sincere *teshuvah* will find a moment on Yom Kippur when he is overcome by a feeling of purity and *dveikus baShem*, a moment when he has made contact with the *Kodesh HaKodashim* of his soul. This usually happens during *Ne'ilah*, the concluding tefillah of this awesome day. The word *Ne'ilah* means *closing*, for at that time the gates of Heaven are about to close and we are given a final opportunity to pray for a good year.[15]

---

14. The *gematria* of the word הַשָּׂטָן equals 364, one less than a complete solar year, indicating that there is one day on which the Satan has no power over the Jewish people (*Nedarim* 32b).

15. *Yerushalmi Berachos* 4:1.

The word can also mean *locking*, as to a door. During these holiest of moments, we are "locked up" with the *Ribono shel Olam* in utmost privacy and we experience an unusual level of closeness to Him. It is during these precious moments that we can feel the spark of Avraham Avinu burning inside us.

Today, when there is no Beis HaMikdash in which to perform the Temple service, we recite the service of the Kohen Gadol during the *chazzan's* repetition of the Yom Kippur *Mussaf*. This practice dates back to Talmudic times,[16] and is in keeping with the verse וּנְשַׁלְּמָה פָרִים שְׂפָתֵינוּ, *and let [the words of] our lips substitute for bulls.*[17] The high point of the *avodah* was when the Kohen Gadol entered the *Kodesh HaKodashim*. The high point of every Jew's Yom Kippur is when he makes contact with his own private *Kodesh HaKodashim.* At that moment, every one of us is overcome by an intense desire to return to Hashem with a full heart, to rid ourselves once and for all of the influences that seek to pull us away from that which is holy and pure. Our task is to take that exhilarating, lofty, holy moment and hold on to it so that its effects will remain with us throughout the coming year and for the rest of our lives.

The Pleasures of the Day

Yom Kippur is a day of *yiras Shamayim*, but it is also a day of *simchah,* joy. On Yom Kippur we are commanded by the Torah to engage in five עִנּוּיִם, *afflictions,* the most difficult being abstention from eating and drinking. And corresponding to those afflictions, we have been given five תַּעֲנוּגִים, *pleasures* — the five tefillos beginning with *Maariv* and concluding with *Ne'ilah*. One who has prepared himself spiritually before the fast begins will experience an intense pleasure, a contact with the *Ribbono shel Olam*, as he prays the tefillos of the day.

16. *Yoma* 36b.

17. *Hoshea* 14:3.

There is something unique about these tefillos. All year long, we talk to Hashem when we daven. On Yom Kippur, Hashem also talks to us. In the central blessing of *Shemoneh Esrei* He says, *"I, only I, am the One Who wipes away your willful sins for My sake, and I shall not recall your errors."*[18] And *"I have wiped away your willful sins like a cloud and your errors like a mist — so return to Me, for I have redeemed you."*[19] Hashem pleads to each one of us, "My Jewish child, come back to Me."

Can there be anything more beautiful, more pleasurable? How unfortunate when someone spends Yom Kippur glancing at his watch, waiting for the day to end! One should want to hold onto this precious day, to remain forever bound to its spiritual bliss.[20]

Two people can be sitting in the same shul on the same bench throughout Yom Kippur. Both are fasting and davening, observing all the laws and customs of the day. One is totally wrapped up in the day's awesome spirituality, a day that is a Gan Eden on earth. The other is looking at his watch every so often, waiting for the day to end. Night descends and the two break their fast at the same time. In Heaven, their efforts are light years apart.[21]

The Stainless Suit

Sefer Yismach Moshe offers a parable. A man was granted an audience before a king; in preparation for that meeting, he purchased a handsome suit. One day, a roofer came to his house and

18. *Yeshayahu* 43:25.

19. Ibid. 44:22.

20. Reb Nissim Pilchik was a Stoliner chassid whose soul was aflame with love of Hashem and His mitzvos. (See "Mizmor L'Sodah" [ch. 10].) Toward the end of his life, Reb Nissim spent Yom Kippur in Jerusalem's Stoliner beis midrash. The day was torridly hot; even young people found fasting more difficult than usual. During the afternoon recess, someone said, "Reb Nissim, only three more hours and the fast will be over." Reb Nissim was visibly upset by this remark. "You consider that good news?" he chided the fellow. "All year long I wait for this *heiliger tog* (holy day). Each moment of Yom Kippur is precious beyond words — and you are trying to make me feel good by telling me that only three hours remain?"

21. Based on *Sefer Yesod V'Shoresh HaAvodah, Shaar HaEisan* ch. 10.

accidentally got some tar on the suit. The man quickly applied turpentine, which succeeded in removing all but a vestige of the stain. The suit was fit to wear in public — but not in the king's presence. For that, it had to be perfectly clean, in brand-new condition.

The man searched until he found a chemist who had invented a cleaning agent that succeeded in removing any trace of tar. Now, the man was ready for his audience with the king.

During the days preceding Yom Kippur, a Jew engages in *teshuvah* and cleanses his soul of the sins that sullied it throughout the year. Often, he is successful — up to a point. As hard as he tries, he may not be able to rid his *neshamah* of every last vestige of *tumah* that his sins have wrought.

Fortunately, we have an "Expert" Who is capable and stands ready to cleanse our souls completely, to the point that they are restored to their original purity.

Rabi Akiva said: Praiseworthy are you, Yisrael! Before Whom do you purify yourselves? We engage in *teshuvah* from Rosh Chodesh Elul as we prepare for "our audience" with the King of kings on Rosh Hashanah and again on Yom Kippur. We need to do our best, even though, despite all our efforts, we often fall short of our goal. But we need not despair. *Who purifies you? Your Father in Heaven, as is said, "And I will sprinkle pure water upon you, and you shall be cleansed";*[22] *and it also says, "The mikveh of Yisrael is Hashem."*[23]

Sometimes, a person who sincerely wants to change feels overwhelmed by past misdeeds. "Can I truly be forgiven?" he wonders. "I have sinned so grievously. How will I ever achieve atonement?"

He should not despair. *Who purifies you? Your Father in Heaven.* Our task is to repent with a full heart, with true regret, with sincere resolve to improve. Once we have done our best, we leave the rest to our great, compassionate Father in Heaven. He will cleanse us on the great, awesome day of Yom Kippur, a day on which holiness, goodness, and purity reign.

---

22. *Yechezkel* 36:25.

23. *Yirmiyahu* 17:13.

CHAPTER THIRTY-SIX

Yom Kippur — The Ketores Service

When the Beis HaMikdash stood, the *Kohen Gadol* performed the special Yom Kippur service, which we recite in the *chazzan's* repetition of the *Mussaf Shemoneh Esrei* on Yom Kippur. Of all the myriad parts of the service, the greatest was the offering of *ketores* (incense), which, in *Rashi's* words, "is the most precious of all *korbanos*."[1] Only on Yom Kippur was the *ketores* offered in the *Kodesh HaKodashim*. As we say in the Yom Kippur *Mussaf*:

> *... In his right hand he would place the shovelful of coals and his left hand the ladleful of ketores. He would spur*

1. *Rashi* to *Bamidbar* 16:6.

himself and enter the Kodesh HaKodashim until he would reach the Aron (Ark). He would place the shovel between the staves of the Aron ... In his cupped hands he would scoop up all the ketores in the ladle and pile it on the coals ... and he would wait there until the entire chamber filled with smoke ...

The Torah states: *"He shall place the ketores upon the fire before Hashem."*[2] Our Sages derive from this verse that the *ketores* must be prepared in the *Kodesh HaKodashim,* as stated above.[3]

The Tzedokim,[4] a heretical group during the Second Beis HaMikdash era who denied belief in the Oral Torah, disputed this law. They claimed to have Scriptural support showing that the *ketores* must first be placed upon the coals and only then brought into the *Kodesh HaKodashim.*

Talmud Yerushalmi tells us that the Tzedokim put forth an argument to support their opinion. They reasoned: One serving a mortal king his meal would surely not prepare it in the king's presence, as this would be disrespectful. How, then, can one consider it proper to prepare the *ketores* in the *Kodesh HaKodashim*? Certainly the proper way is to prepare it *before* entering that holiest of chambers![5]

We do not find that the Sages responded to this argument, which on the surface seems quite logical.

"We Are Your Mate"

There is a very basic difference between Rosh Hashanah and Yom Kippur. While only the Jewish people observe Rosh Hashanah, it is a day on which the entire world stands in judgment before Hashem. *"On Rosh Hashanah, all who walk the earth pass*

2. *Vayikra* 16:13.
3. *Yoma* 53a.
4. Their leader's name was Tzadok.
5. *Yerushalmi Yoma* 1:5.

before Him like young sheep."[6] But Yom Kippur is a day of atonement for the Jewish people alone. It is a day of *dveikus* (attachment) between the *Ribbono shel Olam* and His beloved, chosen nation, a closeness represented by the relationship between *chasan* and *kallah,* husband and wife.

On Rosh Hashanah, again and again, we refer to Hashem as our *Melech,* King. On Yom Kippur, in each of the five tefillos we say: אָנוּ רַעְיָתֶךָ וְאַתָּה דוֹדֵנוּ, *We are Your mate and You are our Beloved.*

The Tzedokim argued: "Is this how one serves a king, preparing his meal in front of him?" The Sages had no need to respond to this argument, for it was fundamentally flawed. True, one does not serve a king this way, but the Jewish people's relationship with Hashem on Yom Kippur is not that of a servant before his king, but of a wife before her husband.

In the presence of their subjects, a king and queen must behave with the majesty and formality that their positions demand. However, this is not the case when they are alone. Then they are husband and wife, and there is nothing wrong with the queen preparing a meal in the king's presence. To the contrary, when the king keeps the queen company as she busies herself in the kitchen, their relationship is enhanced, for it shows how close they are.

The Torah states: *"And any person* [אָדָם] *shall not be in the Ohel Moed (Mishkan) when he [the Kohen Gadol] comes to provide atonement [on Yom Kippur]."*[7] Our Sages teach that even a heavenly angel, of whom it is said פְּנֵיהֶם פְּנֵי אָדָם, *their faces were like a human face,*[8] cannot be present when the *Kohen Gadol* enters the *Kodesh HaKodashim.* That chamber, the place of the *Keruvim*[9] which represent a *chasan* and *kallah,* is the place of *yichud,* union, between Hashem and His people. It is the place that is represented by our joyous declaration on Yom Kippur of אָנוּ רַעְיָתֶךָ וְאַתָּה דוֹדֵנוּ.

---

6. *Mishnah Rosh Hashanah* 1:2.

7. *Vayikra* 16:17.

8. *Yechezkel* 1:10.

9. Two winged figures atop the *Aron,* one with the face of a boy and the other with that of a girl.

A Fundamental Dispute

An important aspect of the Jewish people's status as the *kallah*, bride, of *Hashem Yisborach* is the power vested in the Sages to expound the Torah according to the 13 principles transmitted at Sinai.[10] The Tzedokim's false ideology was based on their denying the validity of the Oral Torah. They denied that *We are Your mate and You are our Beloved,* and consequently did not believe that the Sages could expound the Torah.

The Tzedokim disagreed with any teaching of the Sages that was at variance with the most basic understanding of the Written Torah. The dispute over the *ketores*, by contrast, was not a mere dispute over how to interpret a specific verse and apply it. This argument encompassed the entire ideology of this wayward sect. Therefore, the Sages did not respond to it.[11]

Heavenly Aroma

Sefer Bnei Yissoschor, citing earlier sources, writes that when Adam and Chavah ate from the Tree of Knowledge, they sinned with, and thus spiritually damaged, four of the five senses. Adam *listened* to Chavah's words that they should heed the Serpent's advice; they *saw* that the tree was good for eating; *touched* the tree and then took its fruit; and *ate* from it.[12] However, they did not sin with their sense of smell, and therefore this sense remained in its pure, original state. The sense of smell is the one most closely associated with the days of Mashiach.

---

10. These are the י״ג מִדּוֹת שֶׁהַתּוֹרָה נִדְרֶשֶׁת בָּהֶן, as delineated in the *Braisa of R' Yishmael* that is recited at the conclusion of *Korbanos* each morning.

11. *Talmud Yerushalmi (Yoma* 1:5) relates that during the Second Temple Era, a Tzedoki *Kohen Gadol* died after he prepared the *ketores* outside the *Kodesh HaKodashim* and then brought it inside. According to one version in the Gemara he died immediately, and worms were discharged from his nostrils. He risked his life to perform the service his way, said Rav Wolfson, precisely because the Yom Kippur *ketores* service was so fundamental to the dispute between the Sages and the Tzedokim. The way he died indicated that by offering the *ketores* the wrong way, he had misused the sense of smell.

12. *Bereishis* 3:6.

Of Mashiach, Yeshayahu HaNavi says: וַהֲרִיחוֹ בְּיִרְאַת ה׳, which means *He will be imbued with great cognitive powers because of his fear of Hashem.*[13] The word וַהֲרִיחוֹ is related to רֵיחַ, *smell.* As the Gemara puts it, דְּמוֹרַח וְדָאִין, *he will "smell" and judge.*[14] Because of Mashiach's great level of *yiras Shamayim*, when litigants will come to him for judgment, he will instinctively "smell" the truth and know who is right.

As we have mentioned, the most important part of the *Kohen Gadol's* Yom Kippur service was the *ketores,* a service of fragrance, an offering that was untainted by the sin of Adam and Chavah. The eternal love that Hashem has for *Klal Yisrael* was represented by this special offering. Just as the fragrance of the *ketores* was pure and unblemished, so too is the love of Hashem for His people eternal and is not diminished by our failings.

The Holiest Song

As we have mentioned, the *Kodesh HaKodashim*, the place of the *Keruvim* which represent a *chasan* and *kallah*, is the place of union between Hashem and His people. There is a Scriptural book that is this holy chamber's counterpart:

> *Rabi Akiva said: The entire universe was not worthy of the day on which Shir HaShirim was given to the Jewish people. All the Kesuvim (Writings) are kodesh (holy), but Shir HaShirim is kodesh kodashim.*[15]

Shir HaShirim, in depicting the love between a *chasan* and *kallah*, is a metaphor for the love between Hashem and His beloved nation. The song was written with Divine Inspiration by Shlomo HaMelech.

Its opening verse is שִׁיר הַשִּׁירִים אֲשֶׁר לִשְׁלֹמֹה, which literally means, *A song of songs of [King] Shlomo.* Our Sages interpret שְׁלֹמֹה as

13. *Yeshayahu* 11:3. Translation is from R' Shimon Schwab's work on *Sefer Yeshayahu* published by ArtScroll/Mesorah.

14. *Sanhedrin* 93b.

15. *Mishnah Yadayim* 3:5.

referring to Hashem: מֶלֶךְ שֶׁהַשָּׁלוֹם שֶׁלּוֹ, *the One to Whom peace belongs.*[16]

It would seem, though, that according to this interpretation the word שְׁלֹמֹה should have been spelled שְׁלֹמוֹ, alluding to the male possessive שֶׁלּוֹ *(His)*. We can explain this by looking at a verse in the Torah regarding Avraham Avinu's travels which reads: וַיֵּט אָהֳלֹה, ... *and he pitched his tent.*[17] The Midrash notes that the Torah should have written אָהֳלוֹ, in the masculine form; the letters אהלה are usually pronounced אָהֳלָהּ and mean *her tent. Rashi* explains: First Avraham pitched his wife's tent, then he pitched his own, for a man should honor his wife more than himself.

And so it is in *Shir HaShirim*. While the word שְׁלֹמֹה is pronounced in the masculine form, referring to Hashem, its written form is feminine, for Hashem wants to honor His beloved nation even more than Himself.

Fragrance is a recurring theme in *Shir HaShirim. For fragrance your oils are good; a bag of myrrh is my Beloved to me; the vines in blossom give forth fragrance; perfumed with myrrh and levonah of all the powders of the merchants* ... The song closes with *Flee, my Beloved, and be like a gazelle or young hart upon the mountains of spices.*

As in the *Kodesh HaKodashim* on Yom Kippur, the *kodesh hakodashim* of *Shir HaShirim* uses the pure, untainted metaphor of fragrance to depict the eternal love of Hashem towards the Jewish people.

On Yom Kippur, we are alone with Hashem in the *Kodesh HaKodashim,* the holiest day of the year. To make the most of this special union, to derive the most from our unique relationship on this day filled with Heavenly love and compassion, we need to focus on those powerful words that we fervently declare on both Rosh Hashanah and Yom Kippur:

---

16. *Shevuos* 35b and *Shir HaShirim Rabbah* 1:11. In *Mishlei* and *Koheles*, Shlomo is identified as בֶּן דָּוִד, *son of Dovid.*

17. *Bereishis* 12:8.

וּתְשׁוּבָה וּתְפִילָּה וּצְדָקָה מַעֲבִירִין אֶת רֹעַ הַגְּזֵרָה.

But teshuvah, tefillah, and tzedakah remove the evil of the decree!

Let us strive to use the days beginning with Rosh Chodesh Elul, and especially the *Aseres Yemei Teshuvah*, to improve, and in so doing draw closer to Hashem. In this way, we will perceive His eternal love with yet greater intensity and be granted a year of blessing and all that is good.

APPENDICES

APPENDIX A

A Unique Generation in Unique Times

In *Parashas Vayigash,* following Yosef's revelation to his brothers, Yaakov Avinu and his family descend to Egypt. The Torah enumerates the members of Yaakov's family and concludes, *"All the souls of Yaakov's household who came to Egypt — seventy."*[1]

The Midrash[2] notes that the names listed in that *parashah* add up to only 69. Who is number 70? The Midrash offers four

1. *Bereishis* 46:27.

2. *Bereishis Rabbah* 94:9.

possible answers. The first, cited by *Rashi*, is that Yocheved, the daughter of Levi and mother of Moshe Rabbeinu, is the 70th soul. She is not mentioned in the Torah because she did not actually "descend" from the Land of Canaan; rather, she was born as her mother entered the gates of Egypt.

The other three answers are:

The 70th is *Hakadosh Baruch Hu.*

The 70th is Serach bas Asher, a granddaughter of Yaakov.

The 70th is Chushim ben Don, a grandson of Yaakov.

The last two answers in particular demand explanation, for the list of 69 in the Torah includes both Chushim ben Don and Serach bas Asher!

Yefei To'ar explains that because of his or her special importance, either Chushim or Serach is counted as two.

What was so special about these two individuals?

When the sons of Yaakov returned to Canaan after their reunion with Yosef, they were concerned as to how to break the incredible news to their aged father. The solution was found in the person of Serach bas Asher, a young *tzadekes* who played the harp. Serach played a joyous tune to which she sang the words, "Yosef still lives." Yaakov's spirit was revived and Serach was rewarded with unusual longevity; she subsequently entered *Gan Eden* alive.[3]

The Gemara relates that when Yaakov was brought from Egypt to the Cave of Machpeilah for burial, Esav interfered, claiming that the remaining spot in the cave was reserved for himself. The fleet-footed Naftali raced back to Egypt to get the contract which stated that Esav had relinquished his rights to the cave. Chushim ben Don, a deaf-mute, could not follow the conversation, but he understood enough to know that Esav was holding up the burial of his righteous grandfather. Chushim took a stick, hit Esav on the head, and killed him, and Yaakov was then buried without delay.[4]

---

3. See *Targum Yonasan* to *Bereishis* 46:17.

4. *Sotah* 13a.

True, both Serach and Chushim had achieved something great. But did this make them more important than Yaakov and his sons? Why should either of them be counted as two?

Pesach and Tishah B'Av

In *Megillas Eichah* we read: הִשְׂבִּיעַנִי בַמְּרוֹרִים הִרְוַנִי לַעֲנָה, *He filled me with bitterness; sated me with wormwood.*[5] The Midrash links בַּמְּרוֹרִים, *with bitterness,* to מָרוֹר, the bitter herb eaten on the *Seder* night. The night of the week on which the first *Seder* falls is always the same night of the week as Tishah B'Av of that year.

The Midrash is telling us that there is a deep connection between Pesach and Tishah B'Av. On the surface this is quite perplexing, for as we know, Pesach is the Yom Tov of *geulah,* redemption, while Tishah B'Av represents *galus* and *churban.*

The answer to this is simple and instructive. A fundamental truth of Judaism is that all that the *Ribbono shel Olam* does is for the good. This is especially true of the *galus* experience. Scripture is replete with Hashem's expressions of His great, unconditional love for the Jewish people. And as we say in *Shacharis* every morning, אַהֲבַת עוֹלָם אֲהַבְתָּנוּ ה' אֱלֹהֵינוּ, *With an eternal love You loved us, Hashem, our God.* Hashem did not send us into *galus* to be rid of us, Heaven forfend. *Galus* serves an important, positive purpose.

The Gemara teaches that the Jewish people were sent into exile so that *geirim*, righteous converts, could be brought under the wings of the *Shechinah*. While this statement is certainly meant literally, it has a broader meaning as well. Throughout this world there are *nitzotzos*, sparks of *kedushah*, that have been separated from their source and are in need of "redemption." When a Jew in *galus* studies Torah, engages in prayer, or performs other mitzvos, he redeems some of the *nitzotzos* in that particular place.

---

5. *Eichah* 3:15.

This is only one purpose of *galus*. When the Final Redemption comes, we will be given to understand why this long *galus*, with all its great difficulties and tribulations, was necessary and ultimately for our benefit. Until that time, we live with the firm belief that all is for the good.

Maharal teaches that the words גְאוּלָה (*redemption*) and גֹלָה (*exile*) are phonetically related. He explains that *galus* is the preparation for *geulah*. We need the *galus*; we could not merit *geulah* without it.

This is the symbolism inherent in the linkage of the *Seder* night with the night of Tishah B'Av. Tishah B'Av, with all its sadness and tragedy, contains within it the roots of redemption. And, as the Midrash informs us, Mashiach is born on Tishah B'Av.

Yosef and the Brothers

The story of Yosef *HaTzaddik* and his brothers mirrors the *galus* experience and subsequent redemption. From the moment they first descended to Egypt, the brothers were being unfairly singled out by the ruler of Egypt, Tzafnas Paneiach, who, unbeknownst to them, was their brother Yosef. He accused them of being spies; demanded that they bring their youngest brother Binyamin to him; imprisoned their brother Shimon; planted money in their sacks; and finally, planted his silver cup in the sack of Binyamin and said that Binyamin would have to remain in Egypt and serve as his slave.

At that point, the situation became intolerable for the brothers; realizing this, Yosef could no longer restrain himself from revealing his identity. "I am Yosef!" he declared, and suddenly, the picture changed for the brothers. With those two words, אֲנִי יוֹסֵף, everything suddenly made sense. As Yosef explained, the entire story that began with his being sold into slavery was actually Hashem's way of providing for Yaakov's family during the years of famine. Furthermore, the family of Yaakov knew of

Avraham's prophecy at the Convenant Between the Parts, when Hashem informed him that his descendants would be slaves in a foreign land. Now, after Yosef's revelation, it became clear that his slavery and subsequent ascension to the throne was Divinely orchestrated so that Yaakov and his family could descend to Egypt with dignity.

Similarly, the time will come when Hashem, in His infinite wisdom, will decree that this *galus* must end. And just as Yosef declared אֲנִי יוֹסֵף, *I am Yosef,* Hashem will declare, "Behold, I have redeemed you in later times as in earlier times ... אֲנִי ה' אֱלֹהֵיכֶם, *I am Hashem, your God.*" At that time, we will view the *galus* in retrospect and perceive what we accomplished over the course of time, and we will be happy with what we have achieved. At that time, the nations of the world will also perceive that all along, the *Ribbono shel Olam* was doing that which was for our ultimate good, and they will praise Him for this, as we say in *Hallel,* *"Praise Hashem all nations ... for His kindness has overwhelmed us ...."*[6]

Yehudah and Shimon

Tur[7] writes that the twelve months of the year correspond to the Twelve Tribes, in the order of how they traveled in the *Midbar* and in which their *Nesi'im* (Princes) offered sacrifices at the *Mishkan's* inauguration. Yehudah corresponds to the first month, Nissan, the month of Pesach and redemption. Shimon corresponds to the fifth month, Av, in which Tishah B'Av falls.

In *Tanach,* we find a close association between the tribes of Yehudah and Shimon. At the end of his life, Moshe Rabbeinu blessed each of the tribes — with the exception of Shimon. *Rashi*[8] explains that Moshe did not want to bless Shimon because of

6. *Tehillim* 117:1-2.

7. *Hilchos Rosh Chodesh.*

8. *Devarim* 33:7 ד"ה ועזר מצריו תהי'.

the terrible incident of Zimri and the Midianite princess,[9] but Shimon was included in Yehudah's blessing; the words שְׁמַע ה' קוֹל יְהוּדָה are an allusion to Shimon. Furthermore, when Yehoshua bin Nun apportioned Eretz Yisrael among the tribes, Shimon's portion was found within the portion of Yehudah.

Yehudah and Shimon, Nissan and Av, are intertwined. The blessing of Av/*galus* is rooted in the blessing of Nissan/*geulah.*

As long as the *galus* lasts, the hidden blessing of Av is no more than an allusion. But when the Redemption arrives, we will perceive that Av is, in fact, a month of redemption — on a par with Nissan and even greater, for the holy *sefarim* teach that Tishah B'Av is destined to become the greatest of all *yamim tovim.*

At the Gateway to Egypt

In Midrash and other sources, we find the concept that Hashem prepares the "cure" before the "malady." For example, Providence placed Esther in the position of queen in Achashverosh's palace before Haman's ascension to power. In a similar vein, Hashem does not send the Jewish people into exile until the seeds of redemption have already been sown.

Let us return to the four explanations of how the total of 70 souls was completed.

Yocheved, the mother of the redeemer, Moshe Rabbeinu, was born at the gateway to Egypt. Even before the Jews had entered their place of exile, the Divine plan for their redemption had already been set in motion. There is an added message in this. It is as if Hashem was saying, "Do not think that your exile is a punishment. In fact, it is a preparation for redemption, a redemption that will bring you to a spiritual level you have never before attained. And the seeds of that redemption have already been sown."

9. See *Bamidbar* ch. 25.

Serach bas Asher

In the *zemiros* of Motza'ei Shabbos we sing of Eliyahu HaNavi: אִישׁ פָּקִיד עַל כָּל בְּשׂוֹרוֹת טוֹבוֹת, *the man appointed over all good tidings. Sefer Meor Einayim*[10] writes that whenever someone relates good tidings, he is accompanied by the spirit of Eliyahu. This is why people want so badly to be the first to relate good news. The soul yearns to attach itself to the spirit of Eliyahu. Furthermore, the moment when good tidings are conveyed is a most opportune time for both the bearer and the recipient to engage in *teshuvah*. As *Sefer Malachi* says of Eliyahu, *"He shall return the heart of parents to children and the heart of children to parents."*[11]

The previous verse states, *"Behold! I send you Eliyahu the Prophet before the arrival of the great and awesome day of Hashem."* Eliyahu's primary mission is to bring the news of the Final Redemption to the entire Jewish people.

As the three *Avos* of our people, Avraham, Yitzchak, and Yaakov each encompassed within himself the entire Jewish people. When Serach bas Asher sang to her grandfather Yaakov that Yosef was alive, she was not bringing good tidings to an individual. She was paralleling the future action of Eliyahu in bringing tidings to the entire Jewish nation. And like Eliyahu's, her message was one of redemption. From Yosef will come Mashiach ben Yosef,[12] whose arrival will precede that of Mashiach ben Dovid. Serach was informing the Jewish people that, indeed, the day would come when Mashiach ben Yosef would appear. Her tidings, therefore, allowed her not only to be *momentarily* accompanied by the spirit of Eliyahu, but to have the spirit of

10. By the chassidic master R' Nachum of Chernobyl.

11. *Malachi* 3:24.

12. At the time of the future redemption, the Mashiach descended from Yosef will appear first to save the Jewish people. However, the full redemption will be brought about solely through Mashiach descended from Dovid (see *Targum Yonasan* to *Shemos* 40:11, *Succah* 52a, and other sources).

Eliyahu remain with her forever. Therefore, like Eliyahu, she merited unusual longevity and ascended to Heaven alive.

Because she was accompanied by the spirit of Eliyahu, she is counted as two among those who descended to Egypt. And like the message inherent in Yocheved's birth, Serach's completing the count of 70 alludes to the fact that the impending *galus* was rooted in *geulah*.

With Us in Our Suffering

When Hashem spoke to Yaakov prior to his journey to Egypt, He said, *"I shall descend with you to Egypt, and I shall also surely bring you up."*[13] *Pirkei d'R' Eliezer* states that Hashem completed the total of 70 when Yaakov descended, and He completed the total of 600,000 when the Jews were redeemed from Egypt. As it is written: עִמּוֹ אָנֹכִי בְצָרָה, *I [Hashem] am with him in distress.*[14]

That prophecy was told to Yaakov בְּמַרְאֹת הַלַּיְלָה, *in visions of the night,* and Hashem called his name twice, "Yaakov, Yaakov." As *Rashi* states, the double use of Yaakov's name is לָשׁוֹן חִבָּה, a sign of special love, as if to say: "Do not fear the darkness that is *galus.* My love for you is as strong in *galus* as it is in times of *geulah,* and I will be as close to you then as I was in brighter times. I am the 70th member of your family as you descend, and I will be the 600,000th member when your descendants depart."

A Jew must believe and internalize that when he is experiencing the travails of *galus,* be they personal or communal, the *Ribbono shel Olam* is with him, suffering as well, as it were. He was with the Jewish people throughout their sojourn in Egypt, and He has been with them — and continues to be with them — in every exile. As Dovid HaMelech says, *"Though I walk in the valley overshadowed by death, I will fear no evil, for You are with me."*[15]

13. *Bereishis* 46:4.
14. *Tehillim* 91:15.
15. Ibid. 23:4.

Chushim ben Don

In the Torah, the Tribe of Don appears to be most inferior. While Don led one of the *degalim* (tribal formations) in the Wilderness, it brought up the rear as the Jews marched from one encampment to another. *"The division of the camp of Don ... they shall be the last to journey."*[16] The Midrash relates that because of their sins, members of Don were not afforded the protection of the Clouds of Glory that enveloped the Jews, and thus Amalek was able to attack them soon after the Exodus from Egypt.[17] During the First Beis HaMikdash era, the city of Don was a place of idol worship.

Throughout their 210 years in Egypt, the Jewish people, despite their being enslaved, maintained their high standards of morality — with the exception of one person. Shlomis bas Divri of Don was lax in maintaining the crucial barriers of *tznius* (modesty),[18] and this led to a tragic sin.

And who was the sole offspring of Don ben Yaakov? Chushim ben Don, a deaf-mute.

Chushim ben Don is a metaphor for our generation. In comparison to previous generations, we are spiritually impoverished. We are consumed by our troubles and by distractions which we bring upon ourselves, wittingly and unwittingly. We find it very hard to express a word of tefillah with proper intent, to comprehend a *daf* of *Gemara* with our minds fully focused.

Yet this is the unique mission of our generation, the generation of *Ikvesa D'Meshicha,* the period that heralds the arrival of Mashiach. Previous generations suffered all forms of terrible persecutions, but they had one advantage. Their awareness of Hashem was clear, their minds were focused. These generations possessed scores of great *tzaddikim* endowed with *ruach hakodesh*

16. *Bamidbar* 2:25,31.

17. See "Tefillah — An Expression of Faith" (ch. 2).

18. See *Rashi* to *Vayikra* 24:11.

who imbued their fellow Jews with a deep awareness and connection to the *Ribbono shel Olam.* Our generation, though it does have its outstanding *tzaddikim* and Torah leaders, lacks the spiritual state of mind that was typical of the average Jew in days gone by.

We are beset with worry over our financial situation, health issues, problems with *shidduchim,* children at risk, and other serious matters. We live under the threat of terrorism and concern for our brethren in Eretz Yisrael. Yes, we are "Chushim ben Dons." Nevertheless, as Chushims, with our limited focus and our many tribulations and distractions, we relentlessly carry on and strive to serve Hashem with devotion to the best of our ability. Precisely because our service of Hashem is performed amid such difficult obstacles, every mitzvah that we do, every tefillah that we utter, every word of Torah that we study, is very precious to Hashem.[19] Because of the many spiritual obstacles that we face, including the immoral society that surrounds us, our *avodas Hashem* is even more precious than that of previous generations. We are the generation to whom Hashem calls "Yaakov, Yaakov" with special fondness.

Of all the members of Yaakov Avinu's family, it was Chushim ben Don who killed Esav and made Yaakov's burial possible. There is a deep symbolism in this. Chushim ben Don brought about a redemption of sorts, and therefore merited, according to one opinion, to be counted as two and to complete the total of 70. We, the generation of "Chushim ben Dons," will be the ones to merit greeting Mashiach. We will bring about the fulfillment of the verse *"The saviors will ascend Mount Zion to judge Esav's mountain, and the kingdom will be Hashem's."*[20] חֻשִׁים has the same letters as מָשִׁיחַ.

---

19. Rav Wolfson frequently exhorts his *talmidim* to make every effort to minimize the distractions and dangers to *avodas Hashem* that modern technology presents. Inside Beis Medrash Emunas Yisroel cell phone use is strictly banned, even for learning purposes.

20. *Ovadiah* 1:21.

Hashem's Unconditional Love

As mentioned above, it was Don whom Amalek attacked soon after the Exodus. Of that attack, the Torah states:

> *Remember what Amalek did to you … that he happened upon you on the way, and he killed among you all your weaklings at your rear …*[21]

Regarding the words כָּל הַנֶּחֱשָׁלִים אַחֲרֶיךָ, *all your weaklings at your rear, Rashi*[22] writes: "[This refers to] those lacking in strength because of their sin. For the Cloud [of Glory] ejected them [and therefore they were vulnerable to attack]."

However, *Targum Onkelos* translates נֶחֱשָׁלִים as מִתְאַחֲרִין, *those who came late*, meaning that they were not protected by the Cloud simply because they were lagging behind the other Jews as they traveled. On the surface, there seems to be a disagreement between the Midrash and *Targum.*

We suggest that there is no disagreement. These members of *shevet Don* were indeed sinners, as the Midrash states. However, Hashem did not actively eject them from His Divine protection. Rather, their sins caused them to lose their excitement for *avodas Hashem.*

Journeying from place to place in the *Midbar* was not just any journey. As the Torah states, *"According to the word of Hashem would they encamp, and according to the word of Hashem would they journey."*[23] Moreover, the Jews' encampment in the *Midbar* had the spiritual status of the holy city of Jerusalem. This is why a *metzora* had to leave the encampment, just as he would have to leave Jerusalem until his *tzaraas* healed and he underwent the purification process.

21. *Devarim* 25:18.

22. Citing *Midrash Tanchuma.*

23. *Bamidbar* 9:23.

Yet, when the trumpets sounded throughout the encampment signaling that it was time to pack up and move on,[24] these members of *shevet Don* were in no hurry. This lethargy was due to their sins. Only sin could have robbed them of the zeal and excitement that they should have experienced. And so, when the Jews broke camp and began their journey, these stragglers found themselves outside the protective shield of the Clouds of Glory — and vulnerable to an attack by Amalek.

And it was for the sake of these sinners that Hashem instructed Moshe to wage war against Amalek. For Hashem's love for us is unconditional. Even when a Jew has sinned grievously and in so doing feels no connection to his Creator, his Creator is still connected to him, watching over him and waiting for him with open arms, as it were, to return to Him.

Every year on the Shabbos of *Parashas Zachor*,[25] we fulfill the mitzvah to read from the Torah scroll the command to remember Amalek's attack on our people. This is the only Torah reading of the year that according to all opinions is a Biblical mitzvah. Each year, we read publicly those verses in the Torah that declare Hashem's eternal love for every Jewish soul.

Faith in These Times

We are living through difficult times, when there is much that we do not understand. It is at such times that a Jew must strengthen himself with the words of Dovid HaMelech: אֶשָּׂא כַנְפֵי שָׁחַר, *If I were to take the wings of the dawn,* אֶשְׁכְּנָה בְּאַחֲרִית יָם, *and dwell in the uttermost part of the sea* — an allusion to אַחֲרִית הַיָּמִים, *the End of Days,* the period before Mashiach — גַּם שָׁם יָדְךָ תַנְחֵנִי, *Even there Your hand would lead me,* וְתֹאחֲזֵנִי יְמִינֶךָ, *and Your right hand would hold me.*[26]

24. Ibid. 10:2.

25. The Shabbos before Purim.

26. *Tehillim* 139:9-10.

The Chofetz Chaim and other great *tzaddikim* of his era declared that in their time, the period of *Ikvesa D'Meshicha* had already begun. No one knows how long this period will last, but the signs given at the end of *Masechta Sotah* for *Ikvesa D'Meshicha* are all here.[27]

This is a time when a Jew must strengthen his *emunah*, his faith in Hashem. In earlier times, the simplest Jew possessed rock-firm *emunah*; in our generation of Chushim ben Dons, in our world of troubles and confusion, this is not always the case. One should note that the onslaught of travails in our time should give us reason to hope that Redemption is near. "If you see a generation in which numerous troubles come upon it like a river, expect him [Mashiach], as it is written, *'For distress shall come like a river with the spirit of Hashem devouring within it,'*[28] and next to that it is written, *'A redeemer shall come to Zion.'*"

A Jew is required not only to believe that Mashiach will come and that he can come at any time, but to *await* his arrival. *"For there is yet another vision about the appointed time ... though it may tarry, await it, for it will surely come; it will not delay."*[29] And as our Sages teach, when a Jew departs this world, one of the first questions he is asked by the Heavenly Court is, "Did you wait in hope for the salvation [of the Final Redemption]?"[30]

There are individuals who are plagued by fear that their *emunah* is lacking; they are burdened with *sfeikos*, doubts, concerning the fundamentals of Jewish faith. This is another device of the Satan, to depress a Jew by making him think that he does not truly believe.

27. "In *Ikvesa D'Meshicha* insolence will increase, inflation will soar, the vine will give its fruit but wine will be expensive, the government will turn to heresy, there will be no rebuke, the meeting places of the wise will be used for immorality, the Galil will be destroyed and the Gavlan will be desolated ... those who fear sin will be despised and the truth will be hidden ... the face of the generation will be like the face of the dog ... on whom do we have to rely? On our Father in Heaven."

28. *Yeshayahu* 59:19.

29. *Chavakuk* 2:3.

30. *Shabbos* 31a.

A Jew once came to the author of *Tzemach Tzedek* and poured out his woes. "Rebbe," he wailed, "I have *sfeikos* in *emunah*! What should I do?" The Rebbe appeared not to comprehend the problem. "*Nu,* so you have *sfeikos* in *emunah*. So what?"

The chassid became more agitated. "Rebbe — *sfeikos* in *emunah* ... in *emunah* ... and I cannot rid myself of them!"

The Rebbe responded softly, "Do you see how much it bothers you that have these *sfeikos*? Isn't that the biggest proof that, in fact, you *do* have faith?"[31]

Escaping *Chevlei Mashiach*

People are fearful of the *chevlei Mashiach*, the "birth pangs" that our Sages say will herald Mashiach's arrival. The Gemara teaches that to escape these troubles, one should busy himself with Torah study and acts of *chesed*.[32] Now is the time to strengthen one's commitment to Torah, tefillah, and *gemilas chasadim*.

The economic crisis that has hit America and the rest of the world has caused people to watch their money carefully and to spend less. As a result, some have also cut back on their *tzedakah*-giving. This is a mistake.

When Hashem decreed that Sodom be destroyed, He sent Lot two angels disguised as wayfarers. Lot welcomed these wayfarers into his home at risk to his life, for the policy of Sodom was to persecute guests, not welcome them. As the Midrash relates, those who acted kindly toward strangers were liable to be killed by the people of Sodom.

Zohar states that the two angels who appeared before Lot were a "gift" to him from Hashem, for they presented him with the opportunity to earn the merit he needed to escape the destruction

---

31. It should be noted, however, that lack of vigilance in matters of *kedushah* can cloud one's *emunah*. This topic has been dealt with by Rav Wolfson in a *shmuess* that has been rendered into English and can be obtained by contacting Rabbi Mordechai Brown at 917-613-0824. (It is discussed briefly in "Tefillah — An Expression of Faith" [ch. 2].)

32. *Sanhedrin* 98b.

of Sodom. Hashem was granting Lot a chance to risk his life to fulfill the mitzvah of *hachnasas orchim*. Lot rose to the challenge and thus was saved.

It is the same in our times. The economic crisis makes our *tzedakah*-giving even more potent in Heaven. We should seize the opportunity and give *tzedakah* with *mesiras nefesh*.[33]

There is another mitzvah that is a primary means of escaping *chevlei Mashiach*: "Whoever observes the three meals [of Shabbos] will be spared three tribulations: *chevlei Mashiach,* the judgment of *Gehinnom,* and the war of Gog and Magog."[34] One should experience the Shabbos meals in the proper way, combining culinary delights with *divrei Torah, zemiros,* and avoiding conversation that is contrary to the spirit of Shabbos.

We should take a lesson from the Satan. The Satan knows that when Mashiach arrives, his job will be over, and so he is using every means at his disposal to try to draw us away from anything spiritual. Each day we see the appearance of some new technological device that in moments can, God forbid, wreak havoc on one's *neshamah.*

Let us respond to the Satan's final onslaught by going about our *avodas Hashem* with renewed energy and joy. In this merit, may the Jewish people soon witness the arrival of Mashiach and the building of the Third Beis HaMikdash, *amen.*

33. Rav Wolfson delivered this *shmuess* during the Gaza war at the end of 2008. He mentioned the daily miracles that the Jews in Southern Israel were witnessing, with so many rockets missing their target or causing minimal damage. He suggested that this may be in the *zechus* of the *hachnasas orchim* being performed by the scores of families in other parts of Eretz Yisrael who opened their homes to the Jews of the South, despite the difficulties involved.

34. *Shabbos* 118a.

APPENDIX B

A Mission Fulfilled

The following letter was written by Rav Wolfson to a woman who had lost the child she was carrying. It was translated from the original Yiddish.[1]

I would like to express a number of thoughts which I hope will, to a certain degree, ease your situation. It is possible that my words will offer you nothing new, but my feelings of sympathy impel me to try.

Each morning we recite the *Elokai, Neshamah* blessing, in which we refer to Hashem as רִבּוֹן כָּל הַמַּעֲשִׂים **אֲדוֹן** כָּל הַנְּשָׁמוֹת, *Lord of all works,* ***Master*** *of all souls.* Later, at the conclusion of the *Pesukei D'Zimrah* portion of *Shacharis,* we speak of Hashem as **בּוֹרֵא** כָּל הַנְּשָׁמוֹת, ***Creator*** *of all souls.* Why is it that in reference to

1. This translation was originally published in *The Jewish Observer* (summer 1995) and later in *Vistas of Challenge* (ArtScroll/Mesorah). Over the years, numerous people have requested copies of the letter; thus it is being reprinted here as a public service.

the *neshamah,* soul, Hashem is referred to first as an אֲדוֹן, *Master,* and then as a בּוֹרֵא, *Creator?*

To answer this question we must first understand the following teachings of our Sages which are explained in the writings of the great *tzaddikim* of earlier generations.

In Heaven there is a *Heichal HaNeshamos,* Sanctuary of Souls, the source from which all *neshamos* come. The Final Redemption will not come until all souls have left this *Heichal* and descended to this world.[2]

Each *neshamah* has its own unique mission to fulfill on this world, and is allotted the life span necessary to fulfill that mission. Some *neshamos* belong to a very exalted class. They are of such a sublime nature, so holy, sparkling, and brilliant, that they simply cannot bear to exist in this world for even a short time. However, they too must leave the *Heichal HaNeshamos* so that it will be emptied, and for other reasons known only to Hashem.

And so Hashem chooses a particular couple that will draw such a *neshamah* down to this world. It departs its place near the Throne of Glory and is immediately placed in an environment in which it is at home — an environment which is Divine in nature. A woman who is with child carries within herself not only a child, but an entire *Gan Eden* as well. A flame from the hidden light of Creation shines above the child's head, and by that light the child sees from one end of the world to the other. A heavenly angel learns the entire Torah with the child. All this occurs with every Jewish child.

However, those special *neshamos* of which we have spoken cannot bear to separate themselves from their sublime existence and sully themselves by living on this earthly world. And so they are spared this discomfort and are returned to their Father in Heaven, having fulfilled their mission by leaving the *Heichal HaNeshamos,* and residing within their mother, thus bringing the world one step closer to the Final Redemption.

---

2. *Yevamos* 62a.

And what of the mother, who had endured, hoped, and in the end was so terribly disappointed? She is of flesh and blood and her feelings are understandable.

However, in loftier moments, in moments when her intellect can overcome her emotions, the mother can free herself of her earthly thoughts and share in the elation enjoyed by her *neshamah.* Then she will become infused by a feeling of true joy — the joy of a wealthy person who takes reckoning of all his business endeavors and sees that his profits far outweigh his losses. She has merited to have had as her guest a pure, holy *neshamah,* accompanied by a Divine light, a heavenly angel, and a heavenly Torah. The *Ribbono Shel Olam* had created a beis midrash for this *neshamah* within her. And when this *neshamah* left her, some of the *kedushah* (holiness) that had entered her remained, and will not leave her for the rest of her life.

She has merited to bring Mashiach's arrival closer by offering a sacrifice for this purpose. She is not left with a mother's usual compensation; all that she has endured has been for the sake of Hashem and His people, not for her personal joy and satisfaction. She has served not as a worker who awaits immediate payment, but as a loyal soldier, who is ready to suffer wounds in battle, if necessary, solely for the glory of the King.

Was it all worth it?

In painful moments when disappointment sets in and normal human feelings dominate one's mood, the answer may be negative. However, when holiness breaks through, when the intellect of the *neshamah* speaks and the joy of the Jewish soul bursts forth, then there is an answer of an entirely different nature. This answer is accompanied by the song of triumph, the joy of the victor, the deep-rooted satisfaction of one who has earned something of immeasurable value.

In the *Heichal HaNeshamos,* the Jewish souls are, figuratively speaking, בָּנִים לַמָּקוֹם (children of Hashem). That sanctuary is their source, and their Father in Heaven is their Creator. When they descend to this world clothed in human form they are seen as servants, with Hashem as their Master.

In the morning, when we arise from our slumber and are still mired in our earthliness, when the physical part of our beings prevails, we say מוֹדֶה אֲנִי לְפָנֶיךָ ... רִבּוֹן כָּל הַמַּעֲשִׂים אֲדוֹן כָּל הַנְּשָׁמוֹת, *I gratefully thank You ... Lord of all works, Master of all neshamos.*

In effect we are saying, "You, *Ribbono Shel Olam,* Who directs this world with exacting Providence, a world in which every occurrence is a part of Your eternal plan, You are the One Who determines the destiny of every *neshamah,* in harmony with Your Master Plan."

However, following the recitation of *Pesukei D'Zimrah* and *Az Yashir* (the Song at the Sea), we raise ourselves above the אֲנִי — there exists no "I." Then the *Ribbono Shel Olam* is not seen as אֲדוֹן, the *Master* over His servants, but rather as בּוֹרֵא, the *Creator* of us, His children. Then we can also perceive Hashem as Creator of certain special *neshamos* — those who fulfill their mission without having to be seen as servants, clothed in earthly bodies.

In the early morning, our frame of mind permits us only to recite a *berachah* for a *neshamah* that resides within a body. It is only later, in the midst of the *Shacharis* prayers, when we are in an uplifted state, that we can express a blessing even for those sparkling *neshamos* that are too sublime to enter into this earthly world.

One should realize that the term "miscarriage" is not found in a believing Jew's dictionary. The term implies that one's efforts have ended in failure, that all has been in vain. This is incorrect, for when a Jewish woman conceives it is never in vain.[3]

May the *Ribbono Shel Olam* grant you *nachas* and good health. May you merit to bring into this world and raise healthy children and grandchildren who will toil in Torah study and *mitzvos.* May you and your husband derive much joy and satisfaction from your family and together escort your children to the *chupah* with joy and feelings of gratitude to the One Above. May you, along with all of *Klal Yisrael,* merit to greet Mashiach — whose arrival you have brought closer.

---

3. Moreover, a child will merit *techias hameisim* (Resurrection of the Dead) even if its life was terminated immediately following conception; see *Igros Moshe, Yoreh Deah* III, §138.